D1179853

Twayne's English Authors Series

EDITOR OF THIS VOLUME

Bertram H. Davis

Florida State University

Arthur Murphy

TEAS 258

ARTHUR MURPHY

By ROBERT DONALD SPECTOR

Long Island University

TWAYNE PUBLISHERS
A DIVISION OF G. K. HALL & CO., BOSTON

Published in 1979 by Twayne Publishers,
A Division of G. K. Hall & Co.
All Rights Reserved

Printed on permanent/durable acid-free paper and bound in the
United States of America

First Printing

Library of Congress Cataloging in Publication Data

Spector, Robert Donald.
Arthur Murphy.

(Twayne's English authors series ; TEAS 258)
Bibliography: p. 185-92
Includes index.
1. Murphy, Arthur, 1727-1805
—Criticism and interpretation.
PR3605.M9S6   822'.6   78-24242
ISBN 0-8057-6751-7

In memory of Max Spector

Contents

About the Author

Professor of English and director of the Division of Humanities and Communication Arts at Long Island University, Robert Donald Spector is the author of four books and editor of ten others. He has published more than 400 articles and reviews in scholarly and commercial journals and collections. Recipient of fellowships from the Huntington, Folger, and Newberry libraries and of a travel grant from the Swedish government, he was named as a 1978 winner of the first annual Long Island University Board of Trustees' Award for a Lifetime of Scholarly Achievement.

His study of the English novelist Tobias Smollett in the TEAS was described as an "excellent critical introduction" (*Studies in English Literature*) and his book on Pär Lagerkvist in the TWAS was hailed as a "major contribution" (*Choice*). His earlier analysis of *English Literary Periodicals* was acclaimed as "the most uniquely useful scholarly study of 1966" (*Studies in English Literature*).

Preface

Arthur Murphy was an important writer in his own time. Not only was his creative production enormous, but it was generally highly professional and on occasion outstanding. Murphy turned his skillful hand to most of the contemporary genres. He proved himself a capable polemicist in the *Test* and *Auditor*. As a literary critic he demonstrated his ability with the *Gray's Inn Journal*, one of the superior essay periodicals of the second part of the century. His poetry, in and out of his dramas, displays his competence. His translations, particularly of the work of Tacitus, are as respected by modern critics as they were by his contemporaries. In his biographies of Fielding, Johnson, and Garrick, Murphy provided a storehouse of information and insights for later generations of writers.

But Murphy's particular contribution to the culture of his own age was as a dramatist. He was an adept craftsman for the eighteenth-century stage. In the popular genre of afterpieces, few authors could rival him in talent or popularity. His full-length comedies included some that had continued success well into the nineteenth century. His reputation as a comic playwright stood alongside that of such contemporaries as George Colman, Oliver Goldsmith, and Richard Brinsley Sheridan. In a period not known for great tragedies, Murphy's nevertheless ranked as examples of the best—offering evidence of his learning, taste, and artistry.

Yet, for all that, Murphy's memory faded quickly after his death, and if it did not altogether vanish, it barely retained its identity. To be sure, scholars at times have found his biographical work useful if not truly satisfactory. Literary and political historians have had to recall his journalistic efforts, and those who compile accounts of the theater of his time have not been able to ignore him. Nevertheless, the Murphy his contemporaries knew has been all but eclipsed. In that area where he genuinely excelled, the field of comic drama, little has survived beyond the interests of communities of scholars, and even there it has yielded its importance to the works of Goldsmith and Sheridan. Murphy's work deserves better treatment. Whatever the genre, he was an entertaining and engaging writer, and his comedies, especially, are still capable of providing considerable enjoyment. Two modern scholars have recognized Murphy's importance and have heroically attempted to resurrect his reputation. In 1946 Howard H. Dunbar and James Pike Emery brought forth impressive books on the dramatist, concentrating particularly on his biography, and Emery subsequently made available six of Murphy's plays in a modern edition. Those works suggested a stirring of interest not only in Murphy, but in the theater of his time, and since that revival of concern for eighteenth-century drama, scholarship has made important advances, most evident in the bibliographical work of Carl J. Stratman and in the colossal achievement of the *London Stage.* For Murphy himself, perhaps as a natural development from these major works of scholarship, some recent articles suggest an awakening of interest.

The time, then, seems appropriate for a new look at Murphy. With great indebtedness to all of the above works, I have attempted to do just that. I have focused my attention on Murphy's writing, and I have sought to give the reader a full account of his achievement in each of the genres in which he wrote. Although I have naturally emphasized his dramatic work, I have discussed virtually everything that remains to posterity. My basic text has been Murphy's *Works* of 1786 for everything that appears there. However, I have examined and compared each state of Murphy's plays—from the existing acting copies, through the various editions, to their final form in Murphy's lifetime. For Murphy's *Gray Inn Journal* I have referred not only to his *Works,* but to the 1754 and 1756 editions. My notes indicate the sources I have used for the remainder of Murphy's writings.

Over the years I have incurred many personal debts to scholars and institutions, which I am pleased to acknowledge. I am grateful for the various help of Professors John Pike Emery, Simon Trefman, James L. Clifford, John H. Middendorf, Donald J. Greene, Arthur H. Cash, Morris Golden, and Thelma Mielke. I owe much to the support and generosity of my friend and colleague Professor George Economou. To the Huntington

Preface

Library and the Folger Shakespeare Library I am most appreciative for fellowship awards that enabled me to use their resources and to call upon the cooperative services of their staffs.

Chronology

1727   Born December 27 in Clooniquin, Roscommon, Ireland. One of two surviving children of Dublin merchant Richard Murphy and Jane French.

1729   Father lost at sea. Lives with elder brother James and mother at St. George's Quay, Dublin.

1735   Family moves to London.

1736   Lives in Boulogne with Mrs. Arthur Plunkett, mother's sister.

1738   As Arthur French, studies at English college of St. Omer, Jesuit monastery in France.

1744   Completes studies and joins mother in London. Enters Webster's Academy to study mathematics and accounting.

1745–   Reads extensively in English literature.
1746

1747   Meets William Havard, an actor, and Samuel Foote, playwright and comedian. In August uncle sends him to Cork to clerk for two years for Edmund Harrold, a merchant.

1750   Becomes bookkeeper in London banking house. Meets literary figures, including Christopher Smart and Henry Fielding.

1752   Under pseudonym of Charles Ranger, on October 21, publishes first of forty-nine numbers of *Gray's Inn Journal* in the *Craftsman*.

1753   Publishes first independent number of *Gray's Inn Journal;* runs for fifty-two numbers until September 21, 1754.

1754   Prologue for Foote's *The Knights.* Garrick rejects first version of *The Apprentice (The Young Apprentice).* Publishes volume of last fifty-two numbers of *Gray's Inn Journal.* On October 18 appears as Othello at Covent Garden, first of eight roles for the season. Fights duel with Macnamara Morgan.

1755   On March 18 plays in Aaron Hill's adaptation of Voltaire's *Alzire*. Writes *Englishman from Paris*. Plays various roles for Garrick at Drury Lane. Possible affair with Peg Woffington.

1756   On January 2 *The Apprentice* staged at Drury Lane (published January 5). Anonymous publication of *The Spouter, or, The Triple Revenge*. Drury Lane presents *Englishman from Paris* for one performance on April 3. Publishes two-volume edition of 104 essays of *Gray's Inn Journal*. Quits acting over disputes with Garrick. Begins publishing the *Test* in political support of Henry Fox, later Lord Holland. Writes first version of *Orphan of China*. Contributes, through 1757, to Johnson's *Literary Magazine*. Writes *The Foundling*, comedy now lost.

1757   Gains admission to Lincoln's Inn. Writes *The Upholsterer*.

1757–   Writes "The Theatre," articles on drama and acting, for
1758   the *London Chronicle*.

1758   *The Upholsterer* appears at Drury Lane on March 30 (published on April 7). Writes first version of *The Way to Keep Him*.

1759   On April 21 presents *The Orphan of China* at Drury Lane (published April 3). *A Letter from Monsieur de Voltaire*—not by Voltaire—attacks Murphy.

1760   Presents *The Desert Island* at Drury Lane, January 24 (published shortly after). Also on January 24, the three-act version of *The Way to Keep Him* (published same year). In October responds to attack by Thomas Francklin with *A Poetical Epistle to Samuel Johnson*.

1761   Five-act version of *The Way to Keep Him* at Drury Lane on January 10. Prologue for Henry Brooke's *The Earl of Essex*. Death of mother on February 4. Begins affair with Ann Elliott. Management of Drury Lane with Foote presents three new plays: *All in the Wrong*, June 15; *The Old Maid*, July 2 (both published in 1761); *The Citizen*, in three acts, July 2 (not published until 1763, in two acts). On June 12 responds to Charles Churchill's *Rosciad* in *An Ode to the Naiads of Fleet Ditch*. In November answers *The Murphiad* with *The Examiner* (originally *The Expostulation*).

1762   In May edits Fielding's works, with *Essay on the Life and Genius of Henry Fielding*. Called to the bar on June 21.

On July 15 begins support of Lord Bute in the *Auditor,* which runs to May 16, 1763. First performance in two acts of *The Citizen* at Covent Garden. Writes *Alzuma.*

1763   Publishes two-act *The Citizen.*

1764   On January 9 presents three-act *No One's Enemy but His Own* at Covent Garden (published same year, shortened to two acts in 1774). Also on January 9, *What We Must All Come To.* Later changed to *Three Weeks after Marriage, or, What We Must All Come To* at Covent Garden on March 30, 1776. Completes *The Man Does Not Know His Own Mind* (later, *Know Your Own Mind).* Begins law practice.

1765   Introduces Johnson to the Thrales in January. On March 23 presents *The Choice* at Drury Lane. In December appointed commissioner of bankruptcy in London.

1767   On January 10 presents *The School for Guardians* at Covent Garden (published same year). Publishes translation from Jean François Marmontel's *Belisarius* in March. On April 22 musical version of *What We Must All Come To* (as *Marriage à la Mode)* appears at Drury Lane.

1768   Presents *Zenobia* at Drury Lane on Feburary 27 (published March 3).

1769   Death of Ann Elliott on May 30. Takes case of Robert Taylor against publisher Andrew Millar for more equitable copyright law.

1770   Renews quarrels with Garrick about *Alzuma.*

1772   Presents *The Grecian Daughter* at Drury Lane on February 26 (published same year). Renewed difficulties with Garrick. Writes *Hamlet with Alterations,* unacted, but dated December 15 (published in Jesse Foot's biography, 1811).

1773   *Alzuma* opens at Covent Garden, February 23 (published same year). Advertisement announces plans to retire. Begins paper war with George Steevens.

1774   *No One's Enemy but His Own* in two acts at Covent Garden on October 26.

1776   Presents revision of *What We Must All Come To* as *Three Weeks after Marriage* at Covent Garden on March 30 (published same year). Also on September 23 at Covent Garden offers *News from Parnassus, a Prelude* (published in *Works,* 1786).

1777   *Know Your Own Mind* opens at Covent Garden on
        February 22 (published in 1778). Revision of *The Orphan
        of China* at Covent Garden on November 6. Reconciles
        with Garrick.
1778   Resigns London commissionership of bankruptcy, Febru-
        ary 10.
1779   Elected recorder of Sudbury in Suffolk. Meets Fanny
        Burney.
1780   Draws Henry Thrale's will. Actively opposes mob during
        the Gordon Riots.
1781   Writes epilogues for Frances Brooke's *Siege of Sinope* and
        John Delap's *The Royal Suppliants.*
1783   Serves as senior counsel on the Norfolk circuit. Writes
        The Rival Sisters (published in *Works*, 1786). In Decem-
        ber becomes member of Johnson's Essex Head Club.
1785   New edition of *The Way to Keep Him.*
1786   In June publishes seven-volume edition of his *Works.*
        Writing for *Monthly Review.*
1787   Contributes to *Gentleman's Magazine*. Reviews Sir John
        Hawkins's *Life of Johnson* in *Monthly*. Resigns from
        Norfolk Circuit.
1788   Retires from the bar.
1789   Resigns as recorder of Sudbury.
1791   Publishes *Seventeen Hundred and Ninety-One*, imitation
        of the thirteenth satire of Juvenal, dedicated to Johnson's
        memory.
1792   Publishes *An Essay on the Life and Genius of Samuel
        Johnson*, separately and as an introduction to his edition.
        Meets Jesse Foot, later his executor and biographer.
1793   Edits Macklin's *Love à la Mode* and *The Man of the
        World*. Presents *The Rival Sisters* at the King's Theatre,
        Haymarket, on March 18 (originally published in *Works*).
        Publishes four-volume translation, *Works of Cornelius
        Tacitus*, dedicated to Burke.
1795   Publishes translation of Sallust's *The History of Cataline's
        Conspiracy; with the Four Orations of Cicero.*
1796   Serves briefly as Commissioner of Bankrupts.
1797   Beginning of long illness. Estranged from Hester Thrale
        Piozzi.
1798   Publishes *Arminius*, a tragedy attacking French Revolu-
        tion.

Chronology

1799   Publishes *The Bees*, a translation from Vanière's *Praedium
       Rusticum*, and translates Addison's *A Letter from Italy*
       into Latin.
1801   Reconciles with Mrs. Piozzi. Publishes *The Life of David
       Garrick* in two volumes.
1802   Called to the bench of the Society of Lincoln's Inn. Sees
       The Way to Keep Him in last attendance at a theater.
1803   Receives 200£ per year pension from George III.
1805   Writes autobiographical sketch included in Foot's *Life*.
       Dies on June 18 and buried at St. Paul's Hammersmith
       Church.
1807   Murphy's *Works of Sallust* edited by Thomas Moore.
1835   "Anecdotes of Murphy" added to Boswell's *Life of
       Johnson*.
1876   Publication of Murphy's translation of Vida's Latin poem,
       The Game of Chess.

CHAPTER 1

A Man of Letters

I Background

A N Irishman whose chances for success in London seemed
most probable in a business career, Arthur Murphy emerged
instead as one of the major comic dramatists in eighteenth-
century England. Like the improbable turn of events in a poorly
constructed farce, the bare facts alone of Murphy's youth led
implausibly to his development as a shrewd observer and critic
of the foibles and fashions of contemporary Londoners. Born in
Ireland in 1727, he spent only one year in London before he was
seventeen. His father's death in 1729 set him at the disposal of
generally well-intentioned relatives who sent him from Clooniquin to Dublin and then to Boulogne. Even his education—
contrary to British law—at the English college of St. Omer, a
Jesuit monastery a few miles from Boulogne, suggests an early
alienation from the main currents of English life.

The possibility of any literary vocation seems equally remote
during those youthful years. Jeffrey French, his maternal uncle,
pushed Murphy toward a career in commerce. In 1744, returning
to London, where nine years earlier he had lived briefly with his
mother, Murphy entered Webster's academy to study
mathematics and accounting. At his uncle's urging, he worked as
a clerk in Cork and then as a bookkeeper in London until 1750.
Yet, perhaps aroused by his uncle's parsimonious and dictatorial
nature, Murphy rebelled and almost immediately became
involved in literary activities.[1]

To be sure, outside the main events of Murphy's early
experiences, less noticeable circumstances were shaping the
future dramatist. His classical education at St. Omer's had

19

opened the way to literary interests. For two years in London, even while preparing for a vocation, he read widely in English literature. Moreover, through his older brother James, he had become acquainted with such theatrical figures as William Havard, the actor, and Samuel Foote, playwright and performer. In the lively atmosphere of London's coffeehouses, taverns, and theaters, the provincial youth drew close to the cosmopolitan world of performers and authors, including accomplished writers like Christopher Smart and Henry Fielding, and the aspiring young actress Frances Abington, a twelve-year-old girl performing wherever she could find a stage.[2] Undoubtedly, the excitement of the setting encouraged Murphy's own active participation, and by 1752 he was clearly involved in the literary and theatrical scene and committed to a lifetime of writing.

Perhaps more significant in Murphy's success as a playwright, especially one most adept at treating the mores and manners of his society, were his particular intellect and personality. As a dramatist Murphy insisted that events should arise from characterization, and his own achievement in the theater of the eighteenth century emerges out of his character rather than from any ordinary sequence of occurrences. Murphy was intelligent, but not greatly original. As his and Samuel Johnson's friend Mrs. Thrale noted, he had a remarkable store of knowledge and scholarship, wit and humor, but not much profundity.[3] Well-trained in the classics at St. Omer's, he was able to use his learning in an age that valued classical literature. His years in France and subsequent study of the language made accessible the works of the great French playwrights—tragic and comic—of the seventeenth and eighteenth centuries. He was acutely susceptible and alert to literary ideas and practices and prepared—as his later Commonplace Book indicates—to learn from the artists, critics, and philosophers who preceded him. Classical, Renaissance, and earlier eighteenth century and contemporary names fill the pages of his notebooks.[4] As a writer he adapted, altered, revised, and expanded the variety of sources that his intellect and education made available to him. Murphy, Johnson said, "by some happy Skill displays more knowledge than he really has. . . ."[5] His particular talent was to bring together sufficient invention, feeling, and knowledge to impress an audience, and that was what the theater of his age most demanded.

His achievement as a playwright, one gifted in the comedy of manners, seems most plausible in an examination of his personality. Murphy loved society, enjoyed moving in it, observing it. Impressive in appearance, courtly in address, he was Johnson's ideal of a gentleman,[6] and his social grace made him attractive as a member of any company.[7] His attentiveness to society is evident in his enjoyment of retailing anecdotes. His talent for mimicry suggests his powers of observation and ability to capture the nuances of conversation—qualities essential to the social dramatist. In almost every respect—including a reluctance for genuine emotional involvement—Murphy appears to be a figure drawn from the comedies of the Restoration wits he so much admired, and he had a natural affinity to the kind of drama they produced.

With these attributes, Murphy quickly adapted himself to English society. He was a man capable of social mobility, quick to take advantage of opportunities that would further his career and his art. He could win the trust of a politician like Henry Fox, whose help in gaining Murphy's admission to Lincoln's Inn led the playwright into a successful secondary career in law, where he particularly excelled in matters pertaining to estates and copyright. His social progress is marked by his influence with Lord Bute, through whom he was able to gain a government pension for his friend Johnson, and with the Court itself, where he sought to find an appropriate suitor for one of Mrs. Thrale's daughters.[8]

With equal facility, Murphy made friends within the literary world. His charm could turn potentially disastrous circumstances to success. When he had inadvertently plagiarized a Johnson *Rambler* essay in the *Gray's Inn Journal*—having translated it unwittingly from a French version—his approach to Johnson brought not only forgiveness, but a lifetime friendship, developed carefully through Murphy's tact and understanding.[9] Boswell, no great admirer of Murphy, attests to Johnson's love for him.[10] Through Foote he made his way into the theater; through Fielding, into literary journalism. Even David Garrick must have found him attractive, for he encouraged Murphy's earliest efforts. Their subsequent battles through the years resulted naturally from the efforts of the tight-fisted, practical-minded and vain actor-manager to get whatever advantages he could from an equally conceited and hypersensitive playwright who demanded sufficient compensation along with respect.

Murphy's embroilments with John Wilkes, Charles Churchill, Robert Lloyd, and George Colman were attributable to the normal conflicts engaged in by men involved in the political, theatrical, and literary struggles common in the period. Like Tobias Smollett, the novelist, Murphy engaged in the defense of the government of Lord Bute at the end of the Seven Years' War, and it brought him the political enmity of Wilkes and his followers. Literature was not separate from politics, and arguments that originated in political differences carried into journalism, essays, poetry, and drama.

Journalism, essays, poetry, and drama—these, along with translation and biography, were the province of the eighteenth-century man of letters, and Murphy engaged in them all. Despite his reputation gained as a dramatist, Murphy, like so many of his contemporaries, practiced a variety of forms, and for his time was successful in a good many of them, although his efforts in genres outside the drama, with the exception of his essays in the *Gray's Inn Journal*, now hold little more than historical or biographical interest.

II *Literary Journalism*

Murphy was an accomplished journalist, whether in literature or politics, and his earliest triumph was with the essay-sheet the *Gray's Inn Journal*. Apparently undertaken in opposition to Dr. John Hill's scurrilous newspaper column, "The Inspector," which like Hill himself became a satiric target throughout Murphy's essays,[11] the project proved to be Murphy's first significant literary venture. It originated as a weekly paper in the *Craftsman*, a periodical of which no copies have survived.[12] From October 21, 1752, probably until the termination of the *Craftsman*, Murphy contributed forty-nine numbers. Then on September 29, 1753, he began independent publication of his journal, which ran until September 21, 1754. Its fifty-two new numbers, either gathered or reprinted, were published as a single folio volume before the end of the year.

While it is impossible to reconstruct the format or even to be sure of the name of the eidolon that Murphy used for the *Gray's Inn Journal* in the *Craftsman*, his independent essay-journal clearly adopted the features of earlier representatives of the genre. Like the *Spectator,* which dominated development of essay-journals throughout the century, Murphy's individual papers characteristically center upon a well-developed essay, prefaced by a motto and followed by a brief miscellaneous section, entitled "True Intelligence" and used largely for trivial items of theatrical or social gossip.[13] Charles Ranger, his eidolon named from the popular stage character in Hoadly's *The Suspicious Husband,* is modeled on Mr. Spectator. Displaying enough eccentricity to make him interesting, Ranger has sufficient seriousness and sensitivity to make him a respectable and responsible social spokesman. To broaden the range of his essays, Murphy—like Addison and Steele—employs such devices as clubs, letters, and serial characters so that the point of view is not always Ranger's. For the most part, the essays themselves run the conventional gamut from imaginary dreams and Oriental and allegorical tales to satiric portraits of social types or attacks on social abuses and outrageous fashions. What distinguishes the journal is the quality of its literary criticism, particularly on the drama. While hardly innovative in periodicals, dramatic criticism was not customary, and Murphy's was unusual enough to win the particular respect of Samuel Johnson.[14]

Nevertheless, Murphy was forced to terminate his journal as his desperate financial condition drove him to attempt an acting career.[15] Still, he was far from done with the *Gray's Inn Journal.* In 1756 he published a two-volume edition of 104 numbers, which probably included those that had appeared in the *Craftsman* and three either newly written or expansions of topics in earlier "True Intelligence" sections. While lack of a file for the *Craftsman* prevents examination of changes in later editions, comparison of the 1754 and 1756 volumes reveals extensive revisions in order, dating, and texts, and even extends to the omission of essays included in the first collected edition.[16] Murphy himself in a 1756 advertisement stresses his "Retrenchments, Additions and Corrections."[17] Not least are alterations in style, where Murphy, conscious of a more enduring publication, worked toward removing any signs of coarseness that might blemish his reputation. The same sense of durability brought wholesale changes in the "True Intelligence" section, the most transient portion of the journal. While important in the appeal of the periodical in 1754, topical items about the theater, controversies about Murphy's opinions, and references to such contemporary events as Elizabeth Canning's purported abduction by gypsies no longer had interest in 1756. Although Murphy augmented the section with attacks on the two monthly review journals which had unfavorably criticized *The Apprentice,* his first play, he otherwise reduced the "True Intelligence" to a position of insignificance.

It proved even less necessary when Murphy again revised the journal for his collected *Works* in 1786. Writing now for posterity, Murphy allowed only a few substantial items to remain. While he regarded the *Gray's Inn Journal* as important enough to include in his collection, he was unwilling to mar it with topical trivia. The essays themselves underwent still further revision. Six from 1756 do not appear, while nine new ones are included.[18] The kinds of alteration that had taken place in 1756 are repeated in 1786, and the stylistic changes that give the 1756 edition a more formal character than that of 1754 are extended even further in 1786 so that the essays finally have a truly Johnsonian quality to them.

Murphy correctly regarded the journal as an important achievement. Whatever the edition, the work has significance for his contemporary reputation, for his ideas on drama and society, as a reflection of eighteenth-century attitudes, and as an index to his particular talents. For the literary historian or for the student of Murphy, the *Gray's Inn Journal* offers a portrait of Grub Street, a view of the dramatist's personality, and an insight into his developing craftsmanship. If contemporaries like Johnson recognized in it the work of a genuine man of letters,[19] posterity has come to regard it as among the best periodicals of the century.[20] Not only Murphy's Shakespearean criticism, but also some of his Eastern tales, discussions of diction, and general treatment of drama, acting, and performances have been highly and properly praised.[21]

While brief discussion cannot do justice to the variety and range of topics in the *Gray's Inn Journal,* for an understanding of Murphy's personality, mind, and values it is important to examine, at least, some of his social and literary comments. These do not vary essentially from one edition to another and generally do not have to be distinguished on that basis. Revision improved his technique and expression without affecting his fundamental opinions on society and literature.

Murphy the social critic offers a wide range of notes on fashionable abuses, indecorum, and anticommonsensical conduct. His values are those of moderation, his tone ordinarily not too severe. He aims at "a delicate exertion of pleasantry upon the foibles, the slight indiscretions, the mistaken opinions, or even the virtues of men, when carried to some degree of excess."[22] He places himself in the tradition that extends from Horace through Pope, although an occasional stronger statement has the bite of Swiftian irony, suggesting small hope for the prospects of mankind and despairing of doing much about "the way of the world."[23] Like his Augustan predecessors, Murphy values good sense, derides man's inordinate pride, and warns about the vanity of human wishes.

Generally well-written in all editions, Murphy's essays on society, its conduct, and mores, show more style than originality, offer few surprises, and differ little from the customary fare of eighteenth-century social essayists. As he ranges over misconduct of writers and critics, fashionable excesses in dress, deceptive practices by lawyers and doctors, political chicanery, and the like, Murphy treads the general path of contemporary essayists. His vicious attack on the Jewish Nationalization Act of 1753 conveys more vehement anti-Semitism than theirs, but the difference is one of degree.[24] His treatment of women—making them appear simpletons in need of masculine protection, ridiculing their gambling weaknesses, scoffing at their susceptibility to French fashions—exceeds the number of comments in other journals, but it does not extend much beyond similar coverage in contemporary essays in the *Connoisseur.*[25] What Murphy's work does reveal is his insistently conservative approach to social change, his satiric inclination and his ability to respond to immediate issues in his society—all of which characterize his dramatic writing and particularly foreshadow his comedies.

Murphy's comments on literature and the theater also suggest his essential conservatism and prefigure his dramatic art. Consistent with his inherited Augustan values, Murphy carries on the ancient-modern controversy by asserting the superiority of antiquity. In 1754, 1756, and 1786, he lauds classical achievement and ridicules most contemporary practices. To be sure, Pope, Swift, and Addison are exceptions; his friend Christopher

Smart gains protective praise; Milton stands alongside Virgil,
although well beneath Homer; and Shakespeare ranks eminent
among dramatists. But while Murphy has good things to say about
Ben Jonson, Molière, Congreve, and Vanbrugh, he catalogues
most modern writers as tailors and cobblers, contrasts Aristotle
with the infamous John Hill, Socrates with the Methodist
preacher George Whitefield, Plato's Symposium with the club at
White's Coffee House. As in *News from Parnassus,* Murphy's
dramatic prelude of 1776, the ancient-modern controversy in the
Gray's Inn Journal provides a romp for the writers of classical
antiquity. Murphy's advice to authors is to follow the ancients,
for "those [who] have been accounted classic writers among the
moderns . . . have been most careful to form themselves upon
the *Greek* and *Roman* models."[26] He consistently insists on the
Horatian dictum of *dulce et utile.*

Not surprisingly, therefore, Murphy shows great respect for
genre theory and its attendant principles, a general compliance
to the rules for kinds. Like good eighteenth-century critics
generally, he is not foolish about slavish imitation or strict
adherence to a set of laws. He stresses the importance of
imagination and knows well enough that no one shall "arrive at
the heights of fame by painful vigils and the dint of labour and
application."[27] He warns that it is not enough to say that it is "the
law of *Aristotle,* this of *Horace,* that of *Longinus,* and a fourth
delivered by *Quintilian.*"[28] He recognizes that "one mode of
composition may encroach upon another. . . ."[29] Yet for all his
opposition to arbitrary application, he argues that "there is
scarce one [rule for writing] which may not be accounted for
upon principles of sound philosophy, and reasons drawn from the
constitution of the human mind."[30] Rules can be reasonable when
it is remembered that they emanate from "observations upon the
practices of great writers."[31] And Murphy sees the task of
criticism to discover "the boundaries of each kind," to find "the
peculiar merit of an *Epic Poem,* a *Tragedy,* or a *Comedy*" as well
as the "other subordinate branches of writing."[32]

Most interesting, of course, are Murphy's comments on the
theater and drama. They give clear evidence of his intense
concern even before he had established any formal connection
with the stage. They also suggest how early his principles, values,
and taste had developed and how consistent they were to
remain. No aspect of the theater failed to gain his attention.

He views the theater as both an index to taste and an important force in shaping it. Taste and morality are not separate entities so that appeals through spectacle, tightrope walkers, wire-dancers, and especially pantomime are moral as well as aesthetic sins. To banish Harlequin would make more room for Shakespeare, which ultimately would benefit the "Morals of the British People."[33] From 1754 through 1786, Murphy opposes corrupt theatrical practices that threaten the moral fiber of English theatergoers.

Murphy's remarks on acting proceed appropriately from his demands for instructive drama and lead easily to the relationship between acting and the kind of plays he was to write. To teach effectively, a play must offer fidelity in characterization. "We are interested," Murphy writes, "in the fortunes of persons, who resemble ourselves."[34] To render that resemblance, acting must be natural, and Murphy, who tailored his plays for the needs of the stage, considers the requisites for a good actor in those terms. He argues against false histrionics and artificialities in voice and manner. If "the chief business of actors [is] to express the emotions of the human heart," that can only be done "in as natural a manner, as if they were off the stage."[35] Murphy recognizes the importance of "Manner of Delivery, his Tone of Voice, the Cast of his Eye, his every Gesture and Attitude. . . ."[36] But these must be accomplished while the actor hides his art.

Assessing actors, Murphy uses naturalness as his standard. Good acting demands a combination of physical and mental talents. These come together in a Spranger Barry, Mrs. Cibber, and David Garrick. When Murphy praises Mrs. Pritchard and Mrs. Clive, it is for their ability to get into their roles and lose themselves. He is sensitive to the occasional overacting of Woodward, still guided by the old oratorical methods. Physical characteristics alone are not enough. To render a natural performance, to copy the manners and passions, these require understanding, taste, and sensibility.

For Murphy Garrick especially possessed these abilities. Throughout the three editions of his journal, Murphy lauded the actor-manager through whose efforts and "constant alliance with men of genius . . . the true spirit of dramatic poesy may again revive in this nation."[37] So strong was his support of Garrick that Murphy was unfairly accused of being in his employ and fought a duel to defend his reputation.[38] But Murphy's comments reveal no partisanship, particularly since he pays ample respect to the talent of Spranger Barry, Garrick's foremost rival. For Murphy Garrick truly deserved his stature because the naturalness in his acting allowed him to enter into the very souls of his characters, whether Richard III, Macbeth, or Lear, and to engage the passions of his audience in comedy as in tragedy.

Like his discussion of acting, Murphy's comments on dramatic genres are the attitudes and principles underlying his own plays. The dramatist who demanded that action emanate naturally from characterization and insisted upon verisimilitude or probability reviles the vogue for sentimental or pathetic comedy no less than the popularity of pantomime.[39] Whatever the comic type, "truth should be the foundation."[40] He thinks seriously about the principles of comedy. As in his Commonplace Book, Murphy's remarks in the journal aim at distinguishing wit from humor, burlesque from true comedy. He explores the sources of comedy—making use of Lockean psychology and Shaftesburian theory. His general didactic demand marks as well his expectation of comedy: the improvement of manners and the ridicule of folly. He notes the relationship between comic genius and the age in which it exists, and he deplores its sorry contemporary condition as compared to its virility in the Restoration, whose intellectual comedy Murphy was to use as his own model.[41]

Murphy's comments on tragedy, less numerous than those on comedy, also reflect the principles characterizing his own dramatic works. He insists again on instruction and morality. Tragedy "addresses itself to our humanity: It is the school of virtue, in which we examine the tender and the genuine affections."[42] He is convinced that a didactic purpose can be achieved solely through naturalness, whether in dialogue, setting, or characterization. Characterization, indeed, appears to be Murphy's key to effective drama, regardless of genre. How else can passions be "incited," Murphy asks. Surely, not through "the theatrical apparatus, the bowl, the dagger, the dungeon, or the clash of chains." If an audience is to be affected, it must be through "a faithful portrait of the mind."[43] For Murphy "florid imagery" will not do; "noise and rant [should] be banished." He argues for appropriate diction, objects to "talk in the stile of epigram," and warns against "a false glitter of words, and opposition of ideas."[44] Tragedy, Murphy insists, is produced by mental rather than physical suffering, and conflict should be produced from the feelings and thoughts of a character. His own tragedies often fall short of these ideals, but not for want of his trying.

All Murphy's comments on drama—his concern for moral instruction, his attitude toward the rules and imagination, and his demand for naturalness arising from characterization—come together in his criticism of Shakespeare and his defense of the English playwright against the wrong-headed attacks of Voltaire.[45] Murphy's own dramatic practices were hardly infallible, but he knew well what to value in a play, and he was a most perceptive reader. Before his contemporaries, Murphy recognized some serious misreadings of crucial Shakespearean passages. He cites the need to stress *one red* in "making the green one red" so that the sense should be *"one entire universal red"* in the famous lines from *Macbeth.* On Iago's comment to Roderigo, "I have rubbed this gnat,"[46] Murphy argues against Warburton's reading, supports Theobald's objection, and then provides the correct word, *quat* or *quot,* "a small heat or pimple," which when rubbed becomes "hot and angry." Murphy's interpretation was adopted without acknowledgment by Johnson, who regarded him as a "very judicious critic."[47]

More importantly, Murphy recognized where Shakespeare's real powers lay. If Shakespeare "was not versed in *Aristotle's* art of poetry; . . . he had what was better than art; a genius superior to all mankind."[48] "Nature was *Shakespear's* guide."[49] He was "almost the only poet who has excelled in a masterly power of striking the *imagination,* the *heart,* and our *reason,* all at once."[50] There is praise enough for Shakespeare's poetry in itself, but also recognition of his singular ability "of inserting Poetical Description in the most serious Part of his Drama, with Propriety."[51] That propriety, Murphy knows, comes from the naturalness with which Shakespeare's dramas emerge from characterization—Murphy's own ideal. Whether in comedy or tragedy, "no poet ever understood nature better in the operation of the passions,"[52] and if "the first great Instance of a Dramatic Genius consists in the Formation of Characters," Shakespeare is "unrivalled."[53] It is that strength of characterization that allows Shakespeare to be instructive, to stress morals through tragedy and evoke laughter at absurdity and folly. All this may now seem commonplace in Shakespearean criticism, but Murphy was writing without benefit of the scholarship later critics could depend on; he was among those pioneers who were shifting from "'general criticism' to the [particular] examination of characters and motives."[54]

Nothing in Murphy's journalistic writing matches his achievement in the *Gray's Inn Journal,* and, alongside it, most of Murphy's periodical writing in the 1750s is insignificant, the work of a journeyman in letters who later refused to acknowledge his authorship. If he contributed to Fielding's *Covent-Garden Journal* (1752),[55] his role was menial, important only for advancing his career. If, as seems possible, he wrote the twelve numbers of the *Entertainer* in 1754,[56] the effort was inferior, worth noting only as a sign of his professional interest in the theater. He probably contributed to the *Universal Visiter [sic]* (1756) and perhaps to the *Student* (1751) out of friendship for their editor, Christopher Smart,[57] and he certainly reviewed Burke's essay on the sublime and may have supplied a few more articles for the *Literary Magazine* (1756-58) when his friend Johnson was ill.[58]

Not so a series of articles entitled "The Theatre," which has been ascribed to Murphy on the basis of strong external and internal evidence. Perhaps fifty of the essays in Robert Dodsley's *London Chronicle* from 1757 through 1758 are Murphy's—the first "informed, fair, sometimes brilliant [dramatic] criticism" to appear in an English newspaper.[59] Concerned primarily with current performances, the essays introduced a new mode of criticism, going beyond customary plot summary to acute evaluation of the production. "The Theatre" emphasizes precisely those values that characterize Murphy's own plays and expresses the taste and prejudices that mark his interests throughout his long connection with the stage. The criticism rests on the naturalness and decency that Murphy always demanded in drama. It calls for truthful characterization and the emergence of plot from character, the staples of Murphy's own plays. His distaste for sentimentalism, for the excesses of pantomime; his preference for classical unity rather than the hybrid forms of tragicomedy—these were his views throughout his career, and they are the basis of the criticism in the *London Chronicle.* Acutely attuned to the demands of theatrical performances, aware of the acting techniques that Garrick had introduced, sensitive to the changes in the theater itself, the essays represent a major contribution to the dramatic criticism of the eighteenth century.

Murphy may have engaged in other literary journalism after 1758, but, until his virtual retirement as a dramatist, nothing can safely be ascribed to him. From July 1786 to June 1798, however, he emerged as a leading contributor to the *Monthly Review.*[60] While covering poetry, law, biography, aesthetics, and even novels, he was clearly the *Monthly's* expert on Samuel Johnson and its foremost dramatic critic.

Even before writing his own essay on Johnson's life, Murphy had come to regard himself as the chief defender of his friend's posthumous reputation. Let a writer try to capitalize on Johnson's public image of cantankerousness, and Murphy provides the necessary correctives and counterarguments. When the author is Sir John Hawkins, Johnson's "official" biographer and first editor, Murphy is more vitriolic and more detailed in his defense. How dare a man who pretends to be "the guardian of [Johnson's] fame" write so mean-spirited and wrong-headed an account of the great man's life and writings? Repeatedly Murphy corrects Hawkins's errors of fact, misattributions, and one-sided, unbalanced view of Johnson's character. Murphy rails against what he considers Hawkins's fatuousness and his insinuations about and censure of the man who had been their common friend. He contrasts Hawkins's work with the skillful presentation of Boswell in his *Tour to the Hebrides* and twice recommends Hester Thrale Piozzi's anecdotes and Johnson's own biographies as models that the ill-tempered Hawkins would have done well to follow. For Mrs. Thrale's *Letters to and from Samuel Johnson, Ll. D.*, Murphy has particular praise because "the caricature of Sir John Hawkins may now give way to a better picture. . . ."[61]

While the Johnson reviews are most expressive, those on drama are most numerous. At times Murphy wrote four to six in a single number, the entire "Monthly Catalogue" section on the subject, discussing comedy, tragedy, and the state of the theater. He is the practical dramatist whose values are those of good commonsensical criticism of the late eighteenth century. He recognizes the importance of production and the effect of Garrick, and he differentiates between the printed text and its possibilities as a theatrical script. He scorns bad theater managers who have pandered to the worst taste and offered the most fashionable nonsense.

Common sense governs Murphy's judgment. However much he admires the rules, he warns "the critic not to adopt, with superstition, rules of the drama, merely because they are in Aristotle. . . . [They are] not fundamental, but adapted entirely to the structure of ancient drama." He will not choose between domestic tragedy and heroic because *"whatever is best written is best."*[62] Shakespeare is Murphy's prime example; his achievement in freeing English theater from classical restraints draws repeated praise and defense against Voltaire's obdurate criticism. Murphy asks that a play be plausible, regardless of genre. Let it be an imitation of life and manners; let the dialogue be natural and unstrained; let the action, the fable, arise appropriately from the characters, and let the characters themselves be truly delineated. Such values expressed in Murphy's criticism were the object in his dramatic writing—not always successfully achieved, but, nonetheless, his constant goal.

III   *Political Journalism*

Murphy's political, unlike his literary, journalism was confined to his earlier career. Alert to immediate and future advantages, Murphy willingly undertook the writing of two essay-sheet periodicals during the Seven Years' War, the *Test* in the service of Henry Fox and the *Auditor* in the cause of John Stuart, Earl of Bute. Neither work betrayed Murphy's principles, and both men repaid his labor with favors of their own. After Murphy was denied entrance as a law student by the Middle Temple and Gray's Inn, Fox gained his admission to Lincoln's Inn. In Murphy's serious disputes with Garrick, Fox again interceded on his behalf. Lord Bute, among other kindnesses to Murphy, acted upon his and others' requests for a government pension to their friend Samuel Johnson.

Yet Murphy, desiring in his *Works* to leave his best image to posterity, tried to suppress his connection with such political writing. His judgment was practical rather than aesthetic. He had learned from experience the effects of partisanship on a writer's reputation. Fox himself, a shrewd politician, had warned Murphy not to dedicate *The Orphan of China* to him. However, his advice that Murphy dedicate the play to Lord Bute, together with Murphy's later work on the *Auditor,* whatever its immediate benefits, ultimately brought Murphy enormous difficulty in the theater. Well after his last political essay in 1763, his plays were subjected to rough treatment because of his earlier party affiliations.[63] Omitting the essay-journals from his collected works, Murphy sought a fairer hearing from future audiences than he had received from contemporaries.

In fact, Murphy's political writing, while not in Swift's class, is most respectable. Intelligent and witty, clear and pointed, it served its purposes as well as circumstances allowed, and, at times, rises above the general level of polemical essays. The *Test* was written for Fox, ousted from office with the Newcastle administration after the disastrous Minorcan campaign at the outset of the Seven Years' War. In its thirty-five numbers, from 6 November 1756 to 9 July 1757, Murphy's job was to explain away the deficiencies of Newcastle's ministry, to place the blame for Minorca on the unfortunate, and later executed, Admiral Byng, the commander, and to undermine the new leadership of William Pitt in the ministry he shared with William Legge.[64]

Despite limitations of having to write to Fox's order, Murphy presents a vigorous defense of his cause. Byng's failure at Minorca provides a central point of attack, since the admiral's culpability relieved the Newcastle ministry of direct responsibility. Murphy relentlessly pursues Byng's guilt, whether cowardice or carelessness, and describes efforts to save his life as politically motivated plots. He argues that the administration had no way of knowing that a man of Byng's distinguished family background could have behaved without honor.

Important as the Byng affair was for Murphy's (or Fox's) practical purposes, other arguments in the *Test* more clearly reveal Murphy's fundamentally conservative political philosophy. In the final number, he declares his object to have been "to stand up for the prerogative of the crown, . . . to oppose the democratic faction of a giddy populace. . . ."[65] At a time when party labels were less meaningful than personal loyalties and stands on political issues, he portrays himself as a descendant of the old Whigs, but these particular points he makes suggest his moderate Toryism. Fear of democratic fervor and opposition to England's German alliances were positions that suited Fox's immediate purposes, but they are the constant basis of all Murphy's own political judgments, and he had no difficulty in returning to them later in the war when he was engaged by Bute to argue the peace terms in the *Auditor.*

From a strictly literary point of view, the *Test* bears evidence of Murphy's developing artistic talent. At its best, the essay-sheet makes use of his dramatic ability, his aptitude for farce. Number 24, particularly, deftly plays out an episode in which the key political figures in the controversy—Pitt, William Beckford, and Lord Temple—are ridiculed through a pastiche composed of speeches drawn from a variety of Shakespeare's works. The technique suggests Murphy's earliest successes in the London theater, and the essay ranks with some of Murphy's previous work in the *Gray's Inn Journal*.[66] His literary merit throughout the *Test* is obvious, his style and manner of argument superior to those of his accomplished rival polemicist, Owen Ruffhead, in the *Con-Test*, and his achievement not one to be ashamed of on purely aesthetic grounds.

Aesthetically, if not politically, the *Auditor* is an even more successful venture in journalism, but its purposes were no less tied to the practical concerns emanating from the Seven Years' War. Lord Bute, the unpopular Scottish prime minister and advisor to King George III, had been called upon to bring the war to conclusion and negotiate a satisfactory peace, an imposing task. Having replaced William Pitt at the peak of his popularity, Bute could do no right. A peace that returned any of Pitt's conquered territory would arouse cries of surrender, and yet the French were unlikely to yield to the harsh demands of Pitt's supporters. Meanwhile, every victory of the British and their German allies increased insistence on a hard peace; yet any loss that might have made easier terms more acceptable brought charges of ministerial inefficiency.

Bute needed political propagandists to support his aims and promote his image. To counter the efforts of the *Monitor*, an essay-sheet representing the expansionist interests of the City businessmen, he turned to Tobias Smollett, novelist, editor, and fellow Scotsman, who produced the *Briton*. The opposition responded with the most effective political journal in British history, the ironically named *North Briton*, written primarily by the notorious John Wilkes and the equally infamous Charles Churchill, the best satirical poet of the age. Smollett was in trouble, and Bute quickly turned to Murphy for reinforcement.

Murphy's *Auditor* appeared on 10 June 1762 and ran for thirty-seven numbers until 8 February 1763.[67] Attempting to make palatable an unattractive peace and unpopular minister, he had no more chance of success than Smollett had. Like Smollett, he was an outsider to the true-blue English partisans. Like

Smollett, too, he was given little inside information on the actual peace negotiations, so that he sometimes found himself arguing for terms the government had abandoned, and, even when his services were terminated, he had no advance notice. His denigration of Pitt, his minimizing of contributions by Frederick the Great of Prussia, these had no possibility of appealing to a populace heady with victory. His arguments left the public with a choice between two unappealing images of itself: either it could see its demands as a sign of its own avariciousness and madness or it could regard itself as dupes of leaders working for selfish interests.

Yet the *Auditor,* for all its practical ineffectiveness, is a well-written propaganda sheet. Wilkes himself "balanced a hundred *Auditors* against a thousand *Britons.*"[68] With considerable vitality, Murphy employs those literary devices that had become conventional in eighteenth-century political journalism. Using historical allegory or parallels, he dwarfs his enemies by comparisons with English or classical personages. Reveries, parodies, mock letters provide commentary on political events. The innocent point of view of "foreign observers" or primitives— American savages, Chinese philosophers, Cherokee kings—comments ironically on the practices of Murphy's opponents. Murphy scores the diction, punctuation, spelling, and style of his literary enemies. While none of these is original, Murphy manages it all with a verve that displays his skill as a political writer well above the average.

As in the *Test,* Murphy does not have to compromise his conservative principles in the *Auditor.* He had always believed in the king's prerogative, order, and subordination. Throughout the war, he had opposed the German connection and consistently rejected expansionist arguments raised by trade and commercial interests. It is easy for him to assume the stance of public defender and the Horatian voice of disinterested authority for he honestly regards himself on the side of God and country, legitimacy and order, and he genuinely fears subversion, those who would "throw an entire people into divisions, and thereby threaten danger to the state."[69]

Yet issues and principles prove no more the main interest of the *Auditor* than of any other polemical journal of the time. Personalities dominate, and *ad hominem* attacks characterize the essays of all the participants, Murphy included. In the name

of politics, his opponents ridicule his Irish ancestry, Jesuit
education, playwriting, and acting. For Murphy, Churchill,
Robert Lloyd, and Wilkes, stand as exemplars of tastelessness
and immorality: a hypocritical preacher, a green-room gossip,
and a bawdy parodist of the *Essay on Man*. Wilkes, whose
physical ugliness was an especially inviting target, stands
condemned as "John Squintum," a purveyor of *"squint-eyed
calumny."*[70] Not content with berating Wilkes's politics as
bordering on sedition, Murphy charges him with personal
misconduct, repeating an unfounded anecdote about Wilkes's
intimidation of a nobleman's child in order to get to the boy's
father. Such behavior was inconsistent with Wilkes's character,
despite Murphy's charges about the politician's extravagance
and moral decadence, but for Murphy all that could serve in the
political struggle finds its way into the pages of the *Auditor*.

In the give and take of such personal vituperation, Murphy
shows no disadvantage. He truly faltered only once. Having to
defend his patron's willingness to yield part of the conquest,
Murphy sought to exploit the value of what was to be retained.
Knowing this, his opponents sent a letter, signed "Viator,"
describing the worth of Florida as a colony whose peat bogs
offered a major source of fuel that could contribute handsomely
to trade with the West Indies. Murphy snatched the opportunity
to celebrate the values of such a conquest, and the *North Briton,
St. James's Chronicle*, and *Lloyd's Evening Post*, all conducted by
his antagonists, made the most of his folly.[71]

Although temporarily embarrassing, the episode did not cause
his ultimate suppression of his political writings in his *Works*. A
realistic concern for his reputation did. If the *Test* and *Auditor*
provided him with immediate advantages, they also had a
deleterious effect on his work for the theater. From 1763 to
1767, and even as late as 1773, Murphy's engagement in politics
influenced both his reputation as a playwright and his theatrical
success as his political enemies continued their vendetta against
him.[72] That alone would account for his desire to forget his
polemical journalism, while, for the image he hoped to present to
posterity, his work for the politicians, no matter how respectable
as journalism, could hardly have enhanced his fame.

IV   *Biographies*

Not altogether apart from his journalism were Murphy's three biographical works, written with some sense of topicality about three of his major contemporaries: Fielding, Johnson, and Garrick. His first was *An Essay on the Life and Genius of Henry Fielding, Esq.*, an introduction to the author's works, in 1762. Judged solely as biography, it has serious defects. Murphy is vague on details and careless of specifics. He can hardly have been concerned with dates since he offers only two in the entire essay. Working mainly from his own impressions of a man he had known for a few short years, relying upon anecdotes from colleagues who often had them secondhand, and reluctant to search for materials beyond his immediate grasp, Murphy was no model for later scholarly biographers.

But Murphy's essay cannot properly be evaluated by such standards. Its intention is to introduce Fielding's writings, and its main thrust is critical, not biographical. Murphy seeks, like Johnson in his *Lives of the Poets*, to fix upon those characteristics of the man that helped to account for his creative effort: "the principal features of [Fielding's] mind . . . ; . . . his temper . . . as he transformed [it] into his writings . . ."(7).[73]

If, like most eighteenth-century critics, Murphy regarded an author's character as the shaping force behind his creations, he was working at a decided disadvantage with Fielding. Even eight years after Fielding's death, rumors and gossip were vicious. Murphy, at least, seeks to revise the ugly portrait. Aware that "the curious" among his readers desired gruesome details and spicy tidbits, Murphy refuses to "insult his memory with an unnecessary detail of his distresses, and the actions which resulted from them; to infer the character of his heart from the overflowings of sudden and momentary passions . . ."(7). Murphy could not be expected to reverse contemporary opinion of the man, but his intention, despite some unfortunate effects of his essay,[74] was to put Fielding in the best light and to explain his artistic achievement.

Murphy regards Fielding's character as both beneficial and detrimental to his work. He admires Fielding's "resolution" and "spiritual magnanimity," and he remarks on Fielding's ability to maintain a balanced perspective even after the adversities of his early years (10). If he attributes weaknesses in Fielding's writings to lack of discipline in his youth, to the demands put upon an impecunious author, and to the aggravations and misfortunes of maturity, Murphy also notes the strength that Fielding's work derived from personal anguish. Perceptively, Murphy relates

Fielding's worldly experience to his understanding of men and manners and to his satiric attacks on "vanity," "hypocrisy," and "affectation" (22-23).

Rather sententiously, Murphy exaggerates Fielding's extravagance, dissipations, impetuous nature, and lack of refinement. But Murphy was writing from commitment to the didactic standards and decorum of his age, and Fielding, neither in his life nor work, offered a model of male virtue. Moreover, Murphy's general depiction of Fielding's life and character is not inaccurate. Nobody, including Sir John Fielding, raised a voice about his account's having served his subject poorly. Wrong in particulars, Murphy is accurate overall, and on Fielding's temperament, especially, his remarks differ only in emphasis, not in kind, from modern estimates.

Out of his biographical sketch, Murphy develops a critical evaluation of Fielding's work that remarkably foreshadows modern assessments.[75] If Murphy dismisses Fielding's poetry as unworthy of serious consideration, what later critic could quarrel with his judgment? His evaluation of Fielding's journalism seems equally accurate. For Murphy the genre itself is essentially ephemeral. He cannot regard the hack work, unrevised and unpolished, as serious literature. Yet he does justice to Fielding's more important essays, comparing the *True Patriot* favorably with the political journalism of Addison and Swift and praising parts of the *Covent Garden Journal* as belonging to the same order as the *Tatler* and *Spectator*.

Murphy's appraisal of Fielding's dramas is equally intelligent and knowledgeable. Aware of the realities of writing for the stage, he recognizes the demands placed upon a dramatist that lead to hasty production. He knows, too, the value that fine acting can lend to the performances of pieces that prove less satisfactory in the closet. Although he himself was making his reputation with farces, he refuses to regard them as works "of a higher nature" (14). Murphy does not hesitate to praise Fielding for whatever he finds attractive in his plays. For the news-hungry character in *The Coffee-house Politician*, later adapted in his own *The Upholsterer*, he has kind words, but not so laudatory as his comments on *The Tragedy of Tragedies*, which he describes as "replete with as fine parody as, perhaps, has ever been written" (15). Murphy's overall assessment of Fielding as dramatist seems unexceptionable. Fielding, he says in summary, "did not attain to pre-eminence in this branch of writing," but his works being those of a "genius" "occasionally display the talent of a master" (11).

Alongside that of his contemporaries, Murphy's criticism of Fielding's novels is remarkable. Judgment was so unsettled on even their relative merits that the reviewer in the *Critical*, perhaps Smollett himself, places *Joseph Andrews* above *Tom Jones*.[76] Murphy praises *Jonathan Wild*, particularly its didacticism, but sees it as merely a prelude to Fielding's major works. *Joseph Andrews* approaches "high excellence," but *Tom Jones* "has fairly bore away the palm" (35) while *Amelia* has its "marks of genius, but of a genius beginning to fall into its decay" (45).

On particular points, Murphy judges shrewdly. He recognizes that, in *Joseph Andrews*, "Fielding . . . was employed in the very province for which his talents were peculiarly and happily formed; namely, the fabulous narration of some imagined action, which did occur, or might probably have occurred in human life" (36). Murphy singles out the character of Parson Adams as Fielding's major achievement in the work. He perceives, however, that the scope of the novel is too restricted for "perfection" (37). He accurately compares *Tom Jones* with the epic, and long before the point was conceded, he identifies the unity of its plot. He notes the admirable variety in its characterization, "drawn with truth and humor," conveying "the very manners which belong to it in human life" (41). With good critical insight, Murphy focuses on the role of Fielding's authorial voice and identifies the appropriateness of the novel's language to its fictional purpose. Of a work whose merits were still being debated, Murphy unhesitatingly declares "We shall find it standing the test of the severest criticism, and indeed bearing away the envied praise of a complete performance" (39). If Murphy's metaphorical comparison of the three major works to the progress of the sun is too high-flown, the judgments underlying the image remain impeccable.

His writing itself, however, is not altogether satisfactory. Too much of the essay proves digressive for modern, if not eighteenth-century, taste. Yet the discursiveness raises points that reveal much about Murphy and the aesthetic developments in England after 1750. For example, Fielding's relationship to the Licensing Act of 1737 allows Murphy to discuss censorship, and his remarks suggest the blend of his conservative political

instincts and his large store of common sense. He finds Walpole's
Licensing Act far too sweeping, a threat to liberty. Still, he
himself sets limits indicative of his pyrrhonistic fear of change.
True liberty, he believes, permits action which "shall not injure
the civil and religious institutions of the state, nor be deemed
invasive of the peace and welfare of our fellow-subjects" (13).

Another of Murphy's digressions—his comments on genius,
particularly invention—shows a similar conservatism, but at the
same time reflects the aesthetic developments in the latter part
of the century. Although reluctant to emphasize the importance
of invention to genius, he cannot hide the attraction that the
subject holds for him, and his discussion of invention foreshadows
Coleridge's distinction between fancy and imagination. For
Murphy invention has two faculties: "one, primary and original,
which can associate images never before combined; the other,
secondary and subordinate, which can find out for those ideas,
which had been assembled before, a new place, a new order, and
arrangement, with new embellishments of the most harmonious
and exalted language" (19). Throughout his remarks, Murphy is
greatly indebted to Locke for his distinctions, but his particular
expression and examples suggest the transition between Locke's
discussion of the imagination and the very different conception
that finally emerged at the end of the century.

In all, Murphy's essay, while important for advancing his own
career, [77] had the desired effect of establishing Fielding as a
major author.[78]   According to the standards of the day, the
edition itself was conscientious and remained the standard text
for the next century. Diligently attempting to present Fielding in
the best light, Murphy himself revised it in 1783.[79]

Like his work on Fielding, Murphy's *An Essay on the Life and
Genius of Samuel Johnson, Ll. D.* was a bookseller's job. Called
upon for an edition of Johnson's works with an introductory
essay, Murphy reluctantly accepted, piqued because the publishers had given Sir John Hawkins priority in the field. Yet, once
engaged, Murphy worked at a furious pace to complete his task
and was so successful that the edition, after its first publication
on May 12, 1792, was reprinted fifteen times by 1824 and
appeared as late as 1850. The essay itself was issued separately in
1792 and 1793.[80]

The edition depended heavily upon Hawkins's of 1787–89 [81]
but Murphy's achievement lay in the prefatory essay. In the

thirty years since his work on Fielding, Murphy had matured as a writer, and his essay is "a distinguished example of late Augustan critical biography."[82] Actually, it is no more a modern biography than the Fielding work. Despite his correcting factual errors in Hawkins and Boswell, he offers some of his own, and he aims less at recording Johnson's life than presenting the man's general characteristics as they reflect his moral and literary achievement. Like Johnson, Murphy believed that the "landmarks" of a writer's biography are to "be found in his works" (54, 48).[83]

Resembling his life of Fielding in this respect, Murphy's essay on Johnson differs in tone and attitude. Johnson is a model of decorum, his writings an exemplar, his values the paragon of human virtue. Enraged by Hawkins's account, distrustful of Boswell's particularizing methods, Murphy is determined to do justice to Johnson, "performing the last human office to the memory of a friend, whom he loved, esteemed, and honoured" (189 ff.).[84] He views his task as didactic, since "the best part of [biography's] function . . . is to instruct mankind by examples taken from the school of life" (116). By no means should this mean ignoring the truth, but with Johnson, Murphy obviously felt that he had nothing to worry about because an honest presentation would constitute, in Johnson's own terms, "a moral document," one to edify mankind.[85]

Murphy acknowledges Johnson's weaknesses, but either minimizes their importance or turns them to advantage. Lacking the "exteriors of politeness"(140), Johnson had the more important virtue of honesty. Gruff in manner, "a stranger to the arts of polite conversation, [and somewhat] uncouth, vehement, and vociferous" (50), he was charitable, kind, and soft-hearted. For those who might regard Johnson's melancholy as a sign of his questionable faith, Murphy presents a description of his deathbed struggle, intended to convey the impression of Addisonian assuredness about how a Christian should die.[86] For Murphy, Johnson's life itself offered the epitome of good Christian conduct.

Much of Murphy's essay responds directly to those whose Johnsoniana malevolently dredged up the author's idiosyncrasies. Hawkins led the field. "Professing to be Johnson's friend, that biographer has raised more objections to his character, than all the enemies of that excellent man" (125). Whether explaining the value of Johnson's interest in chemistry or taking on the less

pleasant task of accounting for Johnson's having been duped by
Lauder's infamous forgeries of Milton, Murphy passionately
defends him from what he regards as Hawkins's mean-spirited
calumnies. This defense, in fact, accounts for Murphy's tone,
which is more intimate, more self-consciously insistent on the
writer's relationship to his subject than anything in Boswell's
biography. When Murphy notes Johnson's humor, the point
stands with the authority gained through friendship. His
refutation of Hawkins's account of Johnson's acceptance of a
pension from Lord Bute comes through his personal understanding of the circumstances. For his interpretation of Johnson's
character, for his evaluation of Johnson's melancholy—perhaps
Murphy's major contribution in the work—Murphy appeals to
the reader on the basis of authoritative intimate knowledge, a
sympathetic comprehension which he suggests does not exist in
Hawkins's biography.

Intending his portrait of Johnson to provide an example of
"piety, . . . kind affections, and . . . goodness of . . . heart, . . .
worthy of imitation" (190), Murphy sees Johnson's writing as
serving a similar purpose. Studying Johnson's work, Murphy says,
"authors may learn to grace their style with elegance, harmony,
and precision; they may be taught to think with vigour and
perspicuity; and, to crown the whole, by a diligent attention to
these books all may advance in virtue" (191). Murphy finds little
to disagree with in Johnson's aesthetic values. The congeniality
of their tastes had its basis in a love of classicism, a conservative
response to change, and a high regard for the moral qualities of
literature.

Murphy's literary judgments are shrewd and not simply
encomiastic. He praises the poetic qualities of Johnson's *Irene*,
but, as a knowledgeable playwright, understands its dramatic
limitations. In Johnson's play, Murphy says, "the sentiments are
beautiful, always happily expressed, but seldom appropriate to
the character, and generally too philosophic." The "splendid
language and melodious numbers will make a fine poem, not a
tragedy" (155). Murphy praises *Rasselas* for its "splendour of
eloquence" (168), finds its strength in its "pictures of life, and
profound moral reflection" (167), but acknowledges that
Johnson's interests were not those of a novelist whose purpose it
is to "keep curiosity awake by the artifice of unexpected
incidents" (167). Even Murphy's laudatory comments on the

Rambler wisely connect its sometimes laborious language to the work Johnson was doing on his *Dictionary*.[87]

Yet Murphy's faultfinding is minimal—just sufficient to give greater credence to his praise. For Murphy, Johnson had the makings of a great poet, who, "if he had devoted himself to the Muses, . . . would have been the rival of Pope" (151). The evidence was in *Irene,* the sharp social satire of *London,* but most particularly in the *Vanity of Human Wishes,* where Johnson had excelled Dryden's translation of Juvenal and had approached "nearest to the spirit of the original" (151-52). Johnson's *Dictionary,* according to Murphy, is "the MOUNT ATLAS of English literature," and the conclusion of its "Preface" has the "force of the pathetic and sublime" to move any man of sensibility (169). Not greatly enthusiastic about Johnson's editing of Shakespeare, Murphy admires his commentaries and calls the "Preface" "a tract of great erudition and philosophical criticism" (169-70). Johnson's travel book, *Journey to the Western Islands of Scotland,* Murphy labels "a model for such as shall hereafter relate their travels" and recognizes its particular quality as focusing on "men and manners, modes of life, and the progress of civilization" (172).

Murphy properly fixes upon the *Rambler* and the *Lives of the Poets,* Johnson's major achievements. Despite Murphy's general disdain for the genre, he recognizes that Johnson was no ordinary periodical essayist. He compares Johnson's essays with those of Addison, and while he finds Addison's graceful and charming, a safer "model for imitation," he is awed by the fact that "Johnson is always profound." Murphy knows that Johnson's methods, which forced his readers to "the fatigue of thinking," cost him popularity, but that takes nothing away from his greatness. For Murphy, the *Rambler* made Johnson the "great moral teacher of his countrymen" (158), and Murphy accurately predicted its importance to Johnson's later literary reputation.[88]

For Murphy, however, Johnson's greatest accomplishment was in the *Lives of the Poets,* "the most brilliant, and certainly the most popular of all [his] writings" (174). Murphy devotes more than one-third of his discussion of Johnson's work to the subject. Whatever his small differences with Johnson—particularly on Johnson's overzealous religious treatment of Pope's *Essay on Man*—Murphy clearly shares his aesthetic and political sympathies. Along with Johnson, he opposes the "false wit" and

"Gothic taste" of Abraham Cowley and the Metaphysical poets after John Donne. For Murphy, as for Johnson, "they took pains to bewilder themselves, and were ingenious for no other purpose than to err" (175). To be sure, Murphy does not agree on all of Johnson's judgments. He is more generous with Gray and especially regrets Johnson's unfavorable comments on Prior.

Still, he refuses to acknowledge any malignity in Johnson's criticism. Despite Johnson's known prejudices, Murphy insists that Johnson's life of Swift was "executed with temper and moderation" (177). And for that most crucial of Johnson's judgments, his treatment of Milton, Murphy proves Johnson's staunchest defender. It is the longest single part of Murphy's evaluation, and the defense comes largely from Murphy's common political bond with Johnson. For Murphy, as for Johnson, Milton's politics are abhorrent. Murphy adds to Johnson's attack on Milton's republicanism; he berates Milton's hypocritical conduct, and he finally links him with the regicides of the Puritan usurpers of the royal powers. In his long defense, Murphy clearly indicates those affinities with Johnson's political and aesthetic principles that make his essay on Johnson a very different kind of work from the one on Fielding. With Fielding, Murphy had to find reasons for admiring a man whose principles made him uneasy; with Johnson, as their long friendship suggests, he was most comfortable.

Murphy's final biography, published in 1801, is the work of an old man, perhaps relying too much on a flawed memory, sometimes garrulous and digressive, too often dependent on unacknowledged sources.[89] Yet *The Life of David Garrick, Esq.*, like Murphy's earlier biographies, has an interest other than biographical. Whatever its numerous faults, the work provides an insider's view of eighteenth-century theatrical history, a guide to Murphy's ideas on drama, and an index to his concerns as a playwright.

For Murphy, Garrick is the key to the revolutionary change that took place in the English theaters during his lifetime. Murphy's concern "is the history of Garrick in his profession" (II, 15).[90] Throughout the biography, the actor-manager disappears into his productions, which in turn provides opportunities for comments on the plays themselves, performances, and general discussions of drama and dramatists. Murphy sees in Garrick—his personality and his roles as actor, theater-manager, and author—

a figure around whom an interesting account of eighteenth-century dramatic history may be written.

To be sure, Murphy must deal with Garrick's character to explain his impact on theatrical change. From personal experience he knew Garrick's vices and must have had difficulty in suppressing his personal resentments after the long series of battles they had fought through the years.[91] Yet he minimizes Garrick's most grievous fault, his "love of fame" (II, 13), and lessens the antagonism of his tone in the biography by noting Garrick himself was most victimized by his ruling passion. Instead, Murphy emphasizes Garrick's generosity to playwrights and actors. His willingness to put "his pen at the service of his friends" (II, 144), his support for impoverished authors, his concern for "the welfare of the actors" (II, 127) — all those things which characterized Garrick as "the generous protector of a profession" (II, 128) make understandable his ability to weld together acting companies that under his direction revolutionized drama, giving it a "life and animation" that had all but expired in English theaters in the middle of the eighteenth century (II, 21ff.).

Whatever personal difficulties Murphy had to overcome in dealing with Garrick the man as being of pivotal importance to the eighteenth-century theater, he could be fully at ease with Garrick in his role as actor, theater-manager, and to a lesser extent as author. "As an actor," Murphy writes, "[Garrick] was, with good reason, the idol of the people . . ." (I, 369). He recognizes Garrick's acting genius, its characteristics, and its importance in changing theatrical fashions. Murphy's sole difficulty, as he well knew, is to convey in print "a genius [that] it is necessary . . . should be seen, heard, and felt" (II, 174). How to display those talents of an "actor, who could play before the deaf and dumb, and make them capable"? *"His face was a language!"* (II, 186).

Still, Murphy fixes precisely upon what it was that made Garrick not only the preeminent actor of his age, but the transformer of acting style itself. Murphy describes Garrick's ability to enter a role; he sees that "the power of his imagination was such, that he transformed himself into the very man . . ." (I, 23). The measure of difference between Garrick and his predecessors in the theater was his ability to turn histrionics into natural responses to his characters' situations, and Murphy properly focuses upon Garrick's achievement of "reality." "His look, his voice, his attitude changed with every sentiment" (I, 23). Where other performers concentrated primarily on oratory, Garrick moved out of his characters' innermost feelings. His psychological understanding of his roles led to a more naturalistic theatrical expression, a proximity—as much as the stage allows—to genuine experience.

Garrick's contributions as theater-manager draw equal praise. Forgetting his own battles over money with Garrick, Murphy proclaims, "it was with him a fixed principle that authors were intitled to the emolument of their labours . . ." (II, 171). He raises Garrick to a pedestal; his impending retirement is "a gloomy prospect. The manager, who, during a space of thirty years, had conducted the public entertainment, is on the point of abdicating" (II, 124). Murphy's Garrick is the defender of the faith against the French infidel Voltaire, who had vainly "employed his pen to depreciate the genius of such a poet as Shakespeare; it was in vain that he charged him with monstrous farces; in vain he took upon him to deny all dramatic genius to the English nation" (II, 167). At home the monarch of the theaters had made it his duty "to give variety to the public entertainments" (I, 370), but, more importantly, he had not done so at the expense of values, but instead had "corrected the public taste . . . made the stage the school of virtue and useful knowledge" (II, 164).

Murphy's acclaim for Garrick's achievement accurately evaluates Garrick's contribution by contrasting his management of Drury Lane with that of Covent Garden. At the latter, under Rich, entertainment was assigned to *"Lum* and *Harlequin,"* and then under Beard the theater became an "opera house," terms of opprobrium in Murphy's time.[92] Meanwhile, under Garrick's reign, "Drury-Lane was the seat of the muses. Dramatic poetry was universally in vogue . . ." (II, 172). Pandering to public taste, Covent Garden had sunk into an "abject condition" and had become incapable of producing a good play; its ruling passion was "a general apostacy from good sense . . ." (II, 158). At Garrick's Drury Lane, "dramatic poetry retrieved its honour"; "a new aera opened on mankind." Garrick offered "a just representation of nature" and brought Shakespeare "as it were, from his tomb" (II, 161ff.). "Our great reformer of the stage banished rant and noise, and the swell of unnatural elocution from tragedy, and buffoonery from comedy," restoring "a true taste and manly relish for moral and instructive composition . . ." (II, 163).

Dealing with Garrick's writing—his own plays and adaptations of earlier works—Murphy discusses much of the stage history of the period and reveals his own dramatic values. Murphy's highest praise for Garrick's original composition is in an account of Garrick's various prologues and epilogues, which he compares to those of Dryden, exempt from Dryden's licentiousness. On Garrick's adaptations, Murphy is less favorable because he is generally disturbed by the contemporary practice of "retouching the works of their predecessors." Although Murphy approves of Garrick's removal of bawdy material from Restoration plays, he regards the overall revisions as a lack of "veneration for the best writers of the last century," which "does no honour to [Garrick's] memory" (II, 37). With Garrick's version of *Hamlet*, later to be parodied in a posthumously published play by Murphy, he expresses dismay at "the rage for retouching, and . . . correcting and improving our best authors." Murphy calls it "the very error of the times," lamenting that Garrick "was infected with the contagion" when "he lopped, pruned, and cut away . . . and instead of a flourishing tree, left a withered trunk" (II, 82-83). For Murphy, Garrick's removal of the gravediggers from *Hamlet* capitulates to the French demands for a foolish unity and ignores the fact that Shakespeare replaces the imposed rules with "an exact imitation of nature" (II, 83).

Yet Murphy acknowledges that Garrick's adaptations of Shakespeare brought the greatest English playwright before an audience in a way that kept his reputation alive and made it possible for the public to appreciate his genius. Despite his general attack on adaptations, Murphy praises Garrick's particular contributions. He calls Garrick's *Florizel and Perdita* a triumphant attempt at bringing "a clear and regular fable" out of the confusion of a *Winter's Tale*, "the most irregular production of that great but eccentric poet" (II, 284-85). He praises Garrick's *Catherine and Petruchio* for having salvaged "the precious ore of [the original] without any of the dross" (II, 295), and he acclaims Garrick's treatment of *Romeo and Juliet* for having made "the catastrophe, as it now stands, . . . the most affecting in the whole compass of drama" (152-53).

As his treatment of Garrick's adaptations suggests, the

biography provides Murphy with an opportunity to assess changes in the theater of his time and to express his own values as a playwright. Whether dealing directly with Garrick or making extensive digressions, Murphy's work reveals his critical tastes, dramatic preferences, and theatrical practices. *The Life of David Garrick* is in great part an account of changing aesthetic values in the late eighteenth century and evidence of Murphy's moderately conservative responses to them. Reluctant to yield the old values, he does not deny their inadequacies to explain, for example, Shakespeare's achievement. Murphy will not allow his respect for classical standards to obscure his common sense or to govern his knowledge of dramatic effectiveness.

Shakespeare provides Murphy's best example, and he defends him against the unreasonable demands of French neoclassical criticism, particularly those of Voltaire. Murphy recognizes that for all their adherence to Aristotelian principles, concern for the rules, and regard for the unities, the plays of Racine and Voltaire do not measure up to those of Shakespeare. Without altogether dismissing the importance of classical principles, Murphy argues that they must be flexible and that there are ways of gaining their ends without using their means. Shakespeare's "superior genius gave him a right to be his own legislator . . ." (I, 358–59). Where he does not follow the demand for unity of action in *Macbeth,* "the action is carried on in such a connected train of events, that it appears to be one and entire . . ." (I, 72ff). Whatever the deficiencies in Shakespeare's failure to follow the rules, his "genius triumphed over all inconsistencies" (I, 101–-102), and he succeeded "with all the fire and energy of a superior genius" (I, 42–43).

Throughout his comments on Shakespeare, although Murphy rejects demands for classical unity, he does not dispense with the need for plausibility, which had initially been a concomitant demand of classical criticism. Murphy's arguments on behalf of Shakespeare's practices derive, in fact, from his belief that Shakespeare, by getting to the heart of human passions, had achieved a greater degree of verisimilitude than had any other playwright. In the large bulk of his comment on the theater of Garrick, Murphy insistently seeks that which is natural and probable as the source of his tribute. Whether in farce, comedy, or tragedy, Murphy demands some kind of probability.

As he makes his way through the theatrical seasons during Garrick's career, Murphy naturally singles out for praise those works and performances that most closely adhered to the principles of truth. Whitehead's tragedy *Creusa* receives a full chapter because it is "a model of dramatic fable . . . a regular, a probable, and coherent plot" (I, 260). A revival of Jonson's *Every Man in His Humour* allows Murphy to celebrate a playwright to whom he was indebted, but the encomium rests on Murphy's fundamental values: "The poet does not look for a romantic story, for improbable incidents, and marvellous fictions, such as have of late taken possession of the stage. He had his eye on human life, and thence collected his various characters" (I, 206). Jephson's *Braganza* is approved for that "good sense [that] informed him, that well-known historical truth ought not to be violated by such romantic fictions, as those, with which . . . others had disfigured their exotic tragedies" (II, 12). Where material is added to historical events, "the fictitious circumstances are [to be] with probability, interwoven with the texture of the whole" (I, 287-88). Let people and events, whatever the level of action, be images of truth.

Untruthfulness, whether in a Dryden or a Richard Cumberland, cannot be tolerated. The heroic tragedies of "the great Dryden" "prove nothing but monstrous farces," unnatural "ranting," "nonsense" (I, 51). Murphy criticizes Cumberland's not having "copied nature"; "the author should have considered that no man lives in a perpetual whirlwind of passion" (II, 108). Though Murphy acknowledges the popularity of Cumberland's *The West Indian,* he condemns it for its failure to "copy from life. The foibles, the humours, and the real manners, of a West Indian planter, are not delineated with truth and accuracy" (II, 88). He scoffs as well at Mrs. Griffiths's *The Platonic Wife* as "the idea of a female character that never existed. Platonic love, so opposite to the very ends of matrimony, cannot be supposed to enter the breast of woman" (II, 10-11). Murphy's severest objection to sentimental comedy comes from his belief that this mixture of kinds permits no possibility of artistic truth. Untrue to the nature of either kind, the genre is equally unfaithful to human nature.

Murphy's concern for plausibility has its foundation in his didactic demands. Like most eighteenth-century critics, he regards instruction as a primary function of literature, and his comments throughout the work on Garrick testify to his moralistic views. Characters in tragedy should teach by their very imperfections; comedy provides "moral instruction through laughter"; and even farce must offer a lesson in morality.[93] According to Murphy, "The end which tragedy has in view is to present a true display of happiness or misery resulting from human actions" (II, 165). Historical dramas should enlarge knowledge; farces should attack fashionable vices to cure the public's addictions. If Restoration plays suffer from the indecencies of their times, they should be cleansed for a modern audience. The political message in the "Prologue" to Browne's *Athelstan* is welcomed as a warning to those who may be thinking of "aiding a French invasion" (I, 291), a genuine threat at the time of Murphy's writing. In all, Murphy regards the stage as an effective means of teaching "a lesson to humanity" (I, 93).

V *Poetry*

Like his various prose pieces, Murphy's poetry was the expected endeavor of an eighteenth-century man of letters. He was not a poet, but he did write poetry, much of it competent, some quite artful, and all significant for his personality and character as well as the conditions under which he wrote. His verse was practical, occasional, uninspired by high sentiments or great imaginative impulse, encouraged instead by a need to serve some immediate purpose.

Prologues, dedications, and epilogues especially—a large part of Murphy's poetic work—came from the demands imposed by his theatrical associations. There were expected compliments and expressions of gratitude to players and theater managers, puffs to the abilities of friends and colleagues, and addresses to audiences in support of someone's benefit performance. Some express his genuine sentiments about performers, dramatic kinds, and theatrical customs. For example, his dedication to the printed copy of *The Grecian Daughter* praises Mrs. Barry's talent generally and her particular performance in his play. In the same poem, he celebrates Garrick, whose genius he always acknowledged regardless of their personal differences. As late as 1785, in his prologue introducing Miss Brunton to the stage, Murphy lauds Garrick's tragic and comic genius and describes him as Shakespeare's "best commentator" (VII, 61).[94] At the same time, Murphy expresses gratitude to Mrs. Cibber and Sarah

Siddons, actresses whom he genuinely admired.

More importantly, these genre pieces reveal Murphy's attitudes toward the contemporary theater. To be sure, some statements are no more than conventional criticism of unruly audiences or unconvincing explanations of the function of comic epilogues to ease the pain of tragedy. Murphy himself objected to the practice that he serviceably praises for the sake of the theater managers: "We storm upon the stage th' impassioned breast,/ Then, come, and turn all sympathy to jest" (VII, 55).[95] Yet there is nothing spurious in his promotion of British tragedy, his nationalistic pride in Henry Brooke's *Earl of Essex*, and in his repeated disparagement of Voltaire for attacking Shakespeare.

Of greater significance, however, is the statement Murphy makes about the status of comedy in his "Prologue" to Robert Jephson's *Braganza* (1775). Despite modern debates about the actuality of the profusion of sentimental comedy on the eighteenth-century stage,[96] Murphy's prologue suggests a real struggle between those who desired a return to genuine comedy and the proponents of the "weeping kind," which Murphy and Goldsmith regarded as dominating the theater. Murphy clearly opposes the bourgeois influence on the genre and bemoans the low estate of comedy: "While in these days of sentiment and grace/ Poor Comedy in tears resigns her place,/ And smit with Novels, full of maxims crude,/ She, that was frolic once, now turns a prude . . ." (VII, 51). In 1773 Goldsmith had made the same attack, and although the seriousness of his intentions has recently been challenged, Murphy's comments indicate that the issue was genuine for eighteenth-century playwrights.

Murphy's attitude toward comedy, concern for wit, and conception of poetry continually suggest his affinities to Pope and Swift. In the "Notes Variorum" to Christopher Smart's *Hilliad* (1753),[97] an attack on John Hill, Murphy follows the pattern of the *Dunciad Variorum* and the *Memoirs of Martinus Scriblerus* and makes pedantry and dullness his primary targets. His "To Dr. Johnson, a Poetic Epistle" (1760), employs the methods of Pope and Swift to assail his own collection of "dunces": John Hill, Thomas Francklin, Robert Lloyd, Charles Churchill, and George Colman. The form—mixing styles, varying panegyric with satire—recalls the *Epistle to Dr. Arbuthnot*, and some of the autobiographical lines strongly resemble Pope's self-portraiture: "Again I rave, again I'm all on fire,/ 'Here, bring me paper, boy; bring a quire:/ The God! the God! what bright ideas rise!/ What wit, what fancy sparkles in my eyes!' " (VII, 5).

While contemporary reviewers praised the poem, some modern critics have found its satiric vulgarity offensive.[98] But even less to their taste has been Murphy's *Ode to the Naiads of Fleet Ditch*, a Swiftian attack on Charles Churchill, who had aroused the playwright with charges of plagiarism in the *Rosciad* and who was to continue his vitriol even after Murphy took no notice of it.[99] Murphy himself appears to have been somewhat embarrassed by his poem. Seeking to present a respectable self-portrait to posterity, he excluded the ode from his collected work. Nevertheless, he continued to revise it—altering phrases, rearranging stanzas, improving versification, and changing details—long after its original publication.[100]

In both the original and the revision, it is a clever and effective poem. Murphy primarily attacks Churchill, but neatly includes Lloyd, Colman and William Shirley among the mud-slingers who dwell in the ditch which is the source of Churchill's inspiration.[101] They bemoan the building-over of their cesspool and lament the drying-up of Churchill's muse. The setting allows Murphy a broad frame of scatological references to mock Churchill's defilement of the clerical robes that were the actual garments of his profession. Murphy contrasts the expected piety of the Reverend Charles Churchill with the reality of Churchill's abusive, unchristian, and obscene poetry. He devotes three of the longest sections of the poem to the meanness and lewdness of Churchill's writing, and his revision even omits assaults on the *Critical Review,* Flexney, and Oldmixon to focus more sharply on the impious clergyman and his cohorts, Lloyd and Colman.

Murphy makes the most of his technical energy in his satire. Choosing the ode form because it had recently been made popular by Gray and Mason, who had shared with him the abuse of Churchill and his friends, Murphy nevertheless makes use of *MacFlecknoe* and the *Dunciad* in the satire and borrows the scatological fury of Swift. The original poem, especially, recalls Swift in its nasty brilliance:

> Far other rites your sisterhood employ,
> Far other orgies of obscener joy.
> With ordure fresh his body one anoints,
> And wakes new vigour in his languid joints;

> Another stradling o'er his head, with grace
> Lets fly the briny torrent in his face.

The ode drew an immediate response in the *Murphiad* by the pseudonymous Philim Moculloch,[102] and the battle continued through the political controversy of the next two years.[103] Murphy himself fired a salvo with *The Examiner* (1761), a less vigorous satire than his earlier attack.[104] Returning to his customary use of heroic couplets, Murphy models his poem on Pope's *Epistle to Dr. Arbuthnot*. Carrying on an imaginary dialogue, he assesses his reasons for writing, his recourse to satire, and develops an apologia for his attacks on Lloyd, Churchill, Colman, and Garrick.

His best strokes are again at Churchill's expense. He pictures the rogue-prelate as "a strong, uncouth day-labourer in verse!" He portrays him as Crispinus: "He sanctify'd his scandal with a gown./ Then Tartuff-like, a pulpit he attained. . . ." Churchill the drunkard, Churchill with "pious leer and double chin," Churchill the embodiment of "arrogance and venom"—these are Murphy's targets, and who, he wonders, could fault him for his attack? With the likes of Churchill and the envious Shirley, Lloyd and Colman basting him, what is he to do: "Still must I hear, and never once reply,/ Teaz'd as I am by all the scribbling fry?" Must he ignore the *Rosciad* or Lloyd's libelous fables and epistles? No, like Pope, he can not stand by and watch "all Grub-Street in a rage. . . ."

With these blasts of outrage in 1760-61, Murphy's poetic career, outside his theatrical efforts, all but terminated until 1791, when he published a weak imitation of the thirteenth satire of Juvenal. *Seventeen Hundred and Ninety-One* is an anticlimax to Murphy's earlier satires. All that is interesting is the illustration that it offers of his vituperative response to the French Revolution and his pyrrhonistic, conservative political views which had been expressed as early as his polemical writings in the *Test* and *Auditor*.

VI *Translations*

Despite their significance to Murphy and his contemporaries, less need be said of his work in a final genre, translation. Although skillful and reliable, his translations serve more to remind the twentieth-century reader of the well-roundedness of an eighteenth-century man of letters than to enhance Murphy's ultimate reputation. Rendering classical and French works into English provided him with pleasure and sometimes profit, helped him to fill the pages of his periodical, allowed him to please patrons, and enabled him to express his political views,[105] but in the long run they seem immaterial to assessing his achievement as an artist.

Two works, however, deserve some consideration because they occupied Murphy's attention over a number of years and reveal his talents, interests, and values, as well as the nature of the audience he served. His translation of Vida's *Scacchia, Ludus (The Game of Chess)*, although first published in his *Works*, probably had its origins early in his career and likely appeared in a brief excerpt in the *Literary Magazine* in 1757.[106] Murphy turns Vida's poem into five cantos of heroic couplets in conscious imitation of Pope's *Rape of the Lock*. The work is a curious combination of the heroic and mock heroic. Murphy himself compares Vida with Homer, noting how Vida captures the "passions of human nature" in his tale about "inanimate objects" (VII, 69). Chessmen become armies in battle as Apollo and Mercury engage in war. The game is set up at Neptune's marriage and, through Jupiter's recollections, becomes tied to a war between the gods. Intervention by Venus and Mars is checked by Jupiter, who tries to maintain neutrality throughout the slaughter until Mercury wins. Having gained victory, Mercury teaches the game to a nymph and gives her the board as a token of his love. She, in turn, offers instruction to the Italians. Mixing Georgic and heroic charmingly and effectively, Murphy turns earnestness to jest much in the manner of Pope's poem.

For Murphy the translation of Tacitus was more serious. Its publication in 1793 provided the occasion for his expression of antirepublicanism in response to the French revolution. With the opportunity to gain much needed money from the Earl of Shelburne, he instead maintained his principles by dedicating the work to his old friend Edmund Burke, who, unlike Shelburne, shared his antipathy to the revolution.[107] His interest in Tacitus was long-standing, and the work was a slow and laborious process commencing with his days at St. Omer. As early as 1767 he had sought subscribers, but not until he had put aside his theatrical work could he fully engage in his labor.[108]

The result was worth the time and effort. Murphy was a first-rate classicist and Tacitus was a congenial subject. The translation is a work of scholarship, complete with notes and supplements. Murphy's preface, an "Essay on Tacitus's Life and Genius," recalls his biographical-critical methods in his treatment of Fielding and Johnson. In the translation itself, he finds a convenient middle ground between the literal and free, and offers a generally reliable and eminently readable version of the Latin.[109] Immediately successful, it was reprinted in eight volumes in 1811 and two in 1813 and remained the standard English translation into the twentieth century.

CHAPTER 2

Comedy in Brief: Afterpieces, a Prelude, and a Burlesque

I An Entrance

WHEN Murphy turned to writing for the theater, he came well prepared. His work with Fielding, his essays in the *Gray's Inn Journal,* his friendships (particularly with Samuel Foote), all had brought him close to the theatrical world. As a performer, he had acquired an intimate knowledge of what the stage required. He was aware of what changes in production and acting meant to performances. Better lighting, costuming, and set design, an increasingly more natural acting style in theaters where acoustics allowed a playwright's words to be heard and where theater design permitted gesture and facial expression to be seen,[1] all these Murphy was ready to take advantage of.

His comedies especially—short or full length—were designed to create an air of naturalness; they emphasized characterization, wit, and dialogue beyond the lesser qualities of farce. Farce doats upon the unnatural. Its characterization and situations eschew probability. Its humor is forced, settling for easy laughs and indulging itself in the ridiculous. For Murphy the higher comedic aim was the study of men and manners, the desire to hold up a mirror to life. Understanding that part of his audience demanded farcical exaggeration, he accommodated, but not at the expense of the Restoration humor that he himself prized and found easily adaptable to the conditions of the theater in which he worked.

Coming to the stage when great imaginative power was not a prerequisite to dramatic success, Murphy was fortunate. His inventive talents were not impressive, but he had a fine ability—

as his contemporaries, beginning with Garrick, recognized—[2] to produce plays that were workable theatrical pieces. Lacking inventiveness, he followed the contemporary practice of pillaging the works of continental and earlier English dramatists.[3] Cries of "plagiarism," including Murphy's own, were merely conventional attacks on others, but no hindrance to one's own practices.[4] What mattered was how a playwright used his borrowed material, and in that respect Murphy was unsurpassed.[5] His method was to take what had proved popular and to mold it into something peculiarly his own. In Murphy's hands the grossest borrowing from a foreign play became effectively assimilated "with English manners and English extravagancies!"[6]

Even his debut as a dramatist suggests Murphy's practical professional approach to the theater. His first effort was an afterpiece, a genre most accommodating to theater managers, who used the short plays for a variety of purposes: to fill out a long evening's entertainment; to appease latecomers to the theater, who had either missed part of the mainpiece or were taking advantage of the half-price admission after intermission; to provide a leaven to heavier works of art; to introduce new playwrights and actors; and to present vehicles for actors giving performances for their own benefits.[7] The genre was obviously in great demand: between 1741 and 1776, while the two patent houses offered a total of 124 new mainpieces, Drury Lane alone gave access to 118 original afterpieces.[8]

Yet Murphy did not simply follow the practices of his fellow playwrights. He insisted on greater probability. He scorned the emphasis on farce in the genre, eschewed entirely such popular subgenres as ballad opera, burletta, pantomime, and processionals.[9] He took advantage of the form to refresh the taste for Restoration comedy and to combat the fashionable appeal of sentimental drama.[10] Artistically and commercially, he was enormously successful. Profits from performances and publication temporarily extricated him from his financial morass. Audiences were attracted to performances of *The Citizen, The Upholsterer,* and *The Apprentice* rather than to the mainpieces they accompanied, and whereas most afterpieces had only transitory appeal, Murphy's enjoyed remarkable longevity. Seriously concerned with artistic merit, continually polishing and refurbishing, Murphy rivaled Garrick and Colman in gaining approval for a kind of drama that was trifling in other hands.[11]

Between 1756 and 1765 Murphy wrote nine afterpieces which were largely responsible for his reputation in the theater,[12] while they helped sharpen his skills as a comic dramatist. Together with two other short pieces—*News from Parnassus,* a prelude, and *Hamlet with Alterations,* an unperformed burlesque—they demonstrate not only his talents, but also his consummate interest in the theater and his practical knowledge of stagecraft.

II   The Apprentice

The Apprentice, Murphy's first play, enjoyed initial and long success. Although written primarily to move its author out of the ranks of actors and loaded with topical material for contemporary appeal, Murphy's 1756 afterpiece gained access to the repertories of London and provincial companies and continued on stage until at least 1848.[13] Some immediate charges of plagiarism were balanced by praise for the debut of "the budding Cervantes of the British stage," and as late as 1798, a German visitor to England still pronounced the work delightful and worth a second viewing.[14]

Reasons for the play's appeal and longevity are complex. Murphy attributed its reception to Garrick's production and the remarkable acting skills of Richard Yates and Henry Woodward.[15] Yet his own care and attention with the script partially contributed to its continued viability. Having altered the play from an earlier draft, *The Young Apprentice* (1753 or 1754), to add the devastating character of Wingate, whose parsimoniousness and philistinism he vengefully modeled on his recently deceased uncle, Jeffrey French, Murphy never stopped making changes in his text. Within three months of its production, after having made minor alterations, he added a completely new scene.[16] Changes continued over the years and concluded with his extensive revisions for his *Works* in 1786. For posterity's judgment, Murphy regularized his text, formalized his dialogue, expanded scenes for greater clarity of exposition and characterization.[17]

Yet these things cannot altogether account for Murphy's success because *The Apprentice,* despite changes, remained essentially the same play. Murphy even allowed much of the original topicality to stand. Allusions to Elizabeth Canning, most pertinent to an audience in 1756 still debating the sensational claims of a woman supposedly kidnapped by gypsies, continued to appear in 1786. Various speeches, quoting passages from earlier dramas, were unchanged to reflect shifts in theatrical tastes. In fact, the major concern of the satire—its ridicule of "spouting clubs," amateur theatrical groups whose members were carried away by aspirations for a stage career—hardly retained the same interest at the end of the century as it had in 1756.

To explain Murphy's achievement, then, it is necessary to consider the afterpiece itself. With remarkable skill for a neophyte dramatist, he selected precisely those materials that would be most effective in the theater. He created a clever stagepiece, entertaining in itself and capable of being adapted to future demands. He knew enough to eschew the more transitory elements of farce and to rely upon wit, and he recognized that for his purposes he required special treatment of plot and character.

With plot Murphy understood the necessity of avoiding the complications and convolutions so difficult to follow in a stage production that sought the effects of a kind of Restoration wit. *The Apprentice* moves along simple lines: Dick, an apprentice to the apothecary Gargle, neglects his duties in order to satisfy his obsession with acting. Through his association with players, he is cast into jail. Returning home, he is chastized by Wingate, his father, a man dedicated totally to money and determined on a business career for his son. Mouthing appropriate dialogue from Shakespearean and Restoration plays, Dick reassures him and Gargle, who has come to complain that he is leading his daughter Charlotte astray. However, together with Simon, Gargle's servant, Dick plans a stage career and elopement with Charlotte. He attends a meeting of his spouters' club, which ends in a confrontation with the street watch and the arrest of Dick and Charlotte. At the insistence of Gargle, who believes Dick has seduced his daughter and seeks their marriage, Wingate accompanies him to the sponging house. After a scene in which Dick continues to speak in quotations and Wingate twice knocks him down and threatens to let him go to prison, Gargle, appealing to Wingate's avarice, succeeds in arranging their marriage. Dick promises reform, but refuses to give up going to the theater, and even in his final speech resorts to quotation.

Simplicity of plot is essential to Murphy's purpose. Within the theater, it must have been difficult enough to follow his use of dialogue, cleverly composed of quotations and made appropriate to the particular situation. Murphy avoids the distraction of a complex plot and holds to a minimum even the physical action so characteristic in farcical afterpieces, limiting it to the scene in which Wingate twice knocks down Dick and an earlier one on Dick's difficulties with a ladder at Gargle's window. Murphy's plot—in the tradition of Buckingham's *The Rehearsal*—allows for focusing on the speeches and dialogue to convey his wit.[18]

Characterization serves a similar purpose. Murphy uses "humour" characters because they most readily convey his ideas and allow him free play with satire and wit.[19] Dick clearly represents the madness associated with Shandean hobbyhorses. Down to the very conclusion and even to the moment of his "reform," he persists in his obsessive insanity. Where with Charlotte and Simon Murphy attempts more realistic characterization, he underscores Dick's absurdity. Like Sancho Panza they offer practical commentary on Dick's quixotic fantasy. Simon balances Dick's recklessness by a shrewd self-protectiveness, suggesting that the ladder be kept at Charlotte's window so that he will not be blamed. Murphy draws his character carefully enough to account for his ability to quote from plays; as Simon remarks, "Young master taught me this: I should not know what to say but for he . . ." (45). Charlotte even more deliberately balances Dick's madness. Although prepared for love to go along with him, she expresses a clear sense of impending doom. As Dick romantically quotes from Rowe's *The Fair Penitent*, she deflates it with, "You'll ruin everything. I shall be discovered. Be silent; make no noise. . . ." To his suggestion that they not hurry, but rather "act the Garden Scene first," she wisely responds, "And my next scene will be a prison scene" (42). She prepares to cover their tracks; she knows that his use of a ladder is no more than romantic nonsense. Her plain language undercuts Dick's posturing.

Although Gargle and Wingate were modeled on real people, [20] Murphy casts them, too, in the Jonsonian "humour" tradition. Although clever enough to recognize avarice as the only possible appeal to Wingate, Gargle otherwise behaves as the stereotypical pedant. Discussing Dick's obsession with Wingate, Gargle gets lost in a detailed description of madness. Without having to dwell on characterization, Murphy exploits the witty possibilities of the scene. Pedantry again serves in the play as Gargle, distraught over his daughter's fate, nevertheless can express himself only in terms of his monomaniacal obsession with his profession. "What shall I do?" he asks Wingate. "Consider, Sir, Sir, when the animal spirits are properly employed, the whole system is exhilarated; a proper circulation in the smaller ducts or capillary vessels"—to which the self-centered and practical Wingate insensitively responds, "Look you there now; the fellow is at his ducts again. Ha! ha! What a mountebank of a doctor you are!"(48–49).

Murphy himself describes Wingate as a "humours" character. Working out the resentment that he still felt for his deceased uncle, Murphy casts him as Wingate, who represents the "impotence of a mind whose ideas extend very little beyond the multiplication table, and whose passions are ever in a crazy conflict, unless when they all subside into a sordid love of gain . . ." (9). For Wingate Shakespeare is "a deer-stealer" and Hamlet a Prince of Sweden (19). Confronted by the disappearance and possible death of his son, he questions the value of advertising for his whereabouts: "But then if the young rakehell should deceive me and happen to be dead? Why then he tricks me out of three shillings for the advertisement; there's my money thrown into the fire" (16–17). He responds similarly to Gargle's reported loss of his daughter. Wingate knows the value only of money.

Murphy's characterization and plot suggest his blend of Restoration comedy of manners and Augustan satire in *The Apprentice*, which achieves the form of late-eighteenth-century humor commonly associated with Goldsmith and Sheridan. His indebtedness to seventeenth-century drama is obvious.[21] Quotations by the spouters in their ordinary conversation, when not derived from Shakespeare and other Elizabethan dramatists, come largely from Restoration playwrights. Some of the sexually suggestive playful passages, while mild, may be identified with the Wycherley-Congreve tradition, and Murphy's obvious parody of sentimental comedy in Dick's easy reformation indicates the relationship of *The Apprentice* to survival of the Restoration tradition in the eighteenth century.[22]

And yet nothing of the caustic, biting tone of Restoration comedy is evident in Murphy's satire. Like the late Augustan satirists, Murphy seeks a middle ground between extremes. His simple plot, along with the characterization that sets Dick's quixotic fanaticism against Wingate's materialistic and insensitive realism, marks Murphy's claim to the temperate territory of common sense so dear to Augustan artists. If Dick's final words in the play ("Thus life is but a tragi-comic jest,/ And all is FARCE and MUMMERY at best." [58]) are to be taken as Murphy's own view, they offer an argument—not far removed from Pope's advice to Belinda in *The Rape of the Lock*—that man should not take himself too seriously.

III   The Spouter

Within a few weeks after the appearance of *The Apprentice*, *The Spouter, or The Triple Revenge*, another afterpiece, was published. Its preface claimed it had been rejected by the theater managers, but argued that since Garrick had chosen to produce *The Apprentice*, *"written by a Smatterer in Letters,"* a play not plagiarized from the French, but rather (and far worse) from English, both patent houses were now certainly obliged to perform this superior work.[23] Its playful references to *The Apprentice*, its satiric targets, and its use of Fielding's *Historical Register for the Year 1736* leave little doubt that Murphy, perhaps with Garrick's encouragement, wrote *The Spouter* as a hoax.[24]

Never intended for performance,[25] the play was a calculated assault on Murphy and Garrick's enemies. One of these, Theophilus Cibber, was less Murphy's opponent than Garrick's, and probably Garrick instigated the attack, although Murphy's treatment of Garrick himself suggests that the actor-manager was not intimately concerned in writing the play.[26] Of the two other major targets, John Hill was long an antagonist, but Samuel Foote was an erstwhile friend whose treachery probably provided Murphy's immediate motivation.[27]

Murphy had benefited from Foote's kindness and had reciprocated by promoting his talents, only to be betrayed by him.[28] In the summer of 1755 Murphy had written a sequel to Foote's *The Englishman in Paris* (1753), had discussed it with him, and was planning its production. Foote, meanwhile, had used Murphy's material to write his own *The Englishman Return'd from Paris* and was rushing to bring it to the stage in February before Murphy's could be put on the boards. In *The Spouter* Murphy summarizes his resentment through the character of Dapperwit, who boasts "It's true, a Gentleman told me of the Subject first; and, in Confidence, too! by way of consulting my Judgment. . . . To consult me! A Blockhead!" (26).

But Murphy goes beyond his satire on these three main targets and *The Spouter* assails the various vices he had become familiar with in the theater — the vanity, bickering, and unscrupulousness of its leading figures; the unwholesome symbiotic relationship of playwrights and theater managers, and their joint indulgence of the foolish and pretentious taste of their audience. For all this Murphy designed a freewheeling plot, not unlike that of *The Apprentice*, which allows a discursive view of theatrical men and manners. His hero, Slander (Hill), seeks a stage career against the opposition of his father, Muckworm (Jeffrey French), and makes the theatrical rounds, meeting Patent (Garrick), Lum (John Rich), Squint-Eyed Pistol (Cibber), and Dapperwit (Foote).[29] In the process Murphy provides examples of each man's idiosyncracies and exposes professional rivalries and personal antagonisms.

Designed as a vehicle for satire, the plot of *The Spouter* ranges freely in its attack, and yet the major interest remains in its three main characters, who are used emblematically to comment on the contemporary vices of the theatrical and literary world. While Slander's name has personal significance as a description of Hill's journalistic practices, the character itself depicts the way of life of a Grub Street hack. Its ugliness is mirrored in his squalid surroundings and reflected in his practices. Murphy berates Hill's attempts to bilk the public with senseless literature and useless medicines and equates his bad writing with moral decadence.

Cibber and Foote, through their personal characteristics, represent exemplars of vanity and dishonesty. While the play's proportions emphasize the attack on Foote, the reviewer in the *Critical* correctly notes that Murphy's "virulence" falls upon both men.[30] He describes Cibber with a cruel combination of physical and moral detail. From the opening description of Squint-Eyed Pistol's apartment, Murphy is merciless. On Pistol's table lie *"a List of all his Parts, a Copy of Verses to a Great Man, and his Nose and a Set of Teeth"* (23). Murphy excoriates Cibber's eating habits and his spitting on the floor. He mocks Cibber's custom of "puffing" his own work and meanness to that of others. Finally, by having Cibber boast of family pride, Murphy links him to Colley Cibber, king of Pope's dunces.

Filled with personal anger at Foote's betrayal, Murphy castigates him with vengeance in the character of Dapperwit. Foote's pretentiousness and vanity, his slovenliness and opium addiction, his meanness and dishonesty are catalogued in the play.[31] Like Cibber, Foote is belabored for his physical unattractiveness, as he is described *"plucking his Beard; . . . greasy Night-Cap on, his Nails over-grown . . ."* (26). In the funniest scene in the play, Dapperwit demonstrates Foote's compulsive need to entertain. When Slander comes to him for advice, Dapperwit subjects him to his imitation of a dog, a performance of bow-wows punctuated by Slander's laughs. Vain, unscrupulous, unclean, Foote was made to pay for having plagiarized Murphy's work.

Other satiric portraits in *The Spouter* are less savage caricatures. Murphy scoffs at John Rich's artificial pronunciations, mocks his notions of theater as pomp and pageantry, and laughs at his absentmindedness. With Garrick Murphy is careful to demonstrate his importance, which is underscored by Cibber's jealousy of him. Yet Murphy does have Garrick express "my Love of Money, and My love of Fame" (16), genuine faults in the actor-manager. Perhaps Murphy intended these to cover Garrick's participation in the publication, for Murphy uses the same device to disguise his own authorship as characters denigratingly refer to his talents as an actor, ridicule *The Apprentice,* and mangle his name. Still, Garrick could not have been pleased with the comments, and they suggest that he had no role in writing the play.

There is more to the satire in *The Spouter:* mimicry of the acting styles of Woodward, Garrick, Taswell, and Shuter; some snide comments about the fact that every performer—Garrick, Mrs. Clive, Mrs. Cibber, and Foote—seems to have taken a hand at writing farces. Murphy laughs at the taste that made John Cleland's *Memoirs of a Woman of Pleasure* a best-seller. But it is all rather "inside" material, not merely topical, but, as the *Monthly* reviewer pointed out, too personal even for many of his contemporaries to understand it.[32] Using many of the devices of *The Apprentice, The Spouter* lacks the wit of the earlier work and yields more completely to farce. Serviceable in settling his score with Foote, Hill, and Cibber, it has value today mainly as an

insight into the backstage bickering of eighteenth-century
theatrical society.

IV   The Englishman from Paris

On April 3, 1756, Murphy's *The Englishman from Paris*
appeared at the Drury Lane, one month after the first Covent
Garden production of *The Englishman Return'd from Paris*, the
play Murphy claimed Foote had plagiarized. Murphy's afterpiece "went off well" and provided him with a neat profit, and
yet the premiere production was its last.[33] Apart from its
prologue, which appeared in the *Literary Magazine*, the play
went unpublished until its manuscript was discovered and
printed in 1969.[34]

Publication of Murphy's play now permits judgment of
whether his anger with Foote was justified. He was bitter enough
to continue his attack in the prologue and to add an ironic
passage, using a character from Foote's *The Englishman in Paris*,
to condemn Foote's plagiarism, and the evidence does make
Murphy's resentment seem legitimate. Foote borrowed more
than Murphy's general idea. Dialogue, particular jokes, and even
some of the characterization indicate Foote's indebtedness.[35]

And yet the two plays belong to separate theatrical worlds,
and Murphy's has qualities peculiarly his own. While Foote
depends on physical action to create the impression of liveliness,
Murphy relies on wit, clever characterization, and balanced
argumentation. Unlike Foote's chauvinistic appeal, Murphy's
concern is with the follies and excesses of Englishmen as well as
Frenchmen. Where Foote's play belongs to the farcical tradition
that dominated contemporary afterpieces, Murphy's demonstrates his relationship to those Restoration dramatists whose
works—tempered by Augustan ideals of balance and order—
were the major influence of his later antisentimental comedies.

Murphy's balanced comment required a more fully developed
plot than in his earlier afterpieces. Yet it remains essentially
uncomplicated by the intrigues customary to the genre. Returning from Paris with a French entourage that includes Florid, a
tutor, and the Abbé Millamour, an anti-English writer, Murphy's
hero, Jack—imbued with Parisian ideas—has turned against
marriage to Harriet, arranged by their fathers, Quicksett and Sir

Robert Broughton. Jack's conduct with his old friends Wildfire and Foxchase, his liaison with the snobbish Lady Betty Mockmode, his manners and speech indicate that his experiences abroad have converted him into a Francophile and Anglophobe. Events at home encourage his prejudices. He becomes embroiled with an English mob, scuffles with a pickpocket, and runs for safety to his father's home. Poor Harriet, seeking to win him back, cannot cope with Lady Betty's tutelage in French manners, and Jack joins in ridiculing her. Determined not to marry Harriet, Jack outrages Quicksett by his conduct. However, when Quicksett offers her to Sir Robert, Jack, fearing loss of his inheritance, reconsiders. He drops his French airs and resumes friendship with Wildfire and Foxchase, who vow to improve their own rude manners. Learning of the hypocrisy of Florid, who has coveted Harriet for himself, Jack concludes with a celebration of English virtues and a warning to his audience to follow the dictates of good sense and eschew the extremes of any national characteristics.

Murphy's plot allows him to consider and ridicule the excesses of both Englishmen and Frenchmen. To a surprising degree, at a time when nationalistic feelings were aroused by the outset of war with France, he criticizes many of the most cherished English values.[36] From its beginning, the play mocks John Bull in the character of Quicksett, who not only displays ludicrous insularity, but with English practicality conceives of marriage in terms of estates rather than his daughter's happiness. Even at the climax, Jack himself, in a most antisentimental manner, drops his French affectations not out of love for Harriet, but because he fears her marriage to Sir Robert may produce an heir and put him out of pocket.

Murphy's Englishmen sadly need reform. Wildfire and Foxchase dress so poorly that a French servant mistakes them for coachmen. Murphy ridicules their loutishness, drinking habits, table manners, brawling, and hunting. He equates the addiction to gambling of fashionable English ladies with their empty-headedness. He scorns their conduct in the theater, where they go to talk or show off their foolish imitations of Parisian fashions. With a two-pronged attack, he lashes out at foreign operas and the uncomprehending English audiences that attend them. In Lady Betty's advice to Harriet, Murphy scoffs at manners learned from dancing masters, hairdressers, milliners, and waiting maids.

The lower social orders come off no better. Roger, the servant, resentful of the French inability to speak English, betrays his own language in his dialect. His boasts about English food, servants, and freedom turn into Murphy's ridicule of insular attitudes, servants' demands for tips, and the license for the uninformed to be critical of their government. Returning disheveled to his father's house after his experience with an English mob, Jack ironically comments, "This is it to live in a Country of Liberty" (16). Even the Abbé Millamour's biased criticism makes a serious case against the generality of Englishmen, berating the frenzied appeal of Methodism, delight in public executions, and the inanities of the fanatical debaters in the Robin Hood Society.

But the French character comes off at least as poorly. By their own words and conduct and in the comments of Jack and Lady Betty, who believe they are offering praise, the French are characterized as affectedly effeminate, hypocritical, and treacherous. With Swiftian irony, Murphy turns the intended compliments of Lady Betty and Jack into ridicule of French absurdities. As Lady Betty instructs Harriet in proper behavior according to French fashions— "the way to take Snuff," "how to blow the Nose," "or to cough, or to spit" (21)—not only English gullibility but French customs are depicted as arid nonsense. Harriet's innocent reply enforces the point: "I never cou'd have thought there was so much Consequence in a Trifle" (22). In the same way, Jack's Francophile concern for dress, gesture, and speech offers a disconcerting effeminacy compared to the animal masculinity, whatever their crudeness, of Foxchase and Wildfire. Like Gulliver before the Brobdingnagian king, Jack delivers encomia that prove devastating. "The French," he says, "are a very polite Nation; they never make a Treaty, but with an Interest to break it, when it suits their Conveniency . . ." (19). Or, again, "A Frenchman is the only Person breathing that knows how to give himself Airs—a Frenchman has manners and in short everything. Is a Frenchman in a circle? He takes care neither to say anything nor do anything but what is perfectly obliging" (28).

Florid especially draws Murphy's wrath. Preaching a doctrine of Shaftesburian benevolence, the tutor displays solely evil intentions and masquerades his designs on Harriet behind his hypocritical pedagogy. When he greets Sir Robert with, "I hope I see you with your spirits in due Harmony, and all your Affections in proper ballance," the response deflates the

Shaftesburian and Akensidean rhetoric and sentiment: "I am very well, I thank you, if you mean that. . ." (2). Shaftesbury's "benevolence," the philosophy of sentimental comedy, had no appeal to Murphy, and in Florid's character it stands at the center of his hypocrisy, a symbol of the French affectation of sensibility that Murphy hated.[37]

With the Abbé Millamour, Murphy attacks French snobbery toward English life and letters. Voltaire's comments on Shakespeare as "a Drunken Savage" rankled Murphy, and he sets up his audience's response to the Abbé by referring to Voltaire's remark (8). The Abbé, writing a book intended to display English manners at their worst, suggests the actual work of a French abbé, Bernard le Blanc, *Lettres d'un Francois*, whose appearance in 1745 had aroused British anger.[38] Although Murphy allows Millamour to make some points against English absurdities, he also manages to put the criticism in perspective and to deride French airs of superiority. In a Franco-English dialect, which Murphy manipulates to convey meaning while mocking the pronunciation, the abbé's advice to Jack reveals the instability and dishonesty of the French moral character. Finally, to tip the balanced view of the play to favor his own nation, Murphy brings about the conversion in the abbe's views of England so that he concludes by regretting his return to France and by lauding Shakespeare's genius.

Despite its ultimate British advocacy—through Harriet's simple honesty, Jack's instructions to the abbé to convey a message to his king that England and her ministers are determined to prosecute a just war for their proper interests— the play offers a remarkably broadminded conclusion. Jack's final moral contains a sound statement of Augustan decorum that offers Murphy's own balanced values and takes his play beyond its immediate satire to argue for "Sense alone," rather than the virtues of either nation (34). Murphy's words were unlikely to appeal to his countrymen, aroused by patriotic zeal, and perhaps that as much as any other reason accounts for its disappearance from the stage and Murphy's failure to publish it.

V The Upholsterer

Murphy waited nearly two years before presenting his next afterpiece at Drury Lane on March 30, 1758. Unhappy over his

experiences with Foote and the reviewers, busy with his law
studies and drama criticism, upset by a quarrel with Garrick
about acting roles, he delayed production of *The Upholsterer,*
which was written in 1757. When Henry Mossop, for whom the
first night was to be a benefit performance, argued with his
fellow actors, Murphy to the last minute debated the possibility
of shifting the play to Covent Garden.[39] He appears to have
feared its reception, but despite some initial difficulties *The
Upholsterer* achieved enormous success. Applauded by the
reviewers, it settled into the repertories of both theaters and
played throughout the century.[40]

Perhaps Murphy's anxieties arose partly from an unwillingness
to confront charges of plagiarism, since *The Upholsterer* clearly
borrowed from a variety of sources. As though anticipating such
criticism, Murphy freely acknowledges his indebtedness for his
main character to Addison's *Tatler* No. 155, but the more
sophisticated part of his audience must have recognized his
obligations to other essays in the periodical as well as to
Molière's *Le Malade Imaginaire* (1673), Fielding's *Joseph
Andrews,* and Shakespeare's *Much Ado about Nothing.*[41] The
connection with Fielding's *The Coffee-House Politician* (1730)
was equally apparent. From Fielding's play, Murphy drew his
plot, characters for his love story, a few incidents, and even some
of Quidnunc's speeches.[42]

Yet to accuse Murphy of plagiarism is ludicrous. Throughout
his career, whatever he borrowed he improved upon with his
keen observation of men and manners. In *The Upholsterer* he
demonstrates his ability to appeal to contemporary interests and
to write a lively theatrical piece designed to exploit the talents of
such skillful performers as Garrick, Yates, Woodward, and Mrs.
Clive. He brings to his material a deftness with characterization
beyond that of any of his contemporaries. When Sheridan later
sought a model for Mrs. Malaprop, he turned to Murphy's Mrs.
Termagant rather than Fielding's Mrs. Slipslop, from whom she
had been taken.[43] To Fielding's characters, Murphy adds a lavish
comic array of Pamphlet, Codicil, and Brisk. He develops the
quixotic figure of Razor from his own invention of Timothy Meek
in the *Gray's Inn Journal,* and he turns the familiar literary
character of Quidnunc into a superior comic creation.[44]

As a practical man of the theater, Murphy recognized the
importance of topical appeal, and *The Upholsterer* fixes upon

material with the strongest contemporary interest. Its focus on Quidnunc responds directly to public hunger for news during the Seven Years' War. Pamphlet's remarks on the success to be achieved by "telling the people that they are ruined" (101) ironically mocks the inordinate popularity of John Brown's jeremiad, *Estimate of the Manners and Principles of the Times.* Murphy scoffs at public interest in battles in Saxony, at noble ladies patriotically sweeping the malls in St. James's Park, at the influence of journals like the *Monitor,* and at the farfetched excitement created in London by reports of the death of the emperor of Morocco. Yet while allowing his audience to laugh at its own war-inspired excesses, Murphy comments seriously on more than merely ludicrous behavior. The public passion for news and its manipulation by political journalists, including Murphy himself in the *Test,* had led to the unjust and disgraceful execution of Admiral Byng after the failure of the British expedition at Minorca.

It is precisely that combination of serious satire and risible comedy that accounts for Murphy's contemporary success while setting him apart from the generality of writers of trivial afterpieces.[45] Without yielding to the customary excesses of farce, he uses physical action to appeal to the taste of his audience. Bellmour's beating Brisk in the opening scene and Quidnunc's second-act pursuit of Feeble through the house have farcical effect, but allow Murphy to set character and action. Disguising satiric bitterness behind a love story, itself satiric, Murphy's plot masks his anger through the more readily acceptable image of comedy. Even the exaggerations of the Quidnuncs of the world, who abandon sanity in their personal lives for their grotesque interest in public affairs, are carried out in a framework that allows Murphy's points without alienating his audience.

Murphy's plot is a shrewd mixture of absurd pleasantries and satiric earnestness, a combination of Horatian *dulce et utile.* His hero Bellmour's romance with Harriet, whom he has rescued by carrying her naked from a fire, is frustrated by her father, Quidnunc, whose sole interest is following the nation's affairs and who rejects Bellmour for not sharing his obsession. Quidnunc's madness, resulting in neglect of practical matters, brings him to bankruptcy, but even then he cannot control his passion. He pursues it in mad conversations with Codicil, his pompous lawyer, turning personal discussion into political argument. He carries on with the ill-natured Pamphlet, a man who writes for any remunerative cause and who seeks to resolve his indebtedness to Quidnunc by threatening to libel him. In Razor, a barber released from Bedlam, Quidnunc finds a kindred spirit. Even with Feeble, Harriet's uncle upon whose fortune she depends, Quidnunc cannot act sensibly.

To overcome Quidnunc's opposition, Bellmour uses his rascally servant, Brisk, and Harriet's maid, Termagant, but her confused conduct and malapropisms lead her mistress to believe Bellmour has insulted her. Determined to confront Harriet and put an end to her foolish affectations (built on the prospects of a settlement from her uncle), Bellmour asks his rakish friend Rovewell to accompany him. Rovewell, a cynical adventurer recently returned with a fortune from a West-Indian widow whom he had married, agrees to take him to Harriet's house, but not to witness his romantic capitulation. Bellmour convinces Harriet to elope, but Quidnunc discovers them through Termagant's error. In the ensuing uproar, Razor and a watchman bring in Rovewell, having mistaken him for a thief. Rovewell proves to be Quidnunc's son, and with his fortune and good sense promises to set things right—to unite the lovers and check his father's destructive passion.

More complex than in his previous afterpieces, Murphy's plot represents a change in degree rather than kind. Its primary purpose continues to be a vehicle for satire through characterization.[46] In particular, as Murphy declares, it concentrates on Quidnunc to ridicule "the intemperance of too violent a political spirit, or at least to laugh it into good humour" (72). Through him Murphy berates "the love of news, now grown the ruling passion . . ." (74). From the outset, as Quidnunc ponders the nation's financial problems while neglecting his personal obligations, to the climax, when he proposes to accompany Rovewell to jail because "I may meet a Parliament-man . . . to tell me some news" (121), his obsession dominates *The Upholsterer.* Yet Murphy attacks not the man, but rather the "passion" itself and those who, like Pamphlet, have "fed and inflamed" public feelings with their duplicitous propaganda (72).

But through his relatively complex plot, Murphy develops a series of humours characters to expand his satiric comment to include a more general attack on pride in all its varied forms.

Quidnunc himself desires primacy of information in order to make him cleverer than the rest of society. His daughter Harriet, not in a position to be too selective, refuses to accept Bellmour under what she considers to be charitable terms. Codicil parades his legal knowledge and Rovewell his charm. For Pamphlet scurrilous writing is a means of gaining the world's attention. Mrs. Termagant prides herself on her language and wisdom and demonstrates neither in her suggestion that Quidnunc would do well to follow her practices. "If, instead of his *policies,*" she declares, "he would *manure* his mind like me, and read good *altars,* and improve himself in fine *langidge,* and *bombast,* and *polite* accollishments—" (108). With cunning humor, Murphy repeatedly deflates her affectations by playing upon her scatological and sexual verbal abuses.

While Murphy employs the abuse of language as a means of deriding Termagant's misplaced pride, he does not limit the device to her. When Pamphlet and Quidnunc engage in political discussion, their empty arguments are emphasized by their clichés and platitudes—"Wheels within wheels"; "No smoke without fire"; "Time will tell all" (103). Pamphlet, particularly, reveals how language disguises a lack of knowledge as he explains the meaning of *balance of power:* "The balance of power is, when the superstructures are reduced to proper balance, or when the balances are not reduced to unnatural superstructures" (104). Codicil, too, displays a wonderful aridity of language in his Latin tags and legal citations as he loses all sense of the purpose of his discussion with Quidnunc, an attempt to return him to the proper business of his bankruptcy, and slips into a mad political dispute with arguments as senseless as those of his client.

In yet another way Murphy furthers his satire through a play on language. Although he variously indicates—through his falsely didactic ending, through Razor's identification of Rovewell by "the mole on his cheek" (122), and through Rovewell's pronouncement, "I shall now atone for the irregularities of my youth" (122)—that he is satirizing sentimental drama, the point has sometimes been misunderstood.[47] However, Bellmour's description of his first meeting with Harriet makes clear Murphy's parody of sentimentalism through his love story. Bellmour's language derives its images from the worst romances.

Harriet is an "angel," a "dear naked Venus," with "slender waist" and "limbs 'harmonious, swel'd by Nature's softest hand'" (81). But to Bellmour's rapturous idyllic description of a sensuous scene, Rovewell responds with earthy practicality that terminates the sentimental pretentiousness: "Raptures and paradise!—What seraglio in Covent Garden did you carry her to?" (81).

Despite *The Upholsterer's* broad satiric range, much of its satire and verbal wit were tied to contemporary events, and Murphy over the years altered the play to update it and to improve its diction, dialogue, and design.[48] The first printed version in 1758 is more literary than the acting script. Murphy cuts minor characters and distributes their dialogue among his major figures enhancing the roles of Razor and Quidnunc. He elaborates Quidnunc's madness, develops Termagant's affected language, and heightens the concluding parody of sentimental comedy.

Changes continued, and the 1763 production for Covent Garden condenses the afterpiece. Brisk and Codicil disappear entirely,[49] which obviously necessitates alterations and transpositions throughout the play. Beyond that Murphy salvages material dropped when the three-act version of *The Way to Keep Him* (1760) expanded to five acts in 1761, and he uses the material to increase Termagant's comic effectiveness. Moreover, with the conclusion of the Seven Years' War, Murphy also updates some topical references, including an allusion to his having been duped by Wilkes and Churchill in their political controversy.

For the *Works* in 1786, Murphy, rewriting for posterity, polishes syntax, grammar, and diction—not contributing much to the comic quality. Even with Termagant, Murphy strikes a more literary tone. Still the revision tightens the plot, makes character relationships clearer, and again updates the topicality. The last point is Murphy's primary concern in his eighteen pages of manuscript changes for the play's production in 1791.[50]

VI The Old Maid

For two-and-one-half years following *The Upholsterer*, Murphy engaged in a hectic flurry of dramatic activity. He presented his first tragedy and a three-act dramatic poem. He brought

forth *The Way to Keep Him* as an afterpiece and quickly
converted it into a full-length comedy, and he produced *All in
the Wrong*, a five-act comedy. Together with Foote, with whom
he had become reconciled, he leased Drury Lane for the summer
of 1761 in order to put on their own productions. His battles with
Garrick, who now had the services of George Colman and no
longer needed Murphy as his primary writer, reached a climax
over their disagreement about the rights to the plays Murphy
had produced with Foote. Their split was complete. After the
appearance of *The Old Maid* and *All in the Wrong* during the
next regular season, Murphy's only new play at Drury Lane until
1767 was performed without Garrick's knowledge during his
absence in 1765.[51]

By the middle of 1761 Murphy had established his reputation
as a playwright, and the venture with Foote enhanced his artistic
stature. Because of Foote's indolence, they enjoyed no financial
success, but Murphy could not have been displeased with the
reception of his three plays— *The Old Maid, All in the Wrong*,
and *The Citizen* (a three-act comedy reduced during its first run
to an afterpiece). *The Old Maid*, with its attractive acting roles,
proved a particularly durable afterpiece, remaining in the
repertory of the two patent houses for the next seventeen years
and continuing to appear as late as 1848.[52] Aging actresses doted
on the role of Miss Harlow, the old maid, and capable character
actors found attractive the part of Captain Cape, her suitor.[53]

Generally applauded on its appearance, July 2, 1761, approved
by later critics, and translated into German, *The Old Maid* drew
only one severe rebuke.[54] While most of Murphy's contemporaries—accustomed to savage stage stereotypes of Jews, Irishmen, and Scots—ignored the cruel treatment of the hapless old
maid in the play, the reviewer in the *Monthly*, perhaps Mrs.
Griffiths, wife of the publisher, condemned the "cruel insult, not
upon vice or folly, but upon misfortune," an attack upon a woman
for "her homely person and stale virginity."[55] To the twentieth-
century reader, the argument is justified, and even in plot
summary, which suggests some of the play's virtues, Murphy's
harsh treatment of Miss Harlow is evident.

Miss Harlow, an old maid, receives a letter of proposal from
young Clerimont, who, though he has never met her, has seen
her walking with her sister-in-law, Mrs. Harlow. Mrs. Harlow,
unable to comprehend the young man's interest in the forty-

three-year old hag and nag, warns her not to give up old Captain
Cape, her betrothed, but Miss Harlow attributes the advice to
envy. Mr. Harlow, delighted at the prospect of ridding himself of
a burdensome relative, welcomes Clerimont's suit. Through a
series of separate conversations between Clerimont and the two
women, however, the audience becomes aware that he has
mistaken the two. Speaking to Miss Harlow, he believes that he is
winning her support for marrying her brother's wife. When Cape
later arrives to protest his dismissal, he becomes embroiled with
her brother. He is followed by Clerimont, whose news that he
seeks the hand of Mrs. Harlow leads to another angry exchange,
and both suitors challenge Harlow to a duel. However, the
arrival of Mr. Heartwell, Clerimont's uncle, restores sense and
order. The Harlows then laugh at the unfortunate old maid;
Cape gloats over her predicament, and Miss Harlow seeks refuge
from their ridicule.

Plot summary merely suggests how harshly Murphy has
actually treated the old maid. His tone and dialogue convey even
greater severity. He paints Miss Harlow in most unattractive
colors: the old hen ludicrously arranged in a peacock's feathers
of pride, a vile jilt appropriately jilted. His stereotype begins
with the notion that an unmarried old woman has no right to
expect anything more from society than what she is fortunate
enough to have offered to her. He regards her virginity with
scorn. In Cape's dismissal of her, cruelty underscores his
remarks, "Upon my soul I think you a most admirable jilt, and so
now you may go and bewail your virginity in the moun-
tains. . . ."[56] Alluding to Pope's lines on Belinda, her sister-in-
law's final comments ridicule Miss Harlow's vanity: "In vain the
FADED TOAST her mirror tries,/ And counts the cruel murders
of her eyes;/ For Ridicule, sly-peeping o'er her head,/ Will point
the roses and the lillies dead. . ." (281). Unlike Pope's, the lines
are not aimed at a complacent Belinda, smug in her pride, but
rather at the pathetic old lady, who Murphy thinks should be
content with whatever crumbs she can gather.

Murphy's major change in his source, Christophe-Barthélemy
Fagan's *L' Étourderie* (1737), reinforces his unwillingness to
show any mercy to his character. In the original, she discovers
the young man's mistake,[57] whereas Murphy's character, far too
self-involved to see the truth, cannot gain the audience's
approval even for a degree of intelligence that might lessen her

ludicrousness. Moreover, her discovery enables Fagan to conclude by keeping the revelation a secret from the old maid's
former suitor, thus permitting the original marriage plans to
remain intact. Fagan's old maid, Mademoiselle Cléonte, emerges
less pathetically, her honor wounded, but not destroyed;[58]
Murphy's Miss Harlow stands helplessly before the taunts of
others. Although Clerimont remarks that Cape will ultimately
"think better of it [rejecting Miss Harlow]" (280), Murphy's
Ovidian motto for his publication holds no such promise: "That
day will come when you, who now shut out your lover, will lie, a
cold and lonely old woman through the night" (247-48).

Despite the dissatisfaction that a modern audience may feel in
Murphy's portrayal of his title character, the play itself has much
to recommend it, and Murphy's method of adapting his source
suggests his real achievement in the eighteenth-century theater.
Although maliciously charged with plagiarism, particularly by
those seeking to have Colman replace him at Drury Lane, he
shaped whatever he borrowed into a play that was very much his
own.[59] Of the French play's twenty-four scenes, Murphy uses
nine—four very brief, two of which are short speeches.[60]
Employing less than half of Fagan's farce, he transforms his
material into an original English theater piece, longer and less
farcical than its source.[61] If its major characters derive from
L'Étourderie,[62] they become naturalized British citizens, whose
dialogue is chiefly Murphy's creation. He turns Fagan's L'As-
sesseur into the more credible, independently wealthy Captain
Cape, who, for all his Jonsonian-humours character, has a more
comic than a farcical function. By eliminating the idiosyncrasies
of Fagan's original of Heartwell, Clerimont's uncle, Murphy
sacrifices further opportunities for laughter in order to bring a
sense of balance and sanity to the conclusion of The Old Maid. In
every way, Murphy's additions to his source are designed to
achieve greater probability and transform it from pure farce into
something closely approximating the comedy of manners.

He clearly was dissatisfied with the simplicity of farce,
common though it was to contemporary afterpieces. Along with
his attempt to make his plot more plausible than Fagan's, he
provides greater depth of characterization than farce cus-
tomarily demands. Despite his focus on Miss Harlow's vanity, he
presents Mrs. Harlow in sufficient depth to use her own vanity as
explanation for her later cruelty to the old maid. Aroused by her

anger, Mrs. Harlow vows that if her sister-in-law marries Clerimont, gains "new equipage," has "greater routs," "I must outshine her there" (254). Mr. Harlow, too, is no mere stick figure. His relationship to his sister, his involvement in her marital plans, his design to use her to his own advantage, all echo the conduct of another Harlow family, that of Samuel Richardson's *Clarissa*. With Cape, Clerimont, and Heartwell, whatever the farcical elements, Murphy adds a dimension of comedy to material that originally belonged wholly to farce.

To be sure, Murphy does not altogether escape the farcical elements characteristic of afterpieces, and the effect, while sometimes serviceable to the play's theatricality, somewhat weakens his effort to achieve a more naturalistic comedy.[63] His swift pace, his setting up of situation and relationships, and his immediate definition of major character traits, all derive from the realm of farce. Individual scenes—like those in which the Harlow women meet separately with Clerimont and therefore his error remains unrevealed or those in which the absurdity of dueling is marked by Captain Cape's blustery conduct—clearly depend on farcical elements. Farce dominates in the misinterpretation of speeches and pronoun references or in the failure of any character at any time to utter the word that would clarify what has gone awry. When, for example, Clerimont tries to convince Miss Harlow to support his cause with her sister-in-law, only in his aside does he speak words which if spoken aloud would give the game away. With Cape, Murphy retains too much farcical exaggeration to produce laughs, but then must use him to reveal the comedy of errors, which incongruously makes him more perceptive than the apparently more intelligent Mr. and Mrs. Harlow.

Nevertheless, *The Old Maid* demonstrates Murphy's generally successful attempt to bring farce within the bounds of comedy, and his revisions for his *Works* in 1786 indicate his continuing effort to achieve a drama with more enduring qualities than the flimsy, farcical afterpieces of his contemporaries. The changes suggest Murphy's striving for greater respectability through improved diction and syntax, more regularity and formality. He drops a good many "Zounds" and "Zoons," fashionable oaths two decades earlier. He embellishes such speeches as Mrs. Harlow's statement to her sister-in-law, "You are not now of that age that becomes giddiness and folly,"[64] which becomes, "You are not

now in that sprightly season of life, when giddiness and folly are
excusable, nay becoming your age, sister—" (251). More subtle
are dialogue changes between Mrs. Harlow and Clerimont on
first meeting, alterations to make more credible his mistake in
identities. Throughout, Murphy moves in the direction of a more
literary work. If, in the process, his changes do not always
enhance the performance possibilities of his play, they clearly
indicate his preference for a form of comedy more serious than
farce.

VII   The Citizen

Despite Murphy's established reputation, he had at least as
many problems and difficulties with the production of his next
afterpiece as he had had with his previous works. In early 1761
Garrick had accepted *The Citizen* as a three-act comedy for
Drury Lane, but Murphy, despondent over his mother's death,
had withdrawn the play.[65] Instead, on July 2, he presented it as
part of his summer venture with Foote, but by August 8 he had
reduced it to two acts, apparently by eliminating some minor
characters and scenes.[66] When he offered his revised comedy to
Garrick for the regular season, however, the manager rejected it.
Garrick seems to have been motivated by personal rather than
aesthetic reasons, for, although willing to produce *The Old Maid*
and *All in the Wrong*, he clearly desired to replace the
recalcitrant Murphy with the more amenable Colman. When
Murphy insisted that Garrick employ Ann Elliott, his new
protégée and mistress, the manager had the opportunity he
evidently wanted to complete their separation. Not until
November 15, 1762, at John Beard's Covent Garden, did *The
Citizen* appear at one of the patent theaters a service for which
Murphy later acknowledged his indebtedness to Beard.[67]

Garrick unfortunately had allowed his emotions to obtrude on
his professional judgment. Despite Murphy's political enemies on
the *Monthly Review* and *St. James's Chronicle*—antagonistic to
the playwright for his support of Lord Bute in the *Auditor*—*The
Citizen* proved his most successful afterpiece.[68] Twenty-nine
years later it ran seventeen times in one season. In somewhat
bowdlerized form, it continued on the American stage during the
next century, and its rich reflection of contemporary manners, its
lively theatricality, and its greatly appealing acting roles kept it

popular in England until at least as late as 1830.[69] So astute a critic as Leigh Hunt called *The Citizen* the best play of its kind in the English language.[70]

It is a fine play, which, like most of his afterpieces, skillfully blends Restoration comedy of manners and farce in a way that defies simple classification.[71] Murphy's plot, use of sources, and satire combine an older dramatic tradition with contemporary practices to produce an appealing theatrical piece for his audience — an actor's vehicle that offers the lively entertainment of confusion and chaos with serious social comment — and, at the same time, provide some enduring interest.

Even in summary, which simplifies action and merely suggests characterization and thematic development, Murphy's plot reveals its serviceability to dramatic entertainment and social criticism. While presenting the rather commonplace situations of lovers outwitting dominating parents and unattractive suitors,[72] it nevertheless does so with some hectic activity and some genuine opportunities for the sharp criticism of Restoration comedy of manners and satire of the merchant class that Murphy consistently rebukes in his works. His conventional lovesick hero, Beaufort, seeks young Wilding's help to thwart the marriage plans arranged by the fox-hunting squire, Sir Jasper Wilding, and the avaricious, mercenary merchant, Philpot. Philpot has agreed to the wedding of Wilding to his daughter Sally if Sir Jasper gives Maria Wilding, whom Beaufort desires, to Philpot's son George. The rake Wilding, although content to wed Sally for her dowry, nevertheless schemes with his sister to force George to reject her, and the devastatingly witty Maria plays the fool to convince George that life with her would be unbearable. Since he has difficulty conversing with intelligent, respectable women, George is pleased until her feigned stupidity proves too much. It is a difficult decision because he needs the dowry. Heavily in debt from gambling and carousing, he has temporarily bilked his father, even as the old man believes he is taking advantage of his own son, but George's scheme falls apart when he visits Corinna, a prostitute, and reveals it to her. Old Philpot, a hypocrite, having been interrupted while purchasing Corinna's favors, has hidden under a table and hears his son's confession. Wilding, who has been keeping her, arrives, argues with George, beats him, and accidentally discovers Philpot. When the Philpots return to the Wildings for another attempt at the marriage, Wilding

discloses the incident to the amusement of his father. But George
has his second meeting with Maria, who this time overwhelms
him with her wit. When George renounces her, Philpot demands
her himself and threatens otherwise to reject Wilding's suit for
his daughter. However, Beaufort, who has been masquerading as
a lawyer, announces that Philpot has already signed the
agreement for Sally's marriage and that he himself has tricked
Sir Jasper into approving Beaufort's marriage to Maria. Sir Jasper
forgives the deception. The lovers are happy, and Wilding
delights in the outcome of his machinations. The quarreling
Philpots carry their disagreement into the play's epilogue, but
conclude by expressing their contrition to the audience.

Even in summary, the farcical elements are apparent. The
disguises of Maria and Beaufort; Wilding's beating George to the
delight of Philpot, hiding under the bed; Corinna's unsuccessful
shuffling of her bedroom visitors—all obviously derive from the
genre of farce. Similarly, Murphy presents George's sneaking
into his home in the morning after a night on the town and
convincing his father that he is up early rather than returning
late. Even the characters—whatever their serious satiric purposes—display the exaggerated typology of farcical figures: the
blunt and honest country squire set against the mean-spirited
city merchant.

Yet combined with such material is the sophisticated detail of
comedy of manners.[73] The union is most evident in Maria's scene
with George. If her masquerade draws its laughs from farcical
excesses, its controlling wit and invention belong to Restoration
comedy. Ready to reverse her earlier role of fool to demolish
George, Maria addresses the audience: "I have all the materials
of an impertinent wit, and I will now twirl him about the room,
like a boy setting up his top with his finger and thumb" (II,
285-86).[74] Her catalogue of metaphors describing his confusion
dumbfounds him: ". . . you look as if the stocks were fallen; or
like London-bridge at low water; or like a waterman when the
Thames is frozen; or like a great lawyer with a brief . . ." (II,
289). Appealing mainly to his London business sense, her images
would do justice to a Restoration heroine.

Her brother, too, could easily have graced the Restoration
stage. With the cynicism of its rakish heroes, he comments
knowingly on his sister's affinities to the heroines of Congreve's
world. He scoffs at the way she teases poor Beaufort: "Though
still in her teens, she can play upon all your foibles, and treat you

as she does her monkey, tickle you, torment you, enrage you, sooth you, exult you, depress you, pity you, laugh at you . . ." (II, 222). His attitude toward marriage comes right out of *Way of the World*. "My dear Beaufort," he says, "one sees so many people breathing raptures about each other before marriage, and dinning their insipidity into the ears of all their acquaintance. . . . And then in a month's time [it is] 'I wish I had never seen his face . . .' [or] 'I wish she had poisoned herself with all my heart'" (II, 219-20). He denies that his own marriage has anything to do with love: "This is a match of prudence, man! bargain and sale!" (II, 218), but he has no objection to it. With the relish of a Restoration schemer, he sets about to wreck the plans of Sir Jasper and Philpot, not out of loyalty to his sister or concern for justice and romance, but rather for the delight in outwitting those he considers less intelligent than himself.

Neither farce nor pure comedy, *The Citizen* draws from its varied sources in order to produce a vehicle that carries out its satire in genial terms so that it entertains even as it instructs. From Philippe Nericault Destouches's farce *La Fausse Agnès, ou Le Poète Campagnard* (1759), Murphy derives his general plot, the scenes between Maria and George, and some small details of wit.[75] Yet, as scholars have noted, Murphy's indebtedness extends to borrowings from seventeenth-century drama.[76] Maria bears a strong resemblance to Angelica in Congreve's *Love for Love*, and scenes like Philpot's hiding under the bed have their origins in the earlier comedies. But none of these is merely imitation, the plagiarism Murphy has so often been accused of.[77] Murphy fuses two forms to achieve a genial comedy that satirizes the very audience he is appealing to. Farce masks the earnestness of jest and makes bearable the comic barbs directed at the social class that constituted the major significant part of his auditors.

It is the middle-class merchant that bears the brunt of Murphy's attack. While playwrights like George Lillo and Richard Cumberland had continued the tradition of Steele's appeal to that very group, Murphy, from his earliest plays, was among those for whom the growing bourgeoisie presented a threat to the old social, political, and humanistic values. Murphy makes those merchants symbols of greed and avarice, insensitive materialists, purveyors and supporters of false fashions, and opponents of learning and literature.

The main business of *The Citizen* is to portray the ugly

characters of the Philpots and their hirelings. The son attempts to swindle his father, who is trying to cheat him. Their servants and workers, like Dapper and Quilldrive, use the hypocrisies and deceitfulness of the Philpots to gain their own advantage. Quilldrive seeks his own fortune by "drudging for the old man, and pimping for the young one" (II, 233). Murphy's poetic justice in *The Citizen* derives from the "shrewd" businessman Philpot's being outwitted in that most conspicuous business arrangement, the marriage compact. Son George gets his proper reward first in the physical beating of Wilding and then in the double verbal lashings by Wilding and Maria.

Murphy offers a full sampling of merchant-class vices. Immediately after Maria's description of Philpot as a "picture of Avarice" (II, 227), the old man enters with words that epitomize his sole interests: "Quilldrive, have those dollars been sent to the Bank, as I ordered?" (II, 230). His world is summarized by the platitudes George uses to win his favor: the synonymous *principle* and *principal* of Philpot's vocabulary. Philpot's ideal business ethic is expressed in his approval of Thomas Inkle's betrayal of Yarico's love in Addison's satirical tale in the *Spectator*, "for there was the very spirit of trade" (II, 238). For Philpot and George comes satisfaction in the misery of Dick Worthy, "who was always cramming his head with Greek and Latin at school," for, as Philpot says, "Let him draw bills of exchange in Greek and Latin, and see where he will get a pound sterling for them" (II, 241).

Perhaps the main thrust of Murphy's satire is his relating their crass material values to the Philpots' attitude toward sex and marriage. For them, love and marriage are to be purchased. George is at ease with women only so long as he buys their favors. Philpot himself finds Corinna convenient and safe because "this is the way, to indulge one's passions and yet conceal them, and to mind one's business in the city, as if one had no passions at all" (II, 247). He deals with her as he would with any commercial enterprise, regarding her in terms of investment value and cheating her by paying "light" guineas for her services. Whether with Corinna or the respectable Maria, Philpot evaluates in commercial terms—measuring in percentages and interest. At the bawdy house or in polite company, he takes advantage through deception.

If *The Citizen* also pokes fun at the country squire and his cynical son, it is with less intensity or bitterness. To be sure, Sir Jasper's bizarre dress and country manners are the subject of mirth and the source of embarrassment to Maria. Sir Jasper and Wilding, no less than Philpot and George, engage in arranged marriages with an eye toward fortune. Yet, these are not the object of Murphy's focus. Sir Jasper's bluff honesty and Wilding's intelligence are in themselves saving graces.

Murphy evidently was well satisfied that his fusion of dramatic forms had accomplished his purpose, for the mixture of farce and comedy of manners is untouched in his later version of the play. After reducing it from three to two acts, he made few changes, and the first printed version remains essentially the same in the *Works*. Apart from minor alterations in diction and outdated references,[78] the omission of about one-half dozen lines at the conclusion stands as the only notable difference between the two texts.

VIII   Three Weeks after Marriage

Together with Murphy's comedy *No One's Enemy but His Own, What We Must All Come To,* his penultimate afterpiece, was driven from the stage by political opposition.[79] John Wilkes and his supporters refused a fair hearing to both works by their erstwhile antagonist in the paper warfare that had accompanied the conclusion of the Seven Years' War. After its opening at Covent Garden on January 9, 1764, the afterpiece disappeared from the stage,[80] and the reviewers, motivated by personal and party considerations, assured the failure of even its publication through their charges of immorality and plagiarism.[81]

Yet Murphy did not despair of the play. With musical airs provided by James Hook, the work assumed a new title, perhaps made its appearance at the Haymarket as early as 1764, and certainly was performed afterwards in Dublin, Edinburgh, and the provinces.[82] As *Marriage à la Mode, or Conjugal Douceurs,* it came to Drury Lane on April 22, 1767. Murphy—with the assistance of Mrs. Abington, who performed it for her own benefit—had connived to outwit Garrick by bringing it to his theater under a title that previously had been used for an unsuccessful play at Drury Lane.[83]

Finally, when political passions had abated, Murphy reintroduced the play as *Three Weeks after Marriage* at Covent

Garden on March 30, 1776. With only minimal changes from its
original production, the work was enormously successful. By June
1, it had appeared fourteen times. It drew immediate praise in
the *Westminster Magazine*,[84] emerged as one of the most popular
afterpieces of the eighteenth century, and remained a theatrical
stock piece in the nineteenth. Unsold copies of its earlier publication appeared with a new title page and a reset advertisement, and within the same year a new edition was
demanded.[85]

Three Weeks after Marriage displays Murphy's adept control
over his techniques of composition. Like his contemporaries, he
borrowed freely from a common stock of dramatic and prose
sources, choosing whatever might be serviceable for his purposes. If his material on the quarreling married couple comes
from Mrs. Sheridan's *Discovery* (1763), [86] the characters were
hardly original with her, for they represented a standard type in
Restoration comedy. His satire on Drugget and the ludicrous
extremes of landscape gardening made fashionable by "Cap-
ability" Brown is a commonplace in early eighteenth-century
periodical literature, and Garrick himself had made use of it in
his afterpiece *Lethe* in 1740. [87] Murphy acknowledges his
inspiration for Drugget's character in Pope's essay in *Guardian*
#173, but the name and description may also be found in
Johnson's *Idler* #16.[88] What ultimately matters, however, is the
result of the playwright's use of his material, and by this stage in
his career Murphy excelled in turning his eclectic borrowing to
his particular artistic purposes.

In *Three Weeks after Marriage* the outcome is a lively drama in
Murphy's characteristic combination of farcical material and a
treatment that owes much to the comedy of manners.[89] On one
hand, the play greatly depends on the farcical tactic of
misunderstood words, on certain features of gross characterization that suggest caricature, and on wildly eccentric situations.
On the other hand, its satire, its social commentary, its grounding
in reality, and its dialogue clearly indicate the transformed
comedy of manners that Murphy helped to create in the late
eighteenth century.

Designing his plot to carry this combined comedic form,
Murphy balances farcical exaggeration with realistic social satire
in a story that juxtaposes fashionable nonsense with common
sense. Desiring to marry intelligent and realistic Nancy Drugget,

Woodley, Murphy's sensible hero, encounters her parents' opposition. Mrs. Drugget prefers the more fashionable Lovelace, while Drugget resents—Woodley's candid rejection of his ludicrous plans to improve his estate by shaping his trees and gardens into unnatural designs. Only Dimity, a servant, guiding Lovelace with misinformation certain to anger Drugget, works for a marriage between Woodley and Nancy. The Druggets' older daughter, recently married to Sir Charles Rackett, arrives with her husband for a visit, and they support Lovelace. Hoping to assure an inheritance, Rackett encourages Drugget's madness. While the parents regard their daughter's marriage as a triumph, things have gone badly with the Racketts. Devoted to social life, with its interests in parties and gambling, they are engaged in a continuing squabble about a recent card game, and their quarrel leads to his storming out of their bedroom and making allegations about her. Her parents believe that he is charging her with adultery and regard her as a ruined woman. Even when Dimity learns the truth and sets matters straight, Drugget decides that one such marriage is enough and vows that Woodley shall have Nancy. However, Mrs. Drugget determines to reconcile the Racketts and marry Nancy to Lovelace. Brought together by her, the Racketts quarrel again and Sir Charles leaves. Although Lady Rackett assures her parents that this is the way of the world and that her husband will return, Drugget, convinced that one such family alliance is sufficient, promises Nancy to Woodley. In turn, Woodley offers no resistance to Drugget's mad plans for further improving his estate.

Murphy's plot obviously is less important for itself than as a vehicle for his satire. With *Three Weeks after Marriage,* he extends his satiric range to include more than a single class, to involve a large part of his audience in his attack, and to comment generally on nature versus art. Through Drugget Murphy ridicules middle-class pretentiousness and bad taste. Drugget's addiction to fashionable nonsense betrays natural beauty. His estate—with sundials, duckponds, leaden images, carved trees, mutilated bushes and shrubs, and hawhaws—defaces nature. Boasting that "I won't have anything in my garden that looks like what it is" (297), he replaces common sense by delusion. To Woodley's quotation of Pope's "First follow NATURE, and your Judgment frame/By her just Standard . . . ," he responds, ". . . Mine is all art; no wild nature here; I did it all myself" (296).

No less a perversion of nature are the Racketts' marriage and their commitment to fashionable life. What Drugget does to his garden in the name of fashion, the Racketts in three weeks do to marriage in their pursuit of the way of the world. "Oh! there's no existing, no breathing, unless one does as other people of fashion do" (305), Sir Charles declares. Their dialogue is a dictionary of society's clichés. Their tastes and interests catalogue the vices of the upper classes. At the center of their farcical dispute is their disagreement about a card game they have played, for they are consumed by the passion for gambling that Murphy throughout his work ridicules as a sign of society's imbalance. It is surely no less unreasonable to destroy a marriage because of the foolishness of card-playing than to take the beauty of nature and turn it into a grotesque scene. Both have their sources in the polluted spring of vanity.

Man's pride, the major target of Augustan satirists, is Murphy's larger concern, and he includes his audience in his assault. The vices he attacks are theirs. To comprehend the Racketts' argument, they had to know the details about the card game over which the couple quarrels. His characters present a wide variety of sins common to the society. Drugget places himself above nature by indulging in fantastic gardening schemes that enjoyed enormous popularity. Who among Murphy's audience was free from a regard for class distinctions and social status? Mrs. Drugget cares less about her daughters' happiness than about the improvement in their status to be achieved through marriage. When Lady Rackett appears to have committed adultery, her parents' concern is for the stigma it will place on the family. The Racketts themselves intersperse their argument about the card game with comments suggestive of the conflict that comes with marriage between two social classes. Lady Rackett boasts of her superiority at the card table as though to demonstrate her personal worth despite her social inferiority. She fears losing her husband not because she loves him, but because it will cost her prestige. Although Sir Charles needs Drugget's money, he abuses his wife's shopkeeper family background. He ridicules her as "low, unpolished, uneducated," and boasts that "my rank in life claims respect . . . from one raised in the world as she has been by an alliance with me" (313). In *Three Weeks after Marriage*, Murphy goes beyond the narrow satire of some of his earlier plays, outside his customary attack chiefly on the merchant class and its unimaginative intelligence.

To reinforce his satire and underscore its seriousness, Murphy includes his norm within the play. Nancy, Woodley, and Dimity speak directly to Murphy's view of the world. In her song rejecting Lovelace, Nancy describes courtship in high life in a manner that equates it with Drugget's foolish tampering with nature, and, at the same time, she provides a gloss on the Racketts' mode and manners:

> To dance, and to dress, and to flaunt it about,
> To run to park, play, to assembly and rout;
> To wander for ever in whim's giddy maze,
> And one poor hair torture a million of ways;
> To put at the glass every feature to school,
> And practise their art on each fop and each fool;
> Of one thing to think, and another to tell,
> These, these are the manners of each giddy belle. (323)

Both Nancy and Woodley reveal the social forces at work in the play, the class conflict that Samuel Richardson had described in his novels. To Drugget Nancy declares: "I know these people of quality despise us all out of pride, and would be glad to marry us out of avarice" (321). Woodley, too, puts the audience in mind of *Clarissa,* as even the use of Lovelace for Nancy's suitor must have done. Desperate because of his frustrated plans, Woodley says, "It is enough to vex a body, to see an old father and mother managing their daughter as they please . . ." (296).

Murphy's use of Dimity must have vexed a good part of his audience. Their resentment at being instructed by a servant may account, as well as the political sabotage, for their rejection of *What We Must All Come To.* While Murphy's advertisement to the play stresses the character of Drugget and his intention *"to shew the passions . . . frivolously agitated, and to point out the ridicule springing from their various turns and shiftings,"* Dimity's comments point their main attack on polite society and its collusion with the upwardly mobile middle class. On the Racketts and their kind, Dimity notes their acquiescence to fashion regardless of the subject, even in the matter of marriage. When the Druggets worry about Sir Charles's accusing their daughter of adultery, she reassures them, "I have lived in polite families where there is no such bustle made about nothing" (317). In her advice to Woodley, Dimity demolishes the conduct

of both the *nouveaux riches* and high society. She scoffs at any
romantic notions he may have about marriage in their corrupt
world. She admonishes him to pay court to the parents who
arrange the contract. Then she outlines a sequence of post-
marital events that comes close to a description of Hogarth's
Marriage à la Mode. In summary Dimity notes that her grim
catalogue, leading to the divorce courts or to a lifetime of
bickering and dissatisfaction, is "the way of the world now"
(294).

Dimity's final words, recalling the title of Congreve's play,
serve as a reminder that *Three Weeks after Marriage* is a fusion of
two dramatic forms—farce and comedy of manners. Like
Congreve's work, it is for all its humor a serious statement about
the mores and conduct of its time.

In what may be his best afterpiece, Murphy had elevated the
lightly regarded genre to the level of significant art. In the
earliest form of the play he had found the essentials of what he
wanted to say, and his revisions from the copy he presented to
the licenser through its various printed editions were largely
improvements in grammar, diction, and style. The one major
change for his *Works* is the addition to the scenes of quarreling
between the Racketts, both at the conclusion of Act I and in the
renewal of their argument in Act II. Murphy recognized where
the strength of his comedy lay, and, intelligent craftsman that he
was, he made the most of it in his final opportunity.

IX   The Choice

Murphy's final afterpiece, *The Choice,* opened at Drury Lane
on March 23, 1765, appeared once more that season, once again
the next, and had a single performance at Covent Garden in
1772.[90] Having severed his ties with Drury Lane after another
battle with Garrick, Murphy had used subterfuge and secrecy to
produce his play anonymously at the theater during the
manager's absence abroad. Despite good personal relationships
with the proprietors of Covent Garden, Murphy apparently
desired to resume his old association with Garrick. The
playwright's *No One's Enemy but His Own* and *What We Must
All Come To* had failed at Covent Garden, and, although political
opposition largely accounted for their reception, Murphy knew
that the inferior acting company had not enhanced his chances of
success.

If Murphy had hoped that word of his authorship would get out and that favorable reaction to *The Choice* would indicate a change in the political climate and encourage his return to Drury Lane,[91] he had to be disappointed. *The Choice* failed so badly that Murphy did not attempt to publish it until he revised it extensively for his *Works* in 1786. He repeatedly minimized the efforts he had given to the work, attributing its composition to his desire to provide a vehicle for Mrs. Yates in gratitude for her acting in *The Orphan of China* and her help in getting his tragedy to the stage.[92] Yet Murphy's explanations seem more an exercise in self-defense than a legitimate description of the genesis of his afterpiece.

The Choice does not quite need such defense. Rather than a bad play, it is simply an ordinary afterpiece, running, as many works in that genre did, to farce, but unredeemed by Murphy's customary infusions from the comedy of manners. Although sometimes described as comedy, *The Choice,* as even its plot indicates, belongs to the lesser genre. Having married Clarissa, a young woman of parts but no fortune, Loveworth, Murphy's hero, comes to the country to seek help from Woodvil in gaining the consent of his ill-tempered father, Sir William. When Sir William arrives, Woodvil and his servant, Watchit, hide Loveworth and pretend that Clarissa, who reluctantly accepts their scheme, is Woodvil's niece. They tell the meddling Mrs. Woodvil that Clarissa is an admirer of Sir William, seeking marriage but concerned for a proper settlement on his son. Sworn to secrecy, Mrs. Woodvil immediately informs the incredulous but flattered Sir William. In ensuing discussions with Clarissa, he mistakes her comments for confirmation of her love. When Mrs. Woodvil becomes suspicious, Watchit tries to keep her from the truth by informing her that Sir William has married his mistress, but is now trying to seduce Clarissa. Mrs. Woodvil remains skeptical and almost surprises Loveworth and Watchit in conference with Clarissa, who has recognized the nature of Sir William's attentions and objects to continuing the deception. When Mrs. Woodvil comes upon Loveworth in a dark room, he escapes, and Watchit convinces her that it was Sir William who tried to attack her. Mrs. Woodvil accuses Sir William and repeats Watchit's story about the planned seduction of Clarissa, but Watchit denies it. Sir William, although he thinks them all mad, gets Woodward's permission to marry Clarissa. As she has done throughout, Clarissa pleads Loveworth's cause to his father, who

agrees to forgive his son and even his wife if she shows merit.
Clarissa consents to marry Sir William if he persists after having
met his son's wife. When all is out in the open, Sir William has no
choice but to accept his son's marriage.

In its details, too, the action of *The Choice* clearly marks it as
farce. Despite two references to "the way of the world" (IV, 305,
342),[93] the play lacks the subtler humor of manners comedy.
Whole scenes—such as that following Watchit's "disclosure" of
Clarissa's love for Sir William and Mrs. Woodvil's immediate
transmission of the secret information—depend for their effect
on a series of asides and all parties' misinterpreting the words
and intentions of others. Clarissa and Sir William's talking at
cross-purposes—she believing he knows of her marriage to his
son and he thinking her responses refer to him—is the material
common to farcical afterpieces, just as Watchit's description of
Sir William's bumbling courtship of Clarissa is commonplace to
the genre.

Characterization, as well, depends on the exaggerated short-
hand of farce.[94] Murphy at once sets forth the types of humour
dominant in Sir William and Mrs. Woodvil. Sir William, described
in terms of "the violence of [his] temper" (IV, 304), immediately
acts out the characteristic in his first real speech. His love of
money, commented upon by his son and Woodvil, is caricatured
in his obtuse question about Loveworth's conduct that reveals Sir
William's own perverted values: "Does not he know that I
married a woman of fortune? That my father did the same? All
my family from father to son have had the table of interest in
view, and not one of us ever did a foolish thing out of generosity.
This booby of mine is the first of the name that ever did a
disinterested thing" (IV, 318-19).

Before Mrs. Woodvil appears, her absence is explained by
there being "some scandal stirring there about farmer ASH-
FIELD'S daughter; and she is gone to make her own enquiries.
. . . You know, if there is a secret going forward, she will have a
hundred eyes, all prying about" (IV, 308-309). On her return,
she immediately bursts forth with queries that support the
description: "Where is your master? Where is Mr. Woodvil? I
left him here: where is he gone? What is he about? Is any body
with him?" (IV, 326). The secrets she is given are not safe for a
moment.

Only Clarissa seems outside the realm of farce. Her seriousness and sincerity appear to balance the farcical world of schemers and manipulators. She repeatedly expresses her displeasure at the deception: "I have no right to pass a trick upon him" (IV, 359); "I dread the end of all this" (IV, 379). And yet she has her own farcical role as a burlesque of sentimental heroines. Her excessive fainting and weeping and her final moralizing offer a farcical rather than satiric comment on the popular genre.[95] Her "I have offended" and her kneeling before Sir William since "this posture is the fittest for me" (IV, 383) exaggerate what all too often was already egregious in sentimental comedy. Her concluding moral plays upon its artificiality and excessiveness, and Murphy underscores his point by reminding his audience that "these [are] light scenes" and then by gravely putting a face of mock seriousness on her: "Each sees his neighbour's back with follies groan,/ But never spies the budget on his own" (IV, 387-88).

While all of this is entertaining and cleverly done, *The Choice* does not differ greatly from the generality of farcical afterpieces of the period. Contemporary critics had no difficulty in citing possible antecedents in Garrick's *The Guardian* and Addison's *The Drummer*, and modern scholars have found relationships to other works by Murphy.[96] But a search for sources is not necessary. Murphy's model is everywhere in the genre, and, despite some sprightly moments and fresh insights, his final afterpiece is essentially common fare.

Murphy's revision for his *Works*, while greatly improving the play, does not alter its overall character.[97] The major change is the addition of Mrs. Woodvil, which adds depth and increases the satiric humor without shifting the farcical emphasis. Her presence alters the role of Watchit, who moves from a stock character, the prime manipulator, to a more complex character, one capable of conjuring up stories to move the action itself. For the theme, the inclusion of Mrs. Woodvil and her own arranged marriage, like that of Sir William himself, becomes a more serious satiric comment on what is at issue. Even Clarissa is changed by the introduction of Mrs. Woodvil and develops into a softer, more concerned character. She provides some necessary balance to the outrageousness of the work, without moving it out of the genre. The farce remains, not only in the derision of sentimental comedy, but in new scenes concerning Loveworth's hiding in his room and the spurious charges of Sir William's attack. In both the original and revision of *The Choice,* Murphy fails to infuse the spirit of the comedy of manners that distinguishes his best afterpieces from the farcical plays of his contemporaries.

X   News from Parnassus, a Prelude

In addition to afterpieces, Murphy wrote two short plays, one of which, *News from Parnassus,* a comic prelude, helped celebrate the opening of the newly expanded Covent Garden on September 23, 1776. Appearing only three times after its initial performance and insignificant as drama,[98] the work retains its importance as an index as reliable as the *Gray's Inn Journal* to the playwright's literary and theatrical interests and values.[99] Its dramatic form, derived from the French *pièce à tisoir,* allows Murphy to present his ideas upon a variety of topics through a series of characters developed in loosely connected episodes.[100] While Murphy does nothing to improve upon the genre itself, he uses it to dramatic advantage and conveys a lively sense of action along with his critical opinions.

News from Parnassus begins on a note of action as a news-hungry crowd storms the door of Boccalini, a critic who has just returned from Parnassus. Vellum, the bookseller, and Rantwell, the actor, slip past La Fleur, Boccalini's French valet. Vellum decries the untruthfulness of newspapers, but immediately offers Boccalini an opportunity to contribute to his own. Rantwell interrupts to present his views on acting, but becomes involved in argument with Vellum, who, at the same time, attempts to extract unfavorable comment on Roscius (Garrick) from Boccalini. When Rebus, the playwright, enters, the two retire to the next room. Rebus provides information on the theater, the vogue of sentimental comedy, and the absurdities of unnatural tragedies. As he concludes, Catcall, the critic, forces his entrance and demands his rights as a theatergoer: free admission and the privilege of interrupting performances. Under duress, Catcall departs and Fitzfrolick, a pantomimist, enters and cavorts and prances mindlessly about the stage until he is carried off. Boccalini responds to each of them in turn: ridiculing libelous newspapers, advising Rantwell to study the demands of audiences and to restrain himself from journalistic controversy, and informing Rebus about the demands of drama. Fitzfrolick returns, goes through a series of quick changes, and once more is chaired from the stage. Finally, Boccalini attempts to convey common sense to each of these type characters.

Murphy's loose form allows him considerable satiric range. He pokes fun at French dialects through the character of La Fleur, puns on the occupations of Vellum and Rantwell, and scoffs at the conduct of theater audiences in the figure of Catcall. He ridicules actors who seek only to please themselves and who are restless when not the center of attraction. Through the character of Fitzfrolick, Murphy takes off on his favorite targets—the inanities of puppet shows and pantomimes, with their ludicrous and unnatural methods and content. Using Boccalini to convey his own views, Murphy defends Garrick from the vicious attacks of Rantwell and Vellum, proclaiming him superior to Betterton and Booth, the best of Shakespeare's commentators. Through Boccalini, too, Murphy deplores the adaptations of earlier dramas which distort the intentions of the original plays. Whatever the right to "lop excrescencies, and remove indecency" in altering traditional stage pieces, Murphy insists that "the form in which the fathers of the drama left their works, shews their own frame of thought, and ought to be respected" (IV, 423-24).[101]

More importantly, through Boccalini's exchanges with Rebus, Murphy expresses his own opinions on tragedy and comedy. Rebus boasts that his new tragedy will mystify with its Eastern setting, exotic customs, and obscure language. He deliberately culls "obsolete words" from Shakespeare, and sprinkles his drama with imps, elves, and goblins. To appeal to his audience, Rebus plans a concluding moral about forgery, which will be "highly useful in a commercial country" (IV, 408). Boccalini's response offers Murphy's intolerance of unnaturalness in tragedy, whether it resulted from artificial dialogue, confusion of genre, or the bathos of bourgeois sentimentalism. Although chided himself by Johnson for the oddities and obscurities in his tragedy *Zenobia*,[102] Murphy recognized the artificialities that marred most late eighteenth-century tragedy.

Boccalini's advice to Rebus on comedy presents Murphy's principles and his opposition to sentimental comedy in terms closely paralleling those of Goldsmith's essay "Comparisons between Laughing and Sentimental Comedy" (1773). For Murphy, it is necessary that the comic playwright make:

an accurate study of men and manners: you have attended to the humours that gather in the mind, and the tinge those humours are apt to give to the imagination. You have pursued affectation through all her stages, and can open with a nice hand the vien [sic] of the ridicule that springs from that source. You have seen life, you know the foibles of the fair; the turns of vanity, pride, love, extravagance, and all the whims of fashion. You know the relative duties of life. . . . (IV, 405)

Murphy ridicules "pathetic comedy" (IV, 406), which sends the audience "away with sentiment and highly delighted with so pathetic a piece" (IV, 407-408). Like Goldsmith and Sheridan, Murphy opposed the fusion of pathos and humor.[103] Comedy was "meant to be the mirror of life. 'The proper study of mankind is man.' True comedy serves that purpose: it helps to develop the discriminations of character, and laugh folly out of countenance. Pathetic comedy is a mere substitute for wit, humour, and the powers of ridicule" (IV, 421).

Although Murphy did not immediately publish *News from Parnassus,* he regarded its views as significant enough to include it in revised form in his *Works.* His additions emphasize his belief that whatever the kind of drama, like all literature, it must follow the Augustan principles that derived from nature.[104] His own revisions to achieve greater clarity and effect better transitions belong to that same tradition that prized correctness and precision in art.

XI Hamlet with Alterations

Written in 1772, never produced, and unpublished until after the playwright's death,[105] Murphy's other short play, *Hamlet with Alterations,* belongs to the Augustan Scriblerian tradition of burlesque or parody. It is a sprightly and cunning attack on contemporary adaptations of Shakespeare's plays, but most particularly David Garrick's version of *Hamlet,* which was then preparing for production.

Murphy sets his scene in Garrick's own theater after the crowds have gone. Making three appearances, Shakespeare's ghost refuses to answer the questions of Garrick's underlings. They threaten him with calling the watch because he has paid no admission and warn that King David will not take kindly to such activities. In their cajoling, they reveal Garrick's promotional techniques and his stinginess with playwrights. When the ghost still refuses to answer, they go to inform Garrick and interrupt him while he is contemplating a surprise performance of his adaptation of *Hamlet* and envisioning Shakespeare's approval. He vows that he himself will watch that night. The ghost appears, and Garrick, officiously rejecting efforts to restrain him, follows the specter. The ghost lectures him about the maltreatment of his works by contemporary playwrights who capitalize on his reputation and genius by mutilating his dramas. He expresses his wrath at French criticism of his works and calls on Garrick to defend him. Although Garrick says he understands and promises to revere Shakespeare's memory, as soon as the ghost departs, the actor-manager plans to increase his productions of Shakespeare's plays in order to avoid paying new playwrights and plots to make ever further alterations in a way that will add to the number of benefit performances from which he can collect. Garrick responds to his friends' questions by telling them that the ghost has praised his efforts and proclaimed him the finest Shakespearian actor. He calls upon them to spread the news in the *St. James's Chronicle.*

The focus of Murphy's attack is evident, and the details of *Hamlet with Alterations* underscore his personal assault on Garrick, with whom he was at odds about the production of *The Man Does Not Know His Own Mind* (presented some four years later as *Know Your Own Mind* at the rival Covent Garden theater).[106] Spurred by his knowledge of Garrick's adaptation of *Hamlet*, Murphy expressed his anger through his travesty. Garrick is depicted as a tyrant in his own theater, a man behaving with false regality. His parsimony and greed are matched only by his vanity. Murphy exploits Garrick's methods of expanding his reputation by packing the house with his friends, by playing up to his audience, and by puffing his performances in George Colman's periodical, the *St. James's Chronicle.* But most devastating is Murphy's praise of Spranger Barry, Garrick's foremost acting rival, whom Shakespeare's ghost describes as "my best Othello" (271).

Yet Murphy was not merely vindictive in *Hamlet with Alterations.* Like Samuel Johnson and many other English critics of the time, Murphy generally disapproved of alterations of Shakespeare's work.[107] While Garrick's adaptation was more faithful than many others to the original and was praised on its first performance,[108] Garrick himself described it as "the most impudent thing I ever did in my life . . . ," and never had it printed.[109] For Murphy Garrick's *Hamlet* represented a practice that he genuinely deplored. Moreover, Garrick's decision to play the title role in a French costume and the changes that he had made in the drama—omitting the gravediggers, dumb show, Osric, and Hamlet's trip to England—appeared to Murphy to be a betrayal of Shakespeare's reputation to the corrupt principles of French critics in their attack on the English genius.[110] At no time in his career would Murphy tolerate that.

Yet despite his commitment to Shakespeare's reputation, his anger with Garrick, and the genuine artistic merit of *Hamlet with Alterations*,[111] Murphy attempted neither to produce nor publish it. He thought the manuscript sufficiently worthwhile to revise it, but he had become too politically practical and too conscious of his own reputation to bring the work before the public. Even in the private manuscript he made changes to soften his attack on George Colman, who was the manager of Covent Garden.[112] Without the availability of Drury Lane, Murphy would need Colman's theater, and, in fact, his next play, *Alzuma*, was produced there. He did not have to publish *Hamlet with Alterations* to make his point with Garrick. Knowledge of its existence was apparently one of the reasons that Garrick did not print his own adaptation.[113] Perhaps most important for Murphy, however, was his desire to present an image of himself as a writer of pure motives, one who had risen above the common controversies of the literary scene. His days of journalistic warfare were over; his spirited battles in print with Churchill and others were behind him. He was already looking to posterity, concerned with how it would regard him. Not only did he not publish *Hamlet with Alterations* at the time of its composition; in 1786, along with his political essay-journals and his Swiftian *Ode to the Naiads of Fleet Ditch*, his parody was deliberately omitted from his *Works*.

CHAPTER 3

Democritus in Full Dress: Murphy's Comedies

I Introduction

DELIGHTFUL and entertaining, Murphy's afterpieces represent a minor achievement in a lesser genre. His major accomplishment is five full-length comedies, three of which—*The Way to Keep Him, All in the Wrong,* and *Know Your Own Mind*—place him in the company of Goldsmith and Sheridan as the most important comic playwrights of their time. Although Murphy's reputation has been almost totally eclipsed by the subsequent popularity of his rivals, their contemporaries recognized that his comedic talents equalled theirs.[1]

Like the plays of Goldsmith and Sheridan, Murphy's belong to the late eighteenth-century rejuvenation of Restoration comedies of manners. While it is no longer fashionable or accurate to describe the works of the triumvirate as a revolution against sentimental or weeping comedy, there is no doubt that the three playwrights offered in their modified Restoration techniques a kind of comedy that ran counter to the popularity of a type of drama that emphasized the pathetic rather than the humorous, sensibility rather than satire, emotions rather than reason. In tone, interests, and emphasis, their works suggest their skepticism of the benevolent view of man's nature, their rejection of the improbabilities of incidents and unnaturalness of language, and their scorn of all the basic premises that dominated sentimental comedy.[2]

Antipathy to sentiment and a predilection for comedy of manners characterize Murphy's theory and practice throughout his career.[3] Whether in his prologue to Jephson's *Braganza* or his biography of Garrick, Murphy deplores what he regards as the

97

debasement of comedy, for "a play made up of grave and moral sentences, does not deserve the name of comedy."[4] His reviews in the *Monthly* and his ridicule of Hugh Kelly's *False Delicacy* berate contemporary examples of the genre.[5] His strong antipathy was sufficient to convince Garrick that he had written Goldsmith's famous attack on sentimental comedy, an "Essay on the Theatre."[6] In fact, in his theoretical opposition to the type and in his practical use of a modified form of the satire of his Restoration predecessors, Murphy outdid both Goldsmith and Sheridan. Whatever the final evaluation of his own achievement, Murphy was the most faithful practitioner of the new form of comedy of manners, and his work unquestionably enhanced the possibilities for the success of Goldsmith and Sheridan.

II   The Way to Keep Him

The Way to Keep Him, Murphy's first full-length comedy, appeared initially as a successful afterpiece. Before its opening at Drury Lane on January 24, 1760, however, Murphy had engaged in another of his many controversies with Garrick, who upset the playwright by refusing to play the role of Ferdinand in *The Desert Island*, Murphy's dramatic poem which shared the bill with his comedy. Murphy argued, threatened to take his plays to Dublin, but Garrick prevailed.

Despite their personal differences, Garrick gave the comedy his usual fine production. He took advantage of Murphy's knack of creating roles for particular performers by wisely starring himself as Lovemore and casting Kitty Clive as Muslin, a part obviously designed for her talents.[7] Under Garrick's direction, Murphy's short comedy of manners emerged as distinctly different from the customary farcical afterpieces,[8] and his maturity in handling exposition, characterization, and topical satire became clear to audiences and critics alike.[9]

Murphy appears from the outset, however, to have planned *The Way to Keep Him* as a five-act comedy, which would bring him greater critical and financial rewards than were possible with an afterpiece.[10] Even in three acts the work was longer than others in the genre, and it differed in manner, intention, and depth. He turned almost immediately to revising the successful play against the objections of Garrick, who apparently feared that the additional subplot with the character of Sir Bashful

Constant would detract from his own attractive role as Lovemore.[11] Despite Garrick's persistent efforts, including the aid of Mrs. Cibber and Paul Vaillant, Murphy's publisher, this time the playwright refused to capitulate, and the new version of *The Way to Keep Him* opened on January 10, 1761.[12]

Garrick again did not allow personal differences to interfere with his production. The revised play was an immediate success, and before the end of the month had been shown eight more times.[13] Within five days of its opening, it had been published, and three more editions quickly followed.[14] Reviewers lavished praise, debating only whether its merits were superior to the original. A triumph at its inception, the play proved Murphy's most enduring comedy, continuing as a stock piece for many years, performed well into the nineteenth century, and appearing as late as 1884.[15]

In general characteristics, themes, and intentions, the two versions of *The Way to Keep Him* are indistinguishable. As a comparison of them indicates, Murphy subsumed the original in his expansion and, by adding an interlocking subplot, simply broadened his mixture of farce and comedy of manners to make a more striking and meaningful social comment.

Even in his afterpiece, Murphy developed a complex plot designed through farcical action to convey the Restoration theme of the difficulties in achieving marital fidelity in fashionable society. Lovemore, the philandering husband, treats his wife with casual disdain and carries on an affair with Widow Bellmour. Through Muslin, her servant, Mrs. Lovemore discovers his activities, but is reluctant to accept Muslin's advice to repay him in kind. Instead, she rejects the advances of Sir Brilliant Fashion, who desires her, although he too is enamored of the widow. Having learned about the widow, Mrs. Lovemore confronts her. Since Lovemore has taken the disguise of Lord Etheridge, the widow denies knowing him, but offers advice on how to thwart a rival. When Lovemore arrives, Mrs. Bellmour sends his wife into the next room to spy on her techniques. Mrs. Lovemore, learning the truth, faints, and when Mrs. Bellmour goes to her, Sir Brilliant arrives, and, alone with Lovemore, realizes they are competing for the widow. With the two men gone, the women plot revenge. The quiet-living Mrs. Lovemore surprises her husband with an unwanted party, a houseful of company. During the evening, he intercepts Sir Brilliant's letter

to her and is outraged. Mrs. Bellmour arrives and unmasks his
deception. While he justly accuses his wife of having failed to
make domestic life attractive, he apologizes to both women. Sir
Brilliant, in turn, asks forgiveness and is forgiven by Lovemore,
but put on probation by Mrs. Bellmour. Lovemore assures him
that she will yield and reminds the widow that she has been
equally at fault in playing off her lovers against each other. All
having been properly chastized and having acknowledged their
guilt, their future seems promising.

For his plot and more in the afterpiece, Murphy owed much to
Alexandre-Guillaume Mouslier de Moissy's *La Nouvelle École des
Femmes* (1758). Even before his enemies could chide him for
plagiarism, Murphy acknowledged his indebtedness to De Moissy
for his plan and to Swift's *Strephon and Chloe* for his original
impulse.[16] Yet Murphy, as he noted, had converted De Moissy's
light farce into a more serious comedy far more realistic in its
intentions. He objected specifically to De Moissy's presenting
the husband (Murphy's Lovemore) as retaining his own name in
his illicit affair and allowing the Chevalier (Sir Brilliant) to make
an "Attempt upon his Friend's Honour, without a proper
Detection of either of them. . . ."[17] Murphy sought to correct
the deficiencies in the original by altering a great many details,
providing "a last Act entirely new," and turning "the whole into
an *English* Comedy. . . ."[18]

Expanding his play, Murphy again followed his customary
practice of reshaping source material to his own purposes. Not
only characters (Sir Bashful Constant and his wife) in his subplot,
but incidents and even phrases have antecedents in Pierre-
Claude Nivelle de la Chausseé's *Le Préjugé à la Mode* (1735).[19]
Murphy's borrowings largely affect Act II, Scenes 1 and 3, Act
IV, Scenes 1 and 5, and Act V, Scene 1,[20] and yet his skill turns La
Chausseé's sentimental material to his own satiric purposes and
welds the adventures and problems of his new characters with
the action of his original three-act comedy. The subplot required
wholesale and subtle changes throughout his revision, but
Murphy managed in such a way that the result is a unified play
bearing scant resemblance to his models.[21]

Murphy's subplot expands his theme of marital difficulties in
fashionable society. Sir Bashful's treatment of his lady further
reveals the cynical Restoration attitudes toward love and

marriage. Deeply in love with her, he keeps it secret for fear of being ridiculed. He abuses her publicly, expresses mistrust of her fidelity, and pretends to his own extramarital affairs. He foolishly confides in Lovemore. An even greater philanderer than in the afterpiece, Lovemore has designs on Lady Constant as well as on Bellmour. Encouraging Sir Bashful by saying that he, too, masks his love for his own wife, Lovemore carries out acts of generosity to Lady Constant as though he, rather than her husband, were bestowing the gifts. At the conclusion, as in the afterpiece, Lovemore and Sir Brilliant are undone by the craftiness of Bellmour, but, additionally, Sir Bashful acknowledges the ludicrousness of his imitation of what he has perceived as the way of the world.

Both the five-act play and the afterpiece present Murphy's particular mélange of farce and comedy of manners to achieve a satiric drama that is very much his own. Having traced the development from the earlier play, it is unnecessary to distinguish between them in their use of the two elements. The three-act work merely offers in miniature Murphy's mode of operation, which can be described more fully by discussing the elements as they appear in the longer comedy.

Murphy uses farce to lighten his social comment, to keep his tone from becoming too severe, and to make his instruction more palatable. As in his shorter plays, he rarely resorts to strong physical comedy, rough-and-tumble stage-play, or simple buffoonery, but depends greatly on mistaken interpretations, confusions in exchanges of letters, and maladroit intervention by meddling servants. The very action of *The Way to Keep Him* depends upon farcical misunderstandings.

Misunderstandings abound, and character relationships depend greatly upon misinterpretations. The ambiguity is often deliberate as one character seeks to take advantage of another. When, for example, Sir Bashful reveals his love for his wife, Lovemore expresses his shock in a way that Sir Bashful interprets as a response to his own situation rather than Lovemore's fear that it will spoil his chances with Lady Constant. Lovemore's promise not to betray Sir Bashful's secret "for my own sake" (175)[22] appears to Sir Bashful to refer to Lovemore's marriage rather than his designs on Lady Constant. When Sir Bashful asks Lovemore to deliver a letter to her and assures him that she will be grateful, Lovemore responds, "I hope she will, and I shall be proud to serve her" (212), words that Sir Bashful fails to recognize as meaning for Lovemore's own advantage.

All this is accompanied by farcical asides or exaggerated stage "business." When Sir Bashful tells Lovemore that he is having trouble with his lady, Lovemore replies, "I am very sorry for it," but adds for the sake of his audience, "I am perfectly glad of it" (147). Lovemore responds to his wife's request to answer one question for her, "With great pleasure," but his aside is, "If it is not inconvenient" (203). Berating Lady Constant, Sir Bashful punctuates his remarks with sotto-voce reassurances of his genuine feeling. From the play's opening, when Muslin tries to discover Lovemore's deception from his servant William, Murphy relies on stage "business" to achieve his comic effects. William interrupts the interrogation with a series of kisses and concludes by announcing to the audience that he has not betrayed Lovemore.

More significantly, Murphy uses farce to sustain his action. His plot depends upon the withholding of crucial words that would clarify the situation. In all his denunciations of his wife, Sir Bashful either does not confront her directly or else does so in terms that manage to add to the confusion. Believing that she has presented his anonymous gift to her to Sir Brilliant as a token of her love—though she has rejected it because Sir Brilliant has affronted her honor—he never specifically charges her with betrayal. When Lovemore substitutes his own letter for Sir Bashful's and Lady Constant accuses him before her husband, their words—about "that letter" rather than "my letter" or "his letter" or "the letter" rather than "my letter" (217, 219)— contribute to maintaining the confusion. Even Lovemore's failure to so much as hint to Mrs. Lovemore, until the very end, that he seeks pleasure elsewhere because she does nothing to make domestic life attractive belongs to the realm of farce—that dramatic territory in which action flows through the force of misunderstanding.

But *The Way to Keep Him* is not a farce, and its most interesting elements derive from comedy of manners.[23] Murphy's opening scenes in the five-act comedy employ settings and minor characters to achieve an atmosphere, tone, and moral climate characteristic of the dramatic world of Congreve. Servants engaged in card-playing suggest a Restoration scorn for the vacuous preoccupations of fashionable society. Tag-names— whether Murphy's own for "Lovemore," "Sir Brilliant," and "Constant" or Muslin's "Mr. Coxcomb," "Mr. Impertinent," and "Mr. Brazen" for William (139)—recall the humours comedy of the seventeenth century. William's defense of Lovemore expresses the values and perspectives of the Restoration playwrights: "A wife has no attraction now; the spring of the passions flies back; it won't do. . . . I tell you a wife is out-of-date . . . a wife is a drug now; mere tar-water, with every virtue under heaven, but nobody takes it" (142).

William's words foreshadow the attitudes of the main characters, particularly Lovemore and Sir Brilliant, who breathe the corrupt air of Restoration comedy. They speak cavalierly of the "tribe of lovers," "the pining herd" (143). They disdain married life. Lovemore scorns his wife's suggestion that they dine together in public with, "If you, Madam, have arranged an agreeable party, for me to be present, it would look as if we lived together like Sir Bashful Constant and his lady, who are always, like two gamecocks, ready armed to goad and spur one another" (157). Sir Brilliant reinforces his argument with the "horrible" example of "Sir Theodore Traffic at Tunbridge taking his wife under the arm in the public rooms, and 'Come along home, I tell you'" (157). Even at the end, as Lovemore lectures his wife on what has gone wrong with their marriage, Murphy's language and sentiments come almost directly from Restoration comedy, and his speech clearly echoes the famous "proviso" scene between Mirabell and Millamant in *Way of the World*.[24]

And yet *The Way to Keep Him* is no pale copy of Restoration comedy,[25] nor is the difference merely its mixture of farce and comedy of manners, a combination not unusual in the earlier genre. To be sure, Murphy deals with the same, boring, predictable qualities of society so that his intelligent characters can forecast the conduct of others in a manner suggestive of how wearisome that world can be. But Murphy's aims differ; his concern is more moralistic. If he uses the methods of Restoration dramatists,[26] he is not guided by their purposes. Like his afterpieces, his full-length play adapts the comedy of manners to prevent his descending into farce or slipping into the morass of the popular sentimental comedy of his day. Instead, he offers a work suited to his continuation of traditional Augustan values, particularly the virtues of common sense.

Like the Augustan satirists, Murphy concerns himself with those foibles of mankind that lead to foolish behavior and turn trifles into matters of consequence.[27] His play presents a commonsensical response to the various weaknesses in his society. In addition to the foolish fashionable disdain for love in marriage, Murphy's targets include the frenzied devotion to gambling, the ridiculous pride that finds its expression in dueling, the absurd practices in political electioneering. Gambling particularly draws his lash. His essays in the *Gray's Inn Journal* and his early afterpieces had mocked the wild passion for the gaming table. Here it becomes the social disease communicated from masters to servants, the metaphor of a sick society in which it can be suspended only for a moment of shock, a choice bit of scandal that can bring about a state in which "whist stood still; quadrille laid down her cards, and brag was in suspense" (174).

More positively, Murphy offers his own kind of Augustan good sense in the character of Widow Bellmour. From her first appearance, reading wittily and appropriately from Pope's *Moral Essays*, to the conclusion in which she sensibly acknowledges her own frailties, Mrs. Bellmour is the embodiment of a Popeian vision of commonsensicality. She knows how to deal with men and women. She maintains her dignity through adversity. With genuine understanding, she advises Mrs. Lovemore on the "art of pleasing," her words recalling Clarissa's worldly wisdom in *Rape of the Lock:* "It is the wife's business to bait the hook for her husband with variety. Virtue alone will not do it. Vice puts on allurements: why should not truth and innocence do the same?" (189). At the most trying moments, Mrs. Bellmour retains her good sense, recognizing that "passion is a bad adviser" (201). When the Lovemores stand at the brink of another catastrophe, she finds the appropriate words to soothe their feelings and does not demand perfection in creatures of this world. "Never stand disputing," she says; "you know each other's faults and virtues: you have nothing to do but to mend the former, and enjoy the latter" (238). Not for her the false fashions and empty language of sophisticated society. Those she parodies. Lovemore correctly describes her "beauty, innocence, and merit" (197). She is Murphy's heroine, whose voice of common sense speaks for the needed balance in a civilized society.

Along with the wit that disguises its didacticism, Mrs. Bellmour's language has the easy naturalistic style that Murphy believed essential for dramatic effectiveness.[28] He worked hard and successfully on the dialogue in his play, revising and refining it through one revision after another. His verbal changes from the acting version to the publication of his three-act play improve the naturalness of expression. While alterations from the 1770 edition of the five-act drama include shifting of scenes to add suspense and additional material to increase dramatic irony, these have less importance than his revisions in the characters' speeches. Everywhere, except in Act V, changes in dialogue abound,[29] almost as though Murphy, aware that his play was a major achievement in late eighteenth-century comedy, sought to polish it to perfection for posterity.

III   All in the Wrong

During Murphy's summer partnership with Foote, his second five-act comedy, *All in the Wrong,* ran successfully for ten performances, and— after his ensuing quarrel with Garrick, who objected to the terms of their agreement and reneged on his promise to perform the role of Sir John Restless—it triumphed again with its regular season opening on November 10, 1761. Unfortunately, its similarities to Colman's *The Jealous Wife,* which appeared at almost the same time, limited its initial run, but its nine performances marked the start of a theatrical life that carried it into the next century on London, provincial, American, and Continental stages.[30]

Public support was immediate. Although Robert Lloyd and Charles Churchill, Murphy's political enemies and Colman's friends, assailed him in print, contemporary audiences, writers, and the press applauded his comedy.[31] For the critic in the *Monthly,* Murphy had greatly improved on his source. The *Critical* reviewer, allowing that more wit might have been desirable, acclaimed its characterization, dialogue, and moral.[32] Even Garrick originally had described the play as "a very pleasant laughing Comedy of business, [which] will have great effect in the acting. . . ."[33] Garrick proved accurate for *All in the Wrong,* whatever its weaknesses, ranks with the best comedies of its time.

As usual, Murphy's inventive powers were set off by someone

else's work. This time it was Molière's *Sganarelle, ou Le Cocu Imaginaire* (1660), itself based on an Italian comedy, *Arlechino Cornuto per Opinione.*[34] From Molière, however, Murphy derived little more than the "first hint" of his comedy.[35] Unlike James Miller, who some years before had faithfully adapted Molière's work, Murphy turned a one-act farce into a complex five-act comedy of manners, which uses about one-third of the basic material in the original twenty-four scenes.[36] Expanding and deepening characterization, Murphy develops the plot, elaborates incidents, and creates additional complications. He provides a variety absent in his source and fashions dialogue and wit capable of sustaining the comic concerns beyond the limits in Molière's light farce.[37]

Even the simplest summary of *All in the Wrong* makes evident its complexity. Murphy's involved tale of jealousy concerns six people: Sir John Restless and his wife; Beverley, who wants to marry Belinda despite her father's insistence on a match with Bellmont; Clarissa, Beverley's sister, who plans to elope with Bellmont. The unreasonableness of the Restlesses entangles the lives of the others. Sir John constantly watches his wife, while she so distrusts him that she charges Marmolet, a servant visiting her own maid, Tattle, with having an affair with him. When Belinda, after a quarrel with her father, runs off to the park and accidentally faints in Sir John's arms. Lady Restless mistakes them for lovers. Belinda drops Beverley's picture, which Lady Restless discovers. Her subsequent actions, together with Sir John's chance meeting with Beverley, convince her husband that Beverley is cuckolding him. Conversations, letters, gestures, all are presumed to be evidence of infidelity. When Beverley learns of the picture and believes Belinda has given it to Sir John, he goes to confront him, but meets Lady Restless, and both conclude that they are being betrayed. Sir John and Beverley talk at cross-purposes, which merely reaffirms their suspicions. When Beverley accuses Belinda, she is outraged and vows that he will return on bended knee to beg forgiveness. He learns the truth from Clarissa and Bellmont and prepares to seek her pardon. However, through Sir John, she now believes that Beverley and Lady Restless are lovers. When Beverley calls at the Restlesses to claim his picture, he again becomes involved in their jealousy. Lady Restless, disguised, has duped her husband into taking her into their home. Beverley, hiding in a closet, believes she is Belinda. Lady Restless unmasks, upbraids Sir John, becomes suspicious about the closed closet, opens it, and brings on her husband's renewed accusations. Beverley goes to Belinda, who, out of pique and without regard for her friends' feelings, has consented to marry Bellmont. She rejects Beverley. To protect himself, Bellmont suggests that Belinda's reputation is blemished, and their aroused fathers insist on the company's going to Sir John's to learn the truth. Beverley, who has returned there, has become embroiled with Sir John before the group arrives to set off a barrage of charges and countercharges that leads to chaos. After Bellmont and Clarissa restore order, the couples are properly united, and all admit that they have been in the wrong.

Such complexity of plot, situations, and incidents, while allowing Murphy to turn Molière's work into a fully developed and interesting comedy, creates problems. Having so complicated and involved his plot, Murphy could not possibly find a resolution that would prove altogether satisfactory. For some critics his conclusion seems too rapid, his denouement too hurried; for others it takes too long to unravel the snarled lines of misunderstanding and to sort out the confused lives of his characters.[38] Actually, it is not so much a question of length as it is of finding a satisfactory comic outcome to an action that has been twisted by farcically inordinate misconceptions and unreasonable delusions.

Setting things right requires bringing enlightenment to characters who throughout have behaved irrationally in a world of farce; it demands the imposition of values belonging to the comedy of manners on events more naturally governed by the principles of a topsy-turvy world. Reading the manuscript of the play, Garrick, for all his praise, sensed the difficulties. He warned Murphy that the last act was too long in getting to the point, but he recognized, too, the danger of excessive cuts.[39] Murphy himself understood the problem and tried desperately to solve it. In revising the play for publication and later for his *Works,* he strives for greater plausibility and attempts to minimize the farcical elements. His reworking of the final text involved a complete reordering of the fifth act — one designed to create a more logical conclusion. To some extent he succeeded, but still the farce intrudes.

It is easy enough to explain the appeal of farce to Murphy for both afterpieces and full-length comedies. He recognized it as the surest means of reaching his audience, and he desired immediate success in the theater. In *All in the Wrong*, it serves to create a lively stage-play.[40] It requires little imagination, for example, to visualize the audience's delight in Lady Restless's scampering from door to door trying to discover her husband's "lover" or rubbing Marmolet's face to remove cosmetics that are not there because she cannot believe that anyone in London could have such a complexion. Similar hysteria must have greeted Sir John's examining Beverley to determine if he is his wife's lover and parading around him so that not only Beverley but the audience must have regarded him as a Bedlamite.

But such laughs are bought at the price of credibility. It is difficult to believe that clever Belinda never associates her lost picture of Beverley with that possessed by Lady Restless. Why, too, should Sir John assume that Lady Restless has hidden Beverley in the closet when she, after all, has insisted that it be opened? Garrick properly objected to "Belinda so readily" agreeing to marry Bellmont and to betraying her friendship with Clarissa in order to spite Beverley. He questioned the "manner of Belinda's fainting in the park" and preempted Murphy's excuse that Molière had used the same device by saying it was no more probable in the French play.[41] Murphy must have agreed, for, among other revisions to achieve greater plausibility, he increased the severity of her argument with her father to account for greater stress on his heroine.

Yet farce serves a purpose beyond slapstick as Murphy uses it to ridicule the sentimental elements that abound in contemporary plays. Even the names of his two young women—Belinda and Clarissa—suggest through their Popeian antiheroic allusions a comment on romantic stage heroines. From that point of view, Belinda's fainting parodies the tradition in the kind of drama that Murphy scorns everywhere in his writing. And Beverley's lament on Belinda—"no more of her beauty: it is external, superficial, the mere result of features and complexion" (III, 296)—leaves no doubt that Murphy is exposing the bathos of bourgeois comedy.

Such use of farce suggests Murphy's real interests. He was committed to Restoration comedy as it had developed in the late eighteenth century. At his best, he could fuse farce and comedy of manners. In *All in the Wrong*, he does not quite succeed, but the most effective elements in his play derive from the Restoration form. In Murphy's period it had undergone changes to include happy endings, to purge immorality, and even to offer some instruction. But the emphasis was still on wit, clever dialogue, and ridicule of social absurdity. More than any of his contemporaries, Murphy follows the pattern. Comparing Belinda with Sheridan's Julia in *The Rivals*, for instance, Bernbaum notes Sheridan's reliance on a sentimentalism altogether absent in Murphy's treatment.[42] The atmosphere in Murphy's play, despite its farcical elements, exudes that of Restoration comedy.[43] Belinda's very first scene with Beverley evokes the world of Congreve, as she sets forth her conditions for marriage. Although too early in the play and less effective because less adequately prepared for than the similar episode in the *Way of the World*, the scene offers the same characteristic wit and subtle suggestiveness and underlying seriousness.

Both characterization and theme belong to the Restoration comic tradition, and their treatment finally goes beyond superficial social comment. As in *The Way of the World*, behind all the frantic action stands the threatening figure of insecurity. Whom to trust becomes a major problem for Murphy's characters. His people, like Restoration cynics, are prepared to believe the worst about neighbors, friends, and lovers, and given the opportunity they jump to the most pessimistic conclusions.

Even the intelligent Belinda cannot trust her own common sense. Like Congreve's Millamant,[44] she suffers from the examples of society around her. She speaks confidently about how she will control Beverley's jealousy: "my future conduct, my regard for him will cure that disease . . ." (II, 309). Yet she knows the weakness of a woman's position in her world, Glibly spoken, alluding comically to Pope's Belinda, her words to Clarissa, who has talked of "resign[ing] my person to [Bellmont]," cannot be taken lightly, for in her world they are the solemn truth: "Why, that is what we poor women, after all the victories of our charms, all the triumphs of our beauty, and all the murders of our eyes, must come to at last" (III, 262).

Insecurity is women's natural state in the society. However clever and charming they may be, they have few options. No more than Belinda can Clarissa, levelheaded and bright, control her future. When, out of pique at Beverley's conduct, Belinda agrees to marry Bellmont according to her father's demands, Clarissa stands defenseless, for, as Sir William Bellmont says of his son's "telling me of his love for Clarissa, it is all a joke . . ." (13). Lady Restless, for all her silliness, expresses perfectly the situation of women in her society: "Cruel laws of wedlock! The tyrant husband may triumph in his infidelity. He may securely trample upon all the laws of decency and order: and it redounds to his credit, gives him a fashionable air of vice, while a poor woman is obliged to submit to his cruelty" (III, 236).

Murphy was no crusader for women's rights, but rather a shrewd observer and critic of his society. He recognized that, under such conditions, jealousy proves the natural child of insecurity and that, for all their dominance, men could be no more secure than their women. Their prestige, social position, and right of supremacy were constantly threatened. Not merely Sir John, who approaches caricature, but Beverley, the attractive hero, moves uneasily in a world where sacred trust seems always challenged. Sir John's fear — "My head aches; my forehead burns; I am cutting my horns" (III, 208) — although a comical outburst, hardly exaggerates the general feelings of men in Murphy's dramatic world. The mere suggestion of Belinda's indiscretion with Sir John becomes Bellmont's surest means of thwarting an unwanted marriage with her, and his and Belinda's father take off like bloodhounds to pursue evidence to determine whether she has betrayed the ideals of womanhood in a man's world.

Beverley, because he is not an eccentric character, provides an even better measure of his society's values. From the outset his insecurity parallels Sir John's. Because of the way the game is played, because of the need for women to mask their true feelings, he must allow his mind to think of the possibility that Belinda prefers Bellmont. Her wit and repartee, the expected badinage of a bright young woman in society, as much expression as the rules allow, cannot satisfy a temperament like his. As Bellmont says, "Though a handsome fellow, and of agreeable talents, he has such a strange diffidence in himself, and such a solicitude to please, that he is every moment of his life most ingeniously elaborating his own uneasiness" (III, 253-54). Insecurity breeds jealousy, and when Belinda angrily declares that she is going to marry Bellmont, Beverley responds, "I expected it would come to this . . ." (III, 342).

As Congreve uses love as a metaphor for his society's insecurity, Murphy uses jealousy. He proclaims his purpose to be to "delineate all the varieties of that passion" (Adv't.), but its function, like Congreve's, extends to a general comment on manners and men. Less entertaining than the great Restoration plays (partly because Murphy's theater demanded a more natural dialogue than the artificial and brilliant epigrammatic language of the seventeenth-century stage)[45] and weakened somewhat by its excessive use of farce, *All in the Wrong*, nevertheless, comes from the same mold. In his second comedy as in his first, Murphy proves himself the most worthy successor to the distant reign of Congreve, Wycherley, and Farquhar.

IV No One's Enemy but His Own

Coming after Murphy's two very successful comedies, *No One's Enemy but His Own* disappoints in almost every way. Its reception in the theater proved so disastrous that Murphy evidently had to guarantee the expenses of its printing.[46] Opening at Covent Garden on January 9, 1764, after a short delay, the three-act comedy ran for a total of only three performances,[47] and was generally treated severely in the press. The *Critical* reviewer limited his faint praise to its dialogue and wit, while John Langhorne, in the *Monthly*, described it as "not wholly destitute of comic humour."[48] Everywhere else in print the decision was all but utterly damning.[49]

Despite efforts by later critics to find redeeming features in the play and to emphasize those characteristics of Restoration comedy that represent its strength,[50] *No One's Enemy but His Own* cannot withstand objective scrutiny. To be sure, its initial reception was doomed by Murphy's political enemies, determined that the defender of Lord Bute and his peace treaty be prevented from having a fair hearing.[51] They provided a loud and unruly audience that forced the closing of the comedy and its afterpiece, *What We Must All Come To*. The afterpiece finally reappeared successfully as *Three Weeks after Marriage*, but Murphy could do nothing to salvage his comedy.

Murphy must have recognized that at best his play was a flawed comedy of manners, insufficiently humorous, lacking in liveliness, unsteady in characterization, and irretrievably mired

in farce. In 1774 he reduced it to a two-act afterpiece, which
appeared at Covent Garden on October 26 and ran for five
performances, only to disappear entirely from the London
stage.[52] Its demise was justifiable, for, despite Murphy's improvement in its diction and his decision to include it in his *Works,* his
revision made a poor job worse. Cutting speeches, paring action,
and rearranging material deprived the work of all sense of
character development and relationships, killed whatever spirit
and charm exist in the original, and gained nothing in theatrical
effectiveness.[53] Worst of all, the two most entertaining characters, Lucinda (written expressly for his mistress, Ann Elliott) and
Hortensia, who have the potentialities for attractive Restoration
heroines, are debilitated by Murphy's curtailment.

Murphy might have done better to have expanded his three-
act comedy to the full-dress Restoration drama that he
apparently originally intended. Apart from adding some farcical
characters—Sir Philip Figurein, Crab, and La Jeunesse—his
treatment of Voltaire's *L'Indiscret* (1725), his primary source,[54]
indicates his concern for creating a comedy of manners. He
moved in that direction with borrowings from Mrs. Centlivre's
Busy-Body, Shakespeare's *Antony and Cleopatra,* and Garrick's
adaptation of Vanbrugh's *The Provok'd Wife.*[55] His own
character, Lucinda, a Congrevian heroine, along with his
dialogue, suggests his desire to turn farce to more serious
concerns in his three-act comedy. Even his prologue, directed to
unfriendly critics who would find in his work another example of
a "French-built" farce, marks his intention to create an
eighteenth-century version of Restoration comedy: "Some
scenes, we hope, he brings to nature true,/ Some gleams of
humour, and a moral too,/ No forms, grotesque and wild, are here
at strife:/ He boasts an etching from the real life. . . ./ By easy
dialogue would win your praise/ And on fair decency graft all his
bays."[56]

But Murphy did not accomplish his purpose, and farce overwhelms what merits the play might otherwise have. His drama
revolves entirely around Careless, a farcical character, and a
summary of its plot suggests the encumbrance its hero places on
any legitimate development into genuine comedy. Despite
warnings from his friend Blunt, Careless cannot keep his affairs
to himself. He has lost Lucinda because of his indiscretion, but
has won Hortensia, a wealthy widow, and, at the same time, is

planning to seduce the young wife of Sir Philip Figurein, a foolish old man obsessed with the art of dance. Careless stupidly reveals all this to Wisely, his secret rival for Hortensia. When he gives Wisely a snuffbox with Hortensia's picture to have repaired, Wisely uses Brazen, his servant, to deliver it to her with the announcement that Careless has changed his mind about her. Brazen arrives while Hortensia and Lucinda are discussing Careless, without Lucinda's awareness that she has been replaced by the widow. Learning the truth, she ironically mocks Hortensia's having assumed an air of innocence and moral superiority. Lucinda leaves her and debates with herself the question of marriage for love to Bellfield, her suitor, or for revenge to Careless. Bellfield himself, being tormented by Lucinda, goes to challenge Careless, but is calmed when Careless tells him of his engagement to Hortensia. To further his scheme for winning Hortensia, Wisely again uses Brazen, disguised, as a messenger to inform Careless that Hortensia has rejected him. Careless blithely plans to straighten things out at Sir Philip's masquerade. Instead, Wisely, together with Bellfield and Lucinda, plots to undo Careless. With the entire company secretly watching, Lucinda pretends to be Sir Philip's wife. To seduce her, Careless scandalously denigrates the characters of Lucinda and Hortensia. Finally, unmasked by Sir Philip, Careless acknowledges his fault, but Lucinda joins with Bellfield, Hortensia with Wisely, and Careless stands as the butt of their jokes.

Like plot, characterization indicates Murphy's unresolved struggle between farce and a more sophisticated form of comedy. The conflict is most apparent in a scene between La Jeunesse, the hairdresser, and Crib, the tailor. When they argue about the superiority of their products (wigs and garments) as means for seducing women, their discussion suddenly turns into an inventive clothes philosophy that speaks to more than the surface issues involved. Yet it lacks appropriateness to their exaggerated characters. Murphy's thumbnail sketches of them deny them the right to wit. They are more suited to his use of dialect humor and are more at home in his world of Jack Tattles and Lady Betty Gabbles—characters who do not appear in the play, but are talked about and create its milieu of cheap farcical laughs.

Especially with the caricatured portrait of Sir Philip Figurein, among the minor characters, Murphy indicates an ambivalence in the play between farcical entertainment and more serious comment. Entirely Murphy's creation, Sir Philip did not have to be developed along the lines of Murphy's source, and yet, working for laughs, the playwright subverts all opportunities to demonstrate the selfishness and unconcern for others beneath Sir Philip's apparently innocuous eccentric behavior. Sir Philip perpetually dances or talks about dancing regardless of circumstances. When Wisely tells him that Careless is after his wife, he replies, in the midst of a dance, "This is enough to put a man out of time."[57] Aroused by Careless's behavior, he responds, "You shall dance to another tune presently."[58] And finally, as Careless is unmasked, Sir Philip triumphantly asserts, "You see what a false step you have made."[59] Much of this, especially in the revision, is clever, suggesting Sir Philip's wit, and yet it gets lost as the dervish twirls around the stage. Moreover, it masks a viciousness in Sir Philip's perverted wit. Any form but farce would lay bare the callousness of a character who cannot lament his daughter's death because she had never learned to dance.

Farce also dominates Murphy's treatment of his major characters. Just as it hides the ugliness of Sir Philip's character, it covers the dangerous and malicious aspects of Careless's. Because he ludicrously blurts out secrets immediately after vowing silence; because he seems ingenuous in his indiscriminate confidences to all the world; because he foolishly entrusts privileged information to Wisely, after describing him as one who has "no heart at all: his affections are all contracted into a narrow regard for self, and his understanding points for ever to schemes of interest," [60] because of all these, it is easy to dismiss Careless as a farcical fool. Yet, as his remarks on Wisely indicate, it is more Murphy's manner of presenting him than the character itself that is either farcical or foolish. Murphy, through his exaggeration and farcical techniques, unfortunately undercuts any serious social comment on a character that might appropriately have displayed some of the more savage aspects in social relations. Developed in the context of manners comedy, Careless, the agressive fortune-hunter who jilts and abuses women and casually betrays friendship, might have served the serious purpose suggested by the intended but ignored irony of Murphy's title.[61]

Well within that Restoration tradition is the character of Lucinda. Her early dialogue with Bellfield, although lacking some of the depth or bite of that of women characters in the earlier drama, has a wit that reveals her emotions without making her vulnerable. She entices without losing dignity. Her discussion with Hortensia about men displays that same shrewd understanding that Restoration heroines could express only in the defensive wit that alone protected them in sexual relationships. She shows the same rather frightening intelligence as she levels the pretentiousness of Careless. However, Murphy sacrifices her development to the farcical context of the play. He never goes deeply into her relationships, motives, or understanding because he is more interested in using her simply as the instrument for Careless's farcical downfall. He does that well enough, but in consequence Lucinda's wit always appears superficial, more a matter of verbal ingenuity than of some genuine intelligence or a defensive weapon in the battle of the sexes.

Caught between farce and manners, Murphy never found a satisfactory resolution in either the three-act or two-act version of his play. The work offers some good examples of wit— particularly the clever use of language for double entendre, such as Lucinda's comment on women's coquettishness, which is "like playing with edge tools, till we cut ourselves."[62] As always Murphy displays a fine ear for the sounds and rhythms of speech, as in Blunt's description of Careless: "Every man you meet is a pleasant fellow: he has picked up a character, an incident, a story, a damn'd high story; he goes to the play with it; tells it in a side box; buzz, it goes round the house; whisks away to the card table, and so flies all over the town."[63] Yet these are minor virtues in a play by a dramatist who could offer more when he had settled properly on his form.

V   School for Guardians

School for Guardians, Murphy's next comedy, was the last of three plays that he presented at Covent Garden during his long exile from Garrick's Drury Lane. Like the previous two, it failed. Opening on January 10, 1767, the work ran six times that season and never again,[64] although in 1777—abridged by Thomas Hull and with music by Arne and others—as *Love Finds the Way,* it gave twelve profitable performances.[65] Anonymous publication in 1767 proved equally unsuccessful, and when the playwright reworked the comedy in 1786, he himself reduced it from five to three acts and made numerous revisions.

Murphy's decision to drastically revise his play acknowledges the weaknesses that his contemporaries immediately recognized.[66] Judgments outside the theater matched the severity of audience responses. With the exception of some kind words in the *Court Miscellany*,[67] critical opinion uniformly condemned the play, attacking its plot and wit and charging Murphy with plagiarism.[68] To be sure, political antagonism still motivated some of the vehemence,[69] but Laurence Sterne, without partisanship, aptly summarizes the general evaluation: "[Murphy's play] could scarse [sic] get thro' the 1st night—'tis a most miserable affair."[70]

With some justification, Murphy blamed Garrick for the fate of his comedy.[71] After he had begun working on an adaptation of Wycherley's *The Country Wife* in 1763, he heard that Isaac Bickerstaffe had undertaken the same task for Garrick. Garrick denied it. Murphy reworked his material, combining it with three plays by Molière, in his desire to create an effective acting vehicle for Ann Elliott,[72] his mistress. Her illness delayed production, but in 1766 Murphy offered his comedy and her services to Garrick. When Garrick rejected both, Murphy turned to Covent Garden, but before his play could appear, Garrick rushed into performance *The Country Girl*, his own adaptation of *The Country Wife*. The similarities between the two plays made Murphy's appear a pale copy and doomed any chances of its success.

Despite its effect, Garrick's action cannot be held wholly responsible for Murphy's failure, and he himself seems to have recognized the truth. The *School for Guardians* is a weak comedy. After all his work on it, Murphy tried to belittle his effort. He trivialized its importance by stressing the fact that his sole concern had been a generous desire to aid Ann Elliott's career. With its publication, he sought the unusual protection of anonymity as though he wanted to have nothing to do with it. Murphy must have been aware that, after his first two, his gift for full-length comedy had forsaken him. Even his surprise recovery in 1777 with *Know Your Own Mind* had its origins in a work first completed in 1760.

Yet Murphy's play is not altogether the disaster that most criticism suggests. Whatever its faults, it has a cleverly developed plot, whose structure, based on parallel stories, the playwright adroitly manipulates. Particularly in its three-act revision, the comedy presents its entanglements without too much confusion—no mean trick, as may be seen from its complications even as they appear in summary:

Oldcastle and Lovibond, two elderly guardians, have raised their wards with an eye toward marrying them themselves. Oldcastle has kept Mary Ann in the country to protect her from fashionable vices, while Lovibond has educated her sister Harriet in town in order to inure her to its temptations. When Oldcastle, disguised as Bildulph, brings Mary Ann to the city, she immediately captures the interest of Charles Brumpton, a reckless gallant. Harriet, at the same time, gains the attention of the more sober Belford. With the women's aid, the two young men pursue them. Brumpton schemes with his clever servant, Brisk, pays off the domestics guarding Mary Ann, and works on her naive sympathy. Even when Brumpton, not knowing that Bildulph is Oldcastle, reveals his secrets to him, Mary Ann rescues him. Oldcastle's warnings about the horrible fate that may befall her merely arouse her curiosity and excitement. When Oldcastle dictates a letter to her to dismiss her lover, she rewords it to encourage Brumpton. Throughout Oldcastle's misfortunes with Mary Ann, Lovibond smugly boasts about his control over Harriet. Confident that he has schooled her to his purpose, he is no less deceived than Oldcastle as she gains access to Belford. When Brumpton succeeds with Mary Ann, Lovibond gloats over his superior system and advises Oldcastle to give up his claims for fear that their abuse of both their stewardships will be discovered. His temporary triumph ends with the announcement that Harriet and Belford have married and that the country girl and her city sister have outwitted their avaricious and lecherous guardians.

Cleared of some of its clutter and unnecessary characters, this three-act revision does not differ from the original in ways that would suggest that it would have been better received had it been the one presented in 1767.[73] In essentials—their fundamental structure and satiric attitudes—the three and five-act versions remain remarkably similar. The development along parallel lines so essential to Murphy's purpose characterizes both.

Murphy handles that development very cleverly, and had he chosen to write a farce strictly along French lines, his method would have been most appropriate. As in a work by Molière, his setting is designed to carry out the balanced structure of the play itself. The two houses—Oldcastle's and Lovibond's—reflect his character pairings. The lecherous and greedy old men, who have contrasting views on how to handle the young girls, are both parallel and antithetical. Mary Ann and Harriet, raised by diametrically opposed principles, work in their opposite ways to achieve their ends. Brumpton, reveling in the description of himself as a "coxcomb," and Belford, a model of "gravity and good sense," "in all things . . . opposite characters" (IV, 193), operate in differently devastating ways to undermine the guardians' unscrupulous plans.

Murphy manages his balance nicely, playing upon it in the very details of his farce. Just as Oldcastle and Lovibond ignore each other's boastfulness about what they believe to be their triumphs, Belford and Brumpton remain unconcerned about each other's victories and revel in their own. With dramatic irony, Murphy plays one story against the other, so that when Lovibond gloatingly describes to Harriet how Mary Ann has tricked Oldcastle by hiding her lover in the closet, she has just performed the same deception on him. In a fine turnabout, Murphy displays Mary Ann, who has been restricted to the simple life, acting without compunction to deceive Oldcastle, while the supposedly worldly-wise Harriet hesitates and rationalizes before duping Lovibond. Scene after scene uses parallelism and contrast to good comedic purpose along farcical lines.

But Murphy refused to settle for farce, and that proves the play's main difficulty. His satire, caught in an unsatisfactory mixture of forms, never coalesces to a single overall effect. His stage business caters to such farcical humor as lazy servants unwilling to respond to a knocking at the door until they discover it is their master and then they stumble over each other anxious to impress him. Murphy depends on farce, with country dialects or the standard confusions of identity and misinterpretation or the hurrying and scurrying to hide lovers in closets. Yet Murphy fails to subordinate these, as he desires, to the more polished humor of the comedy of manners for which he aims. The theme, as Brumpton's servant, Brisk, suggests in his advice to his master—warning him that beauty brings nothing in the market place and raises the threat of cuckoldry—is more ambitious, more a comment on society, but is overwhelmed in the delight in farcical excitement. Mary Ann's epilogue, with overtones of Pope, indicates Murphy's unachieved aspiration to the material and effect of manners comedy: "Be rul'd by reason for your beauty's sake./ Reason still gives to radiant eyes their grace. . . ./ Beauty, ye fair, may forge the lover's chain;/ But the mind's charms your empire must retain" (IV, 298).

Murphy's difficulties with *School for Guardians* resulted from the conception of his comedy and his use of his sources. Rather than concerning himself with a play, he sought to create an effective acting vehicle for Ann Elliott. He began with shaping a role for her from Wycherley's drama. Dissatisfied with that, he ambitiously combined three plays by Molière—*L'École des maris* (1661), *L'École des femmes* (1662), and *L'Étourdi* (1653)—with Wycherley's *Country Wife*. Yet he never seems to have focused clearly on the problems of bringing the two forms together, but instead concentrates on what is necessary to present Miss Elliott's talents to their best advantage in the role of the shrewd country girl. Unfortunately, the effect of his borrowing is a play whose stage business is superior to its overall comedic authority and whose technique is vitiated by an inadequate mixture of farce and comedy of manners.

The major emphasis of the comedy is naturally farcical, since, as Murphy acknowledged, it "consists of three plays by Molière moulded into one."[74] Its narrative basis depends primarily on *L'École des femmes*. Young Brumpton's character and adventures and the complex plot structure belong to the French farce. From the same source Murphy derives the figure of Oldfield, part of Mary Ann, and Peter and Bridget, the corrupt servants. For some incidents and for suggestions for the characters of Lovibond, Belford, and Harriet, as well as the title of the play, Murphy uses *L'École des maris*. Finally, *L'Étourdi* provides him with Brisk and Sir Theodore (the latter dropped in the revision). In all, Molière's works gave Murphy a stockpile from which he drew freely for his characters and situations.[75]

With so much to suggest farce as the appropriate genre for the *School for Guardians*, Murphy nevertheless refused to settle for that. When Oldcastle sees his servants for a second time willing to betray him for money, he exclaims, "The way of the world!" (IV, 264), a reminder of the milieu that Murphy hopes to create for his play. He maneuvers his plot and directs his witty dialogue in a manner that provides a sense of the late-eighteenth-century comedy of manners, including a final moral to replace Restoration licentiousness.[76] But most particularly, Murphy develops the character of Mary Ann so that she seems to have stepped forth from the earlier comedy of manners. If she is not "almost an exact copy of [Wycherley's] Mrs. Pinchwife,"[77] as a contemporary reviewer declared, she comes close enough to be a half-sister. Less knowing than Margery Pinchwife, Mary Ann, in her relations with Oldcastle and in her ability to turn his dictated letter to her own advantage, comes directly out of Wycherley's play.[78]

But this is precisely the difficulty with Murphy's comedy. Mary Ann is not at home in the world of *The School for Guardians*. Seeking to create an impressive acting role for his mistress, Murphy loses control of the play itself. As he proceeds beyond the first act and parts of the second, where he displays his greatest originality, he becomes involved in the complications borrowed from Molière and traditional French farce. His best comedies, like those of the Restoration, proportion farce so that it provides lively action without intruding on the comedy of manners. In the *School for Guardians,* they coexist as two disparate elements. Not content with farce, Murphy makes graceless use of *The Country Wife* and succeeds only in creating, as he originally desired, a vehicle that might display the talents of Ann Elliott or any young actress.

VI   Know Your Own Mind

When *Know Your Own Mind*—Murphy's final comedy and his last play designed for stage production—opened at Covent Garden on February 22, 1777, it received a warm welcome. Its success was immediate and enduring. Staged eighteen times in its first season, seven the next, and three the following, it continued to appear as late as 1848.[79] Despite demurrals by Murphy's enemies—including George Steevens, upon whom he had modeled his villain—unbiased critics hailed it as the finest

comedy since Congreve's day. They acclaimed its wit, characterization, and plot.[80] Even Colman, Murphy's old rival, derided
charges that the work was merely a translation or adaptation.[81]
Having announced his intention to retire, Murphy was urged to
continue as the most eminent playwright of his time.[82]

Yet despite its success and unquestionable merits, the work
proved a trial to Murphy long before its first appearance, and
subsequent events denied it the high place it deserves in theater
history. As usual, Murphy's problems began with Garrick. By
1760 Murphy had completed his first draft, and Garrick
scheduled production in 1761-62, until their disagreement about
Murphy's summer partnership with Foote led the playwright to
withdraw his work. After their reconciliation in 1767, Murphy
again offered the comedy to Garrick. Finally set for production
in 1772, with Mrs. Barry scheduled to play Lady Bell—a role
written for Ann Elliott, who had died in 1769—the comedy again
was set aside because of Murphy's differences with Garrick
about casting. Not until Garrick's retirement, and then at the
rival Covent Garden, was the play produced.[83]

Murphy's difficulties did not end there. Generally fortunate in
the acting and production of his works, Murphy had poor luck
with what may be his best play. Harry Woodward, scheduled to
perform the important role of Dashwould, died, and the less
competent Charles Lee-Lewes replaced him. Instead of a Mrs.
Barry or Mrs. Abington as Lady Bell, the crucial female
character, Mrs. Mattocks played the role without distinction.[84]
The production was poorly cast, and the audience viewed *Know
Your Own Mind* under the least favorable circumstances. Even
the publication of the play, delayed until 1778 because of
Murphy's difficulties with the publishers, whom he had opposed
over the copyright laws,[85] was shoddy and did nothing to
enhance its reputation.

For all that, *Know your Own Mind* might have achieved even
greater contemporary success and might have been better
known today were it not for an unfortunate coincidence of
literary history. Late in the same theatrical season, *The School
for Scandal* opened triumphantly at Drury Lane, and Sheridan's
masterpiece overshadowed Murphy's achievement.[86] It was
Murphy's particular misfortune that not merely the time of its
appearance, but, oddly enough, Sheridan's very indebtedness to

Murphy, enforced comparison of their plays. Sheridan borrowed abundantly from Murphy. Not only did Malvil provide him with strong hints for the characters of Joseph Surface and Mrs. Candour, but Millamour, Mrs. Bromley, Dashwould, and Miss Neville all make their way into his comedy, bringing with them traces of Murphy's dialogue and situation.[87] And yet it must also be acknowledged that Sheridan effectively converts his borrowed material into a play that surpasses Murphy's. Although *Know Your Own Mind* is a fine comedy, it lacks something that Sheridan's play offers to the modern reader even as it did to eighteenth-century audiences—a sentiment that makes the drama appealing even as it carries its bite.

Granted that Lady Bell is one of the most attractive heroines in British stage history, to be compared not only with Goldsmith's Miss Hardcastle and Sheridan's young women, but even with Congreve's Millamant.[88] Granted, too, that Murphy's wit matches that of his competitor and his handling of plot and rendition of reality surpass those of his rival.[89] Still, Murphy's play is less likable and its acerbic manner less calculated to win an audience. Sheridan has been accused of yielding to public taste for sentimental comedy,[90] but, in fact, that enables him to create a warmth in his characters and to generate a concern for what happens to them that is absent in *Know Your Own Mind*. For all Lady Bell's appeal, her invulnerability makes her a figure to be admired rather than loved. Millamour, Murphy's hero, generates even less concern; he has no hard center, no positive qualities to make what happens to him seem consequential.[91] On the other hand, Sheridan's couple—Charles Surface, cast in the mold of Tom Jones, and Maria, softly feminine as well as intelligent—have a charm that makes important their survival in the world of Backbites, Sneerwells, and Snakes.

Nevertheless, Murphy's comedy is an artistic triumph and deserves to be considered in its own terms. Its construction follows perfectly the classical rules that call for a comic fusion in all its parts. Plot and character work together to offer a unified comedic effect. Its comedy begins with its characterization, out of which its situations arise naturally, and nothing interrupts its progress.[92] Compact and intricate, it weaves a tight network of various plot lines. So swiftly does it move throughout and so stunningly do events culminate in its series of short climactic scenes that only a very talented playwright could have made

Know Your Own Mind a successful theatrical piece. Some measure of Murphy's skill can be felt even in a summary of its complex plot.

Sir John Millamour and Bygrove, brothers-in-law, have raised their sons by contrasting principles. Given freedom of choice by his father, Millamour proves incapable of making up his mind. Led either by his friends—Sir Harry Lovewit, Dashwould, and the unprincipled Malvil—or by his own whims, he repeatedly changes his ideas on professions and marriage. Young Captain Bygrove has responded to his father's insistent dictates by continually appearing to consent while determined to have his own way. The young men have reached marriageable age. Bygrove desires Lady Jane, who loves him, but Millamour cannot decide between her and her sister, Lady Bell. He even considers proposing to their aunt, Mrs. Bromley, in which he is encouraged by Malvil, who, while pretending to work in the marital cause of the recently widowed elder Bygrove, schemes with her to ensnare the younger man. Malvil himself, with the help of Mrs. Bromley and his accomplice, Madame La Rouge, hopes to win Miss Neville, Mrs. Bromley's ill-treated ward. Miss Neville, however, desperately loves Sir Harry Lovewit, although unable to believe him interested in someone of her low social position. Through forgery and libel, Malvil seeks to undermine his rival. At Mrs. Bromley's urging, he also works to arrange a marriage between Captain Bygrove and Lady Bell. Captain Bygrove, following Dashwould's advice to pretend a romance with Lady Bell to arouse Millamour's jealousy and spur him to propose, further complicates the situation. Millamour temporarily succumbs, but through Malvil's guile returns to the pursuit of Mrs. Bromley. When it is discovered, however, that he has sent plagiarized verses to the aunt and both nieces, Millamour becomes a target for the young women's torment, particularly that of the acerbically witty Lady Bell. Ultimately, Malvil's machinations are exposed, through both his own drunken carelessness and Dashwould's revelations. Millamour uses Madame La Rouge, betrayed by Malvil, to unmask the hypocrite before the entire company. A chastized Mrs. Bromley reconciles with Miss Neville, who is promised to Sir Harry; Captain Bygrove gets Lady Jane, and Millamour, properly chided to the end by Lady Bell, swears to be forever constant.

Even summary suggests how far Murphy has come in his last

comedy from the farceur of his early plays. He obviously was not content to follow his French source, Philippe Nericault Destouches's *L'Irrésolu* (1713), a five-act comedy.[93] The two plays have altogether different intentions. *L'Irrésolu* belongs to a long tradition of French farce, and, although Murphy borrowed heavily from Destouches, he reworked his material—altering characters, adding Dashwould, Sir Harry, Malvil, Miss Neville, and Madame La Rouge, and changing situations—in such a way as to emerge with a late-eighteenth-century comedy of manners, dependent upon wit for its effects and carefully controlling the proportions of its farce.[94]

Murphy directs his audience's attention to what he is about. His prologue specifically eschews the play's relationship to farce, warning that here there will be "no monsters for ill-judg'd applause," no stereotypes of Welshmen, Irishmen, or North Britons, but rather, "Some plot, some character; he hopes, some wit" (339-40).[95] His second-act song from Congreve reminds his audience of the theatrical world that they are in. Dashwould's comments on the changeable fashions of society, the fickleness of taste, and the clichés of the town portray a weariness with the way of the world. Mrs. Bromley's fear of being buried in a country life shows Restoration disdain for the ways of bumpkins, and Malvil summarizes the sophisticated attitude by ridiculing country manners and rustic pleasures.

In his method of presentation and his characterization, Murphy clearly indicates his allegiance to a form of manners comedy. Like his Restoration predecessors, he has the difficult job of offering his audience a point of view, a way of knowing what to believe in information that comes from satiric characters, whose comments determinedly are cast in wit. What in Dashwould's remarks on Malvil or Malvil's on Dashwould is truthworthy? To be sure, some characters and statements seem wholly reliable: Sir John, despite his failures with his son, presents some kind of norm; Miss Neville offers some authorial voice as she illustrates the deplorable state of dependent young women or helps to reveal Lady Bell's fundamental goodness. But these prove the exception. Murphy must set the characters of Sir Harry Lovewit and Dashwould by presenting Sir John and Bygrove's views of them even before they appear. In that way the audience knows the possibilities to expect and can better judge not only their characters, but the accuracy of their judges' opinions.

Perhaps Murphy's treatment of Millamour provides the best example. Before Millamour has had a chance to display his fickleness, Dashwould gives a detailed and witty description of his changes of mind about professions and marriage. But Dashwould's perceptions are too cleverly expressed to be trusted. Indeed, their very wit puts them in question. They must be bulwarked in a variety of ways: first, by Bygrove's earlier remarks and Sir John's fears about Millamour; then by the testimony of three servants; and, finally, by Millamour's own actions. Murphy's method recalls Congreve's opening of *Way of the World,* where Fainall and Mirabell discuss nine characters— their accuracy is remarkable, but their own characters and circumstances are such that it requires considerably more evidence to be believed.

Further complicating Murphy's difficulties is the fact that, as in Restoration comedy, information comes from characters whose perceptions are delivered in a witty language that allows them to speak truth without seeming didactic. Their comments forcefully express a serious concern without losing the tone of comedy. Here Murphy's polished wit and dialogue surpass anything he had done before.[96] Lady Bell, especially, displays Murphy's effective use of Restoration techniques in conveying his information. She comments tellingly on Mrs. Bromley's abuse of Miss Neville; she gets to the heart of her differences with her sister, and she perceives early where Miss Neville's desires lie. Like a good Restoration heroine, she offers the truth to an audience while entertaining it with banter. Her remarks to Lady Jane illustrate her manner. Chiding her sister, who has claimed moral superiority, she will tolerate no such nonsense: "The difference between you and me, Sister, is this; you deny your love to your female friends, and own it to the man; now I deny it to him, but among ourselves, I fairly own that Miss Neville is not more impatient to be married to Sir Harry than I to—" (371). Only Miss Neville's embarrassed exit prevents Lady Bell's naming Millamour.

Most significant for Murphy's relationship to the Restoration comic dramatists is his characters. They embody the spirit of the earlier comedy. If Murphy falters at times because of the

demands of writing manners comedy in the latter part of the
eighteenth century (the sudden transformation and ability to
make decisions in Millamour, for example; though a similar
change of character in Mrs. Bromley has been better prepared
for), overall he has grasped the essential traits of the characters
for his genre. Lady Bell provides an excellent example. She does,
as critics have suggested,[97] surpass anything offered by Sheridan.
Murphy knows precisely how to set her up, to get across a sense
of her vanity, her delight in the role of participant in the battle of
the sexes. Murphy gives her character by her self-reference to
Belinda; he plays off her forward and outgoing nature by
contrasting her with the sly and cautious Lady Jane. To the very
end, she carries out her part as a Restoration comic heroine,
delightfully tormenting Millamour after having promised to
marry him. Holding out both hands to him, she challenges him
wittily: "which will you have? Puzzle about it, and know your
own mind if you can" (431).

Two other characters—Malvil and Dashwould—come directly
from the world of Restoration comedy. Motivated by different
interests, they provide the vitality of the action, stirring up
trouble, scheming and devising, setting things in motion. Malvil,
as his name indicates, is an instrument of evil. Plotting and
moving toward his own end, he creates with malevolent energy
the events that develop Murphy's story. His insidiousness lies in
his effective hypocritical methods. Without commiting himself,
indeed, while pretending to virtue, he damns Mrs. Bromley in his
report to Bygrove: "Though I am not inclined, with the malicious
part of the world, to suspect her virtue . . ." (367). He conveys
scandal through half-truths or innuendo. Without saying anything, Malvil says everything he wants to say: sowing doubts,
damning without exposing himself. As Dashwould comments,
"He is often present where [his friends'] characters are
canvassed, and is anxious about whispers which nobody has
heard. He knows the use of hypocrisy better than a court
chaplain" (350–51).

Dashwould himself is a Restoration schemer of a different
order. He is the satirist present in the work itself. Modeled on
Samuel Foote, he combines Foote's unattractive habit of placing
opportunities for wit above friendship with Foote's comic energy
that Murphy admired.[98] Dashwould freely takes off at the

expense of the town's characters. His is the cynicism of Restoration comedy, for, as Bygrove remarks, "He put all to death without remorse. He laughs at everything, as if Heaven intended to make its own work ridiculous. He has no relish for beauty, natural or moral. He is in love with deformity, and never better pleased than when he has most reason to find fault" (346). Dashwould, however, distinguishes among the follies of the world. To Millamour he says, "I don't dislike you for your absurdity: that moves to divert me: Malvil excites other feelings" (418).

Murphy uses Dashwould as both primary observer and modus operandus in his work. Dashwould provides the most knowing comment on Miss Neville: "She is a natural character . . . has a heart" (399). He points out the weakness of Sir John's faith in his son, saying, *"Gulliver's Travels* is a true history to him" (351). Looking for weaknesses in the world, he finds them even in his friends, Sir Harry and Millamour, and ridicules them, for, as he believes, "the passion . . . that runs headlong without cause, and will not hearken to reason, is a greater part of society than all the little wit that has been in the world" (417-18). While Murphy may share Bygrove's sentiments—in response to Dashwould's banter— that modern wit has gone awry in scandalous libels, he most certainly does not agree with Malvil's insistence that "Ridicule is a very unfair weapon . . . it is by no means the test of truth" (347). Shaftesbury's maxim, denied by Malvil, lies at the center of Murphy's satire, and no character in the play employs it more than Dashwould. Moreover, Murphy uses his comic energy to set things right in the confused world. His Restoration vigor and cynicism uncover Malvil's deceptions and bring about as much stability as is possible in the world of comedy.

More than any other play of its time, *Know Your Own Mind* carries on the tradition of Restoration comedy.[99] Like Congreve, although less effectively, Murphy broadens his satire beyond the particular circumstances of his action. He condemns as much fashionable vice, as large a part of the evil in the ways of the world, as he can within a single comedy. If this diffuses his focus,[100] it also allows him to make a more meaningful comment on the decadence of his society. He does not restrict himself to the limited nonsense of a circumscribed group, but suggests that their aberrations reflect those of the world around them. They

ARTHUR MURPHY

appropriately belong to the world gone mad over gambling, the
political schemes of Charles James Fox, and the republicanism of
Catherine Macaulay. Their litigious natures plead for the
machinations of self-interested lawyers.

Within his comedy of manners, Murphy employs farce
supportively and sentiment sparingly. Millamour's stumbling,
interrupted "proposal" to Mrs. Bromley and the unmasking of his
plagiarized love notes are no more than Congreve's treatment of
Lady Wishfort. If the characterization of Miss Neville appears to
yield to sentimental taste, her role is too insignificant to affect
the tone of the play. Against such details, Murphy's use of
manners comedy is overwhelming. He places wit above all else.
Dashwould relies on it even at the cost of friendship; Malvil and
Bygrove indulge in it; Lady Bell employs it to deride every
notion of a sentimental heroine. Murphy uses Lady Bell and
Millamour in a manner recalling Congreve's Mirabell and
Millamant. Wherever the situation tends naturally to farce,
Murphy turns it away to a witty social comment. Despite
eighteenth-century changes in decorum, a more moralistic
attitude demanding that marriage appear an attractive state,[101]
Murphy follows closely the pattern of Restoration comedy.

Murphy remains true to that tradition in all three major
versions of *Know Your Own Mind*: the acting copy, the 1778
revision, and the final text in 1786. Apart from his minor
alterations—changing Sir Harry Lizzard to Sir Harry Lovewit,
omitting some poetic quotations—Murphy does some extensive
rewriting in order to add clarity to his plot and characterization.
He reduces the hectic quality of his opening scene and makes it
more formal by eliminating the low comedy of the servants
which originally initiated the action. His complete removal of
Trinket, a servant, lessens the complications of his plot without
losing anything significant. Whether adding, subtracting, or
transposing (all of which are considerable), he aims at clearer
exposition. New dialogue for Miss Neville, bemoaning her
dependence, offers a better picture of her mind and situation.
Her discussion with Lady Jane, added to Act I, provides clearer
understanding of subsequent action. Murphy is at pains to
achieve greater credibility as he changes details concerning
Dashwould, Mrs. Bromley, and Sir John. If, at times, he loses
something through revision—as in his reduction of the climactic

scene between Millamour and Lady Bell, making it less like Congreve's between Millamant and Mirabell — [102] the total effect of his changes produces a more polished and professional drama. Nothing, however, alters its fundamental nature as a late-eighteenth-century rendition of the Restoration comedy of manners.

CHAPTER 4

Heroic Endeavors:
Tragedies and Tragicomedy

I Background

THEATRICAL conditions posed incredible difficulties for any late eighteenth-century tragic drama. Even the best had to compete with the popularity of bathos and sentimental comedy. After their initial performances, Shakespearean and lesser tragedies had to be propped up in their appeal by attractive comic afterpieces or other forms of light entertainment whose effects were inescapably anticlimactic.[1] The time-honored practice of humorous epilogues, as Murphy himself recognized, diminished the impact of any serious drama.[2]

Other theatrical developments also militated against successful tragedy. While Garrick had introduced greater realism to the stage, its development was still transitional, and audiences formerly content with conventions that demanded full use of imagination or simple acceptance of unreality now had neither the older conditions to depend on nor altogether new ones.[3] For comedy, rooted in the immediate society, the problems were less formidable; for tragedy, based on history or classical sources and still devoted to the conventions of classical drama, they were disastrous. Costuming had evolved only to a limited degree in historical accuracy and emphasized the enhancement of character rather than chronological fidelity: faithful enough to suggest historical truth, but false enough to challenge verisimilitude. Scenery, while moving toward greater realism, and lighting, which allowed a greater sense of time changes, had not yet achieved a convincing competence.[4] Even acting methods, undergoing realistic alterations, wavered between Garrick's new style and Quin's oratorical manner, and where unaffected techniques were employed in stylized, formal tragedies still bound to classicism, they proved at odds with the material.

For all that, dramatists like Murphy, who sought to enhance their reputations, turned to tragedy—the highest genre. Murphy himself wrote six tragedies, the last two not intended for production. While all show his fundamental allegiance to classical theory, they also display his willingness to cater to public taste and to take advantage of topical interests or popular fashions. As with his use of farce in comedy, when it suited Murphy's purposes, he laid aside his theoretical principles.[5] He wanted theatrical fame, and if the appeal of *chinoiserie,* or patriotic emotions, or any other momentary interest would gain it, Murphy capitulated. Even when it meant trying his hand at a form he disliked—the tragicomedy of the *Desert Island*— Murphy was willing.

Although, like other eighteenth-century tragedies, Murphy's have lost their appeal, they enjoyed contemporary artistic and commercial success. The *Grecian Daughter* alone remained popular in the nineteenth century, but all of his stage tragedies, with their recognition of what the age demanded, surpassed the competitive efforts of William Whitehead, John Home, Robert Jephson, Hannah More, Richard Cumberland, and Richard Glover.[6] During his lifetime, Murphy's plays received more productions, had more performances than, and outlasted the works of any of his contemporaries and were surpassed only by the earlier tragedies of Shakespeare, Otway, Hill, Rowe, Southerne, and Congreve.[7]

II   The Desert Island

Beginning with *The Orphan of China* in 1759, Murphy sought the tragic muse six times over the next four decades. The first of his tragedies, however, was followed almost immediately by his only tragicomedy, *The Desert Island,* a poetic drama more interesting for its stage history and peripheral matters than for any intrinsic merits. Appearing together with the popular three-act version of *The Way to Keep Him* at Drury Lane on January 4, 1760, it ran eleven more times and then vanished from the London stage.[8] Its failure is understandable, for despite some success as a publication and a measure of achievement in its poetry, the work is an untheatrical, weakly contrived dramatic exercise.[9]

Much of its interest today comes from its history, which displays Murphy as an embattled man of the theater. Together with *The Way to Keep Him,* the play thrust Murphy into a major struggle with Garrick. He threatened to take his work to the Smock-Alley Theater in Dublin unless Garrick agreed to act in the drama, but had to settle for Garrick's writing and presenting an epilogue, which, offered in the character of a drunken poet, ironically proved a successful piece of stagecraft.[10] But that was only the beginning of Murphy's difficulties. First, the play provided the occasion for a scurrilous attack in a pamphlet entitled *A Letter to M. de Voltaire; with Comparatory Descants, on the Extraordinary Composition and Incidents of a Dramatic Poem, Called The Desert Island* (1760). Then it brought the opening assault of Charles Churchill's satirical blasts at Murphy in the *Rosciad* and the *Apology.* For Churchill, *The Desert Island* was sufficient to demolish the reputation of any playwright. Scoffing at what he describes as Murphy's plagiarized fairy tale, with its simplistic treatment of characters and nature, Churchill lambasts the author and his work.[11] And finally, after his literary skirmish with Churchill came a vicious attack on Murphy by the pseudonymous Philom Moculloch in *The Murphiad.*[12]

Apart from its biographical interest, *The Desert Island* reveals much about Murphy's writing that has less to do with the play itself than with such matters as his dramatic practices and intentions. The work displays again Murphy's characteristic approach to creativity, which begins with source material and reworks it into something ultimately far removed from its origins. Here the starting point is Pietro Metastasio's *L'Isola Disabitata* (1752).[13] To turn its fourteen short scenes into a three-act play, Murphy had to do more than merely expand its dramatic speeches. Despite Churchill's jibes, Murphy copies neither Metastasio's work nor its French adaptation by Collet (*L'Isle Deserte*).[14] As Murphy asserts in his "Advertisement" to his publication, he has allowed his "own Imagination" free range in developing a drama appropriate to the English stage.[15] Doubling the length of Metastasio's work, Murphy changes character relationships and improves motivation while providing greater plausibility in the action. Metastasio's thirteen-year-old sister of the heroine becomes a sixteen-year-old daughter, whose response to her father's friend—her awakening sexual awareness—enhances probability, even as she retains her youthful simplicity necessary to the plot. By dropping the vengefulness of Metastasio's heroine, Murphy increases the credibility of her willingness to accept her husband's return, and by allowing her husband rather than his friend to relate the circumstances of their enforced separation, Murphy makes the impact upon the wife more believable.[16] If Murphy rather foolishly permits the characters' names to remain Italian, his decision to Anglicize the characters themselves clearly reinforces his appeal to his English audience. Elaborating and altering, effecting a change in what he calls its "colouring," and working his own poetic and scenic effects and playing to patriotic impulses,[17] Murphy, as always, turns his source material into his own work.

What Murphy does in *The Desert Island* greatly differs from anything he offers elsewhere in his dramas, and perhaps its main interest is in his attempt at a combination of things which for him was unique. Both its genre and theme accord with nothing else in Murphy's work, and very likely its lack of stage popularity accounts for Murphy's unwillingness to venture again outside the conventional paths of his successes. Murphy came to the theater for practical reasons, and despite his growing desire for more than a contemporary reputation, he obviously was reluctant to yield immediate returns for his efforts. *The Desert Island,* in its dramatic kind and in its particular interests, had proven unprofitable, and Murphy returned to types and subjects with which he was more at ease and of whose impact on audiences he could be assured.

Murphy's problems with genre and theme may be anticipated from his simple plot, whose qualities are remote from anything in the rest of his work. For sixteen years Constantia, his heroine, has lived with her daughter Sylvia on a desert island after her husband, Ferdinand, has disappeared while seeking help. Longing to return to her world, but embittered by her husband's apparent desertion, she has instructed her daughter in the cruelty of men and society. She has chosen to live only because of her obligation to Sylvia, whose cheerful innocence turns her mother's thoughts to nature's beauty. Wandering alone one day, Sylvia spies a ship on the horizon and hides near the inlet where two men come ashore. They are Ferdinand and his young friend Henrico, whom he has rescued from pirates. Ferdinand has forlornly returned for some trace of his wife and child. Secretly watching them without understanding her own feelings, Sylvia is

drawn to Henrico. Searching the island, Ferdinand discovers a
rock on which Constantia has been inscribing her story and reads
its message forgiving his supposed betrayal. He vows never to
leave the island on which he thinks his wife and child have
perished. Fearing that Ferdinand will go mad, Henrico goes for
help to remove him, but meets Sylvia and they immediately fall
in love. He sends Sylvia for Constantia, but she has already been
reunited in a pathetic scene with Ferdinand. He has explained
his disappearance, and she has forgiven him, but the bewildered
Sylvia cannot reconcile these men and their stories of society
with her mother's descriptions. Finally, encouraged by her love
for her father and Henrico and their assurances that loyalty,
freedom, and happiness exist in England, Sylvia agrees to return
with them to civilization.

Even in summary, *The Desert Island* is obviously a tragicomedy, a form not only unusual for Murphy, but one
inconsistent with his dramatic theories.[18] Uncomfortable with
the genre, Murphy seeks almost to disguise it by describing it as
"a dramatic poem in three acts." Desiring to move into new areas
in the theater, he seems reluctant to commit himself. To be sure,
he had already tried his hand with tragedy in *The Orphan of
China*, but that play had depended greatly on fashionable taste
for *chinoiserie* and new effects in stage production. So, once
again, in *The Desert Island*, he edges toward tragedy, but
hesitates about his new direction. While some critics have seen
his attempt as audacious experimentation, it appears rather timid
and uncertain, designed more for the closet than the stage,
neither a mainpiece nor afterpiece.[19] Murphy's hand is unsteady
even in maintaining a dramatic effect in such passages as those in
the second act where Ferdinand's and Henrico's accounts of
their experiences suggest a narrative voice in the poem.

Murphy's treatment of theme seems equally indecisive. At ease
while satirizing his society, Murphy chooses another approach in
The Desert Island. His seriously intended comparison of the
virtues of natural and civilized life wavers between classical
restraint and romantic, emotional indulgence.[20] Although Garrick's prologue plays down Murphy's romantic elements and
emphasizes the play's classical orderliness, beginning with his
stage directions, Murphy appeals to a growing popular demand
for the exotic, the mysterious, and the wild: *"rocks, caverns,
grottos, flowering shrubs, exotic trees, and plants growing wild."*

Constantia herself appears *"in a romantic habit of skins, leaves and flowers"* (III, 391), and her opening lines tie together emotion and setting as gloomy, wild, and isolated nature evokes her feelings of despair; even her initial lament describes her story as a "melancholy tale" (III, 382).

Murphy's expression throughout inclines to sentimentalism, which perhaps explains his willingness to retain the romantic Italian names for his English characters. Ferdinand's speeches to Henrico about his lost love derive from sentimental romance. In Ferdinand's meeting with Constantia, Murphy offers Gothic touches like Smollett's scenes in *Ferdinand Count Fathom*. Speech after speech suggests Gothic and sentimental romances. Constantia, responding to Sylvia's delight in regaining her lost fawn, expresses herself in Rousseauistic terms: "Oh! happy state of innocence! how sweet/ Thy joys, simplicity, e'en yet the mind/ With artificial passions learns to glow . . ." (III, 394). Ferdinand's description of himself (before the "grots" and "gloomy cave") combines Gothic and sentimental in a single speech: ". . .it is the doom of love like mine/ To dwell for ever on the sad idea/ Of the dear object lost; to visit oft/ (A lonely pilgrim) ev'ry well known scene,/ Each haunted glade, where the lov'd object stray'd;/ To call each circumstance of pass'd delight/ Back to the soul . . ." (III, 411-12). Without intending parody, Murphy grants Sylvia an outburst of gushy pastoral song. Even in his revisions of the play, although working toward more formal diction and syntax, Murphy increases the pathetic elements.[21]

And yet Murphy never altogether yields to the play's romantic appeal to an audience accustomed to sentimental comedy and tragedy for many years in the theater. He cannot repudiate his own inclination for wit or sophisticated enjoyment of society. In Henrico's meeting with Sylvia, Murphy plays upon her silly simplicity. Constantia, for all her bitterness toward man in society, defends the civilized world through her very longing for it. To be sure, in moments of weakness, she bemoans the fact that "the whole brute creation," except man, can be "forgetful of their cares. . . . Know some repose" (III, 396-97). Yet she regards Sylvia's argument for nature's beauty as being mere sophistry for want of knowledge, for "What is this waste of beauty, all these charms/Of cold, inanimate, unconscious nature,/ Without the social sense?" (III, 399). She longs for civilization, some "faint prospect of my fellow creatures"; and when Sylvia reminds her of her charges against society, she ignores them and replies, "It is "easy to forego/Untasted sweets, pleasures you never knew" (III, 397-98). Finally, there is Ferdinand's argument to convince Sylvia to leave her island paradise for "cultur'd fields." Turning aside "civil discord" and war with assurances of "a happy, venerable king,/ Dispensing justice and maintaining laws" (III, 435), he celebrates liberty and orderly succession and concludes by praising England in terms of bourgeois perfectability.

Murphy simply could not make up his mind about what he was doing in *The Desert Island*. In *The Grecian Daughter*, his most successful tragedy, he would effectively use romantic elements to appeal to his audience and to bolster the sense of passion in his characters. He would even offer a happy ending in his tragedy to placate the demands of a shifting set of aesthetic values. In *The Orphan of China* he had already employed—if not with great artistic merit, at least with popular appeal—romantic emotionalism and primitivistic *chinoiserie*. With *The Desert Island*, however, his difficulty is in his own ambiguous attitude toward his theme and form. Unhappy with his genre and indecisive about his argument, he conveyed his uncertainties to an audience that mistook his intended "simplicity and innocence" in Sylvia's character for "archness."[22] Even his poetry, which drew most of the contemporary praise,[23] has a hollow blank-verse eloquence inappropriate to its sentiments. Where it should be reckless and bold, it is formal and oratorical, and despite its technical virtues,[24] it provides dull dramatic expression. In *The Desert Island* Murphy attempts something different from anything else in his work, but his experiment fails because he lacked faith in his medium and was awkward in his sentiments.

III The Orphan of China

Completed by 1756, Murphy's first tragedy—*The Orphan of China*—because of difficulties with Garrick did not appear at Drury Lane until April 21, 1759. With customary duplicity, Garrick had simultaneously encouraged Murphy and John Hawkesworth to adapt Voltaire's play, but when Murphy's was ready, he attempted to subvert it. Not only did the work require elaborate treatment for which Garrick felt unprepared, but its French *chinoiserie* posed considerable risk. Attacked in 1755 for his *Chinese Festival,* Garrick feared another theatrical disaster.[25] To discourage production, he sought outside opinions on the manuscript, and when that failed, he counted on Mrs. Cibber's refusal to play the role of Mandane to gain a further postponement.[26]

Murphy obstinately pressed for performance. Despite William Whitehead's detailed criticism of the play's weaknesses and Henry Fox's suggestions for revisions (including arming Timurkan with a sword to allow him the semblance of an honorable defeat), Murphy gained their and Horace Walpole's support.[27] He ignored Garrick's problems and rejected the idea that during the Seven Years' War *chinoiserie,* because of its French associations, had declined in popularity and could arouse public indignation. While Garrick relied on Mrs. Cibber's last-minute withdrawal, Murphy had secretly rehearsed Mrs. Yates to replace her.[28]

Murphy prevailed, and with Garrick's help *The Orphan of China* triumphed. Garrick had spared nothing in its staging, including innovative scene changes and folding gates and doors. The play "went off with great applause" and, despite its late appearance, ran nine times, including three author's nights.[29] Revived successfully the next season and later in 1764, it enjoyed success through 1766. Revised by Murphy and with Mrs. Barry in the role of Mandane, it repeated its triumph at Covent Garden in 1777, and it retained its reputation as late as 1798.[30] Its publication brought ample reward. It went quickly to a second edition, and Lord Bute, to whom it was dedicated, responded generously.[31] With his first tragedy, Murphy had emerged as a major dramatist.

Yet the appeal of *The Orphan of China,* like that of most popular eighteenth-century tragedies, cannot be easily understood today. While acknowledging Murphy's competent handling of plot and, to a lesser extent, characterization, modern readers are unlikely to find pleasure in the language and poetic speeches that pleased his contemporaries.[32] The heroic conventions that prevailed from the Restoration through most of the following century now seem unnatural and affected, and the play's grandeur and sublimity, prolix exhortation. Besides, the effect of Murphy's play depended greatly on contemporary circumstances. Not only Garrick and Mrs. Yates's acting, but the recent favorable reception of Voltaire's tragedy, which Murphy had adapted, contributed importantly to its success.

Most significant of all was Murphy's ability to make the most effective use of his *chinoiserie*. Despite its somewhat declining appeal,[33] Murphy revived it through clever allegorical political comment and promotion of patriotic fervor at a time of international strife. He adapts his material to offer a moral story to an English audience. As Mrs. Yates's epilogue makes clear, he does not confuse his Chinese fiction with the realities of Chinese life, but uses the English creation of Confucius as wise philosopher to offer "moral truth" and "moral beauty."[34] His Chinese are English Christians in Oriental dress. In moments of stress, they invoke heaven, call upon angels, and seek a Christian-Judaic mantle for their acts of vengeance and justice.[35] When Zamti refuses to respond to Mandane's request that he take her life rather than permit Timurken, the tyrant, to torture her, Murphy's hero argues in Christian terms against such conduct.

Rather than *chinoiserie*, European thought pervades Murphy's political play. Montesquieu inspires Murphy's passages in defense of liberty. Murphy designs speeches on the rights of man and the spirit of the laws to rally his audience to the defense of the nation in the name of liberty and freedom. Lord Bute himself recognized the political implications and supported Murphy partly because he identified Zamti with his own role as protector of the future George III.[36]

While such matters contributed to its popularity, they should not obscure the fact that, as a tragedy measured by the values and conventions of its own time, the play has genuine merit. For example, while twentieth-century critics have dealt unfavorably with Murphy's language in the play, Goldsmith in the *Critical Review* singles it out for praise. Although unmoved by its *chinoiserie* and acknowledging the importance of its production, Goldsmith, like the reviewer in the *Monthly*, emphasizes Murphy's poetic talents, his "glowing imagery." For Goldsmith, "all the faults of the performance proceeded from vicious imitation," that is, the use of what Goldsmith considered a barren Chinese tradition—"but all its beauties were the poet's own."[37] His review and later essay on the "fame machine" in the *Bee* acknowledge the emptiness of the sentiments in the drama, but Goldsmith repeatedly praises its poetic speeches, especially those between Zamti and Mandane in which the mandarin tries to convince his wife to place loyalty to her country above her personal feelings.[38]

Actually Murphy accomplishes more than Goldsmith's comments suggest. To be sure, he owed much to Voltaire's *L'Orphelin de la Chine* (1755), itself dependent upon a French translation of a fourteenth-century Chinese play.[39] His structure, the relationship between action and characterization, and even some of Murphy's language derive from Voltaire's work. And yet *The Orphan of China* ultimately becomes Murphy's own play. It is not simply the best English adaptation of a Voltaire tragedy or an improvement of its immediate source, but rather, as the reviewer in the *Monthly* recognized, it was "a new English play."[40] With the skillful hand of a professional playwright, Murphy turned a dull, polemical dramatic source into a lively, effective theatrical piece for his contemporaries. He uses stage business, spectacle, and emotional fervor to shape a drama more consistent with Elizabethan melodrama than with the refined, controlled passion of French neoclassicism. At the same time, he converts Voltaire's theme concerned with Chinese history to a political and patriotic call for freedom and liberty.[41] He adds characters—Etan and Hamet, Morat and Mirvan—and changes the motives of Voltaire's conquerer (Timurkan), whose desire is to seduce Mandane, so that he becomes a symbol of political tyranny rather than a headstrong lover. To heighten the action and create a sense of immediacy, Murphy presents Voltaire's infant orphan as a young man heroically set to regain his throne. Voltaire's placid and passive drama, complete with a happy ending, yields to Murphy's impassioned and gory treatment. Blood and battle and continual emotional struggle become Murphy's means of arousing an audience already stirred by the events of the Seven Years' War. So different finally from Voltaire's play was Murphy's adaptation that in 1807 it was translated as a successful tragedy for the French theater.[42]

In a letter "To M. De Voltaire," appended to his text, Murphy details the differences from his source. The epistle cleverly defends Shakespeare from Voltaire's attack in patriotic terms that assure Murphy's support from an English audience.[43] He minimizes his own indebtedness to Voltaire by citing how his interest in the subject had been aroused by Bishop Hurd's comments which compared the Chinese original with the works of classical antiquity and by acknowledging his borrowing from both Corneille and Racine to reinforce his tragedy.[44] More specifically he emphasizes objections to Voltaire's treatment of the subject, those points of disapproval that had led him to construct his play according to principles at variance with Voltaire's

Without descending to servility, Murphy praises Voltaire's superior talents, but then analyzes the weaknesses in the French play that had to be dealt with to succeed on the English stage. Murphy the professional dramatist senses the passive, static, and wordy characteristics of Voltaire's work. He describes Voltaire as talking about action rather than presenting it and deplores the absence of stage business that sacrifices tragic emotion to philosophical discourse. Shrewdly, Murphy observes that Voltaire ignores the natural conflict for parents whose patriotism requires them to sacrifice their child for the safety of their prince. He recognizes that Voltaire's decision to keep the changelings as children eliminated them as responsible moral agents for a motivating force in the play. Citing Voltaire's own warning that love should function as the primary interest or not at all in a tragedy, Murphy censures his allowing Timurkan's amorous interest to detract from the main concern. In all, Murphy rebukes Voltaire, who had abhorred Shakespeare's irregularity and had sought to apply Aristotelian principles to the Chinese play, for not having effectively applied his own rules, and Murphy proclaims his own design for "order and propriety" (I, 102).[45]

The epistle accurately surveys the differences in technique and intention between Murphy's and Voltaire's tragedies. Murphy's plot reveals a political play designed to arouse the audience's patriotic passions through the heroic attitudes conveyed against the splendor of Oriental settings in which the action, as in Greek tragedy, provides a catharsis. He focuses on Zamti and Mandane, a Chinese mandarin and his wife who unselfishly had exchanged their infant, Hamet, for Etan, who is Zaphimri, the orphaned heir to their country's throne. While Etan has been raised without knowledge of his identity, Hamet has been taken from the country by Morat, who believes his charge to be the exiled prince. Murphy's action begins with the capture of Hamet by Timurkan, the cruel, conquering Tartan emperor. Believing that Hamet is the heir, Timurkan plans to kill him, and Zamti and Mandane must decide whether to permit their son to die in order to maintain their oaths. When Octar,

Timurkan's general, convinces his leader to make Hamet a puppet ruler, Zamti and his forces gain time to plot the tyrant's assassination. Zamti gathers his followers and reveals the identities of the youths, both of whom insist on offering their lives for the public welfare. Zamti dissuades them. Unable to ascertain the positive identity of his captive, Timurkan tries to apply pressure to Mandane and Zamti. His threat to execute Hamet leads the distraught mother to acknowledge her son, but neither she nor Zamti, although threatened with execution, will betray the prince. Only the intervention of Mirvan, Timurkan's Chinese counselor, who secretly waits to avenge his parents' slaying by the enemy, prevents their death. Mirvan offers to torture them for the information. A series of subsequent plots to break their resistance—including Octar's rejected suggestion that Timurkan marry Mandane—fail, and the enraged emperor orders the couple and the youths brought to him. As Timurkan sends Hamet to the rack, Etan, who had previously escaped, enters and proclaims his identity, throwing all into confusion and ending the episode. Awaiting torture, Mandane unsuccessfully begs Zamti to slay her with a dagger she has procured. As Zamti is taken to the rack, Mirvan breaks in to announce a rebellion, but deliberately misleads Timurkan on its significance. Etan enters with a saber. Timurkan, seizing Mirvan's, duels with the prince, who slays him. While the palace battle rages, however, Zamti remains on the rack, and Mandane, thinking him dead, stabs herself. She and Zamti die on stage, but not before the patriotic mandarin admonishes the despondent Etan to live for the public good.

It is obvious how intent Murphy is on hewing to his theme, exploring the conflict in loyalties and exalting the virtues of patriotism dedicated to freedom and loyalty. Speech after speech makes explicit Murphy's values. Changing his source so that his two young men become moral agents, he gains two spokesmen for his message. Unencumbered by the conflicts between personal and political responsibilities as Zamti and Mandane are, Etan and Hamet can boldly proclaim Murphy's theme. Hamet vows to die for "the liberties of China" (I, 61). Etan declares, "We'll dare for liberty, or bravely die" (I, 3), and with youthful abandon, he sets the issue squarely: ". . . Better to die/ With falling liberty, than basely lead/ An ignominious life . . ." (I, 32).

Yet Murphy's play draws its greatest strength from the

complex conflict in his adults. Weighing the values of nature and civil demands, Zamti and Mandane have to struggle to decision and their conclusion becomes more movingly dramatic and more meaningful. *Nature* stands as the crucial word in underscoring their dilemma. Mandane especially pleads nature's cause in her desire to save her son at the expense of her civil duties. Repeatedly, she describes "nature's workings in a parent's heart" (I, 52) or emphasizes "a mother's love" (I, 21) and cannot believe that Zamti, who "doats upon his boy" will not provide instruction on "how a father feels" (I, 21).

Nor is she wrong on Zamti's instincts. When he first confronts his son in Timurkan's presence, he reveals his inner conflict and uses the word *nature* to express his sentiments: "Cease your fond conflict Nature!" (I, 29). Yet, from the outset he is determined to protect the heir. He calls upon Mandane to conquer "all the dearest ties of nature,/ To serve the gen'ral weal" (I, 38). He warns her, in words that suggest Murphy's Tory and monarchic loyalties, "Reveal the awful truth; be thou spectatress/ Of murder'd Majesty . . ." (I, 37). When Mandane rebukes him—"Is human nature exil'd from thy breast?" (I, 34)—he responds, "I was a subject, ere I was a father" (I, 35). Within the heroic framework, Murphy offers genuine conflict, and if some modern readers find it unmoving,[46] for Murphy's audience it was an exemplar to suggest that the sacrifices they were being asked to make were minimal by comparison.

So evidently didactic in purpose, *The Orphan of China* required decorative accoutrements to palliate its obviousness. Murphy mixes his elements well, aware of what effective theater demanded. He understood that *chinoiserie* had the advantage of combining exotic attractiveness and classical values. Bishop Hurd and William Whitehead (in his prologue) argued its classical authority, and Murphy himself emphasizes the similarities. Timurkan's first speech contrasts the values of a civilized society with those of "rougher scenes" (I, 22). Murphy stresses classical moderation even within the excessive passion of his drama. His portrait of Timurkan bears the exemplary admonitory characteristics of Johnson's description of Charles XII in *The Vanity of Human Wishes*. Murphy's comment on the tragic ending of Zamti and Mandane ascribes their deaths to "rashness" (I, 90, 92), a cardinal sin of classicism. And yet, he balances all this by appealing to romantic emotions through romantic devices. His use of hidden identities, of princes in disguise, recalls earlier prose romances. But particularly in its setting, combining *chinoiserie* remoteness with Gothic terror and sentiment, the tragedy deviates from the classical formalism of plays like Addison's *Cato.* Examples abound, but the scenic directions for Act III provide sufficient illustration. When Zamti and his plotters meet clandestinely, the scene is a temple with a tomb in its center, and Gothic chill joins with Oriental eeriness amid ". . . the long-winding isles,/ The solemn arches, whose religious awe/ Attunes the mind to melancholy musing . . ." (I, 40). Murphy obviously appreciated the necessity of reaching his audience's emotions while preaching his patriotism.

As with all his work, Murphy did not allow his tragedy to remain unchanged over the years. Although it underwent considerable revision even prior to production, he made alterations for its first publication. Largely verbal, Murphy's changes strive for greater clarity in expression and motivation. He makes stage directions more explicit as though to supply visual detail. Perhaps most important, additions in dialogue— especially, but not solely, for Mandane—seek increased melo- dramatic effect, underscoring the parents' emotional struggle. This spelling-out of feelings appears intended to convey what gesture and movement might have offered in the theater. At any rate, Murphy's changes continued in the same direction for both his revision in 1777 and in his *Works.* As audience sensibility shifted toward a greater taste for melodrama, he accommodates his text. Yet, despite its many alterations, *The Orphan of China* remains throughout essentially the same play. Shifting some scenes, striving for more formal diction, and increasing the emotional content, Murphy seems nevertheless to have been generally content with his initial effort. To be sure, he sought always to present his best image to posterity—even the letter to Voltaire, strengthened in its defense of Shakespeare and in its expression of Murphy's tragic theories, suggests that—but he obviously did not believe his drama had fallen much short of its original purpose.

IV Zenobia

Zenobia, Murphy's next tragedy, opened on February 27, 1768. With the exception of *The Choice,* which appeared anonymously in 1765 during Garrick's absence, it was his first production at Drury Lane since 1761. Having failed with three plays at Covent Garden, Murphy sorely missed the superior acting of Garrick's company, while Garrick, having quarreled with Colman, looked to Murphy as a satisfactory replacement. Both men willingly allowed the playwright Isaac Bickerstaffe to end their long rift.[47]

Despite some further argument about financial arrangements and after delays caused by the odd machinations of the actor Spranger Barry and his future wife, Ann Dance,[48] Murphy's tragedy opened to general applause. It ran well for five seasons, moved successfully to Covent Garden in 1777 to remain on the boards until 1787, and appeared frequently in provincial and American theaters.[49] With three editions of its published texts and generous praise from the critics,[50] Murphy clearly had established himself as a major tragic playwright of his period. Professing delight in both the performance and publication of *Zenobia*, the *Monthly* reviewer expressed the overall opinion of Murphy's contemporaries.[51] And, like Thomas Davies, who in 1784 singled out the play for its superior dramatic situations,[52] modern writers have acknowledged that *Zenobia* ranks among the best tragedies of its time.[53]

As eighteenth-century tragedies go, *Zenobia*, in fact, is a satisfactory work of art. Murphy displays his skill in the carefully structured, tightly bound plot of the heroic drama that he fashioned from the merest suggestion of a story in Tacitus. Complicated by disguised characters and its reliance on events prior to its dramatic action,[54] the plot proves difficult to follow even in outline, but summary makes evident the multiple loyalties involved in its conflicts and the heightened passions that give it power. Whatever the limitations of the genre and its conventions for a modern reader, *Zenobia* has the strength to move through its playing upon universal emotions.

Zenobia, disguised as Ariana, falls captive to Pharasmanes, the Iberian king who has slain his brother and her father, King Mithridates of Armenia. Not knowing she is the wife of his son Rhadamistus, whom he kept from the Armenian throne, Pharasmanes wants to marry her. When a group seeking to join the Romans, at war with Pharasmanes, is captured, Megistus, Zenobia's old protector, is among them. He had saved her and her unborn son from drowning, when she and Rhadamistus had sought suicide together, and her husband had apparently been swept out to sea. During Pharasmanes's pillaging, her child had disappeared, but Megistus informs her of his safety. Through the intervention of Teribazus, Rhadamistus's brother, who also loves Zenobia, Megistus's life is spared. Rhadamistus, bearing the name of Flamminius, arrives as a Roman peace emissary. Learning of the loyalty of Zopiron, an Armenian at Pharasmanes's court and husband of Zelmira, who has befriended Zenobia, he reveals his identity to him as Zenobia had to Zelmira. He discovers that his countrymen, believing him dead, look to Teribazus to oust Pharasmanes. Meeting his father, who does not recognize him, Rhadamistus charges him with murdering Mithridates and Zenobia and refuses to accept him as king. He also meets Teribazus, who does not know his true identity. Although Teribazus refuses to fight against Pharasmanes, he agrees to join the Romans and asks them to protect Zenobia. Teribazus brings Rhadamistus and Zenobia together, but neither one tells him the truth. Then, meeting with Pharasmanes again, Rhadamistus discovers his father's hatred for him and desire for his death. Urged by Tigranes, his evil counselor, Pharasmanes presses Zenobia for marriage, but Teribazus protects her until he feels that she and Rhadamistus have betrayed him. When they try to escape, he captures them, but, learning the truth, vows to kill Pharasmanes. Rhadamistus, to save him from the guilt of parricide, dissuades him. To save her husband's life, Zenobia marries the tyrant. Aroused by jealousy, however, Pharasmanes plans Rhadamistus's execution, but she has poisoned the ceremonial wine, and Pharasmanes dies. Having drunk from the same glass, Zenobia also dies, but first she pleads with Rhadamistus to raise their son virtuously. When Rhadamistus seeks to take his own life, Teribazus successfully intervenes.

Summary suggests Murphy's concentrated effort to bring together noble actions of characters called upon to make sacrifices in the name of conflicting principles. It is Murphy's design and Murphy's intention, and not that of any source. Although he himself cites the *Annals* of Tacitus (Bk. 12, sec. 44-51) as his touchstone and notes that earlier French and Italian writers have used the same story, he also insists on his basic originality, which "takes a play, as Britons takes a ship;/ They heave her down;—with many a sturdy stroke,/ Repair her well, and build with Heart of Oak./ To ev'ry breeze set Britain's streamers free,/ NEW-MAN her, and away again to sea."[55]

Comparison of *Zenobia* and the story in Tacitus suggests that

Murphy's source provided no more than an impulse for his drama.[56] He alters not only action and circumstances, but even Tacitus's characters. For Murphy Rhadamistus must be a noble figure worthy of Zenobia's sacrifice. That required major changes from Tacitus's character: a tyrant over the Arminians after having slain Mithridates; a scheming politician whose attempts to undermine Pharasmanes's authority warranted harsh treatment; a possessive, jealous husband, who, when Zenobia could not maintain the pace of their retreat, wounded her and cast her into the water so that no other man might have her. All that remains of Tacitus in Murphy's *Zenobia* is the heroine's strength and her rescue by shepherds.[57]

Murphy makes minimal use of other sources. From Prosper Jolyot de Crébillon's *Rhadamiste et Zénobie* (1711) — a translation of which was Murphy's original title — he borrows some planks of action and characterization to deck out his British vessel.[58] He read Pietro Metastasio's *Zenobia* (1740), but appears not to have been affected by more than its general tone. For the device by which Zenobia kills Pharasmanes and herself, Plutarch's *Moralia,* either directly or through its use by Corneille or Charles Gildon, probably was Murphy's source.[59] The story and its treatment, as Murphy insists in his prologue, are largely his own.

If, for all that, Murphy's play does not appear strikingly original, the reason is not far to seek. Heroic conventions had hardened into a fixed pattern, and he accepted what was expected in the genre. Some of his practices worked exceedingly well, but others simply met contemporary standards. In *Zenobia,* he adheres to the unities, and his focus and concentration yield a surprising degree of suspense. If his blank verse never rises to genuine poetry, neither does it move to the excesses that would interfere with the relative naturalness of his characterization, a constant danger in the decorum of heroic tragedy. He tempers the cold restraint of the genre with an appeal to popular taste for romantic emotionalism, an effect created less through sentiment and language than through his ability to conceive of the most impressive means of presenting the conflict of his characters on stage. Even Zenobia, given to conventionally excessive weeping and stock responses and attitudes,[60] appears so more in isolation from the other characters than in the context of the tragic action.

Noble gestures, high-flown oratory, these, after all, are the

common characteristics of heroic drama, and if *Zenobia* is not
inspired by Murphy's originality, at least it is informed by his
theatrical knowledge. He knows what he is after: a statement of
the conflict between man's passions and intellect, a need for
balance and order, a warning against unnatural conduct. If
Rhadamistus's desire for "life, . . . love, . . . liberty and joy" (I,
181) is to be satisfied, the theme of Murphy's tragedy stresses the
difficulty of achieving such gratification in a world dominated by
demand for power and its perverse effect on human nature.
Murphy had struggled with the problem in *The Orphan of China*
and was to do so again in *The Grecian Daughter* and *Alzuma*—in
fact, his tragedies offer a community of values and techniques.

Repeatedly, tragedy in *Zenobia* emanates from unnatural
conduct. Teribazus, speaking to Zenobia about love, sets forth
the warning of the consequences of destroying nature's laws.
Rage born of love, he declares, can act to make "all nature
shudder," and "Love despis'd/ Not always can respect the ties of
nature" (I, 135). The result of such extreme behavior, he
acknowledges, destroys nature's harmony and ends in chaos.
While his words comment on the private emotions, they bear
upon the major conflict in which personal feelings have public
consequences and the selfish drive for power that ignores the
demands of nature results in political turmoil. For Murphy, the
conservative polemical writer, dramatic tragedy serves to
illustrate the consequences of individual license.

Pharasmanes, the tyrant whose lust for power ignores the
natural feelings toward his own sons, stands at the center of the
tragedy. In Murphy's changes from Tacitus, Pharasmanes rather
than Rhadamistus has slain Mithridates. That act foreshadows
the tyrant's treatment of his sons, for Mithridates had been
Pharasmanes's brother, and, as Rhadamistus notes, taking a
"brother's blood" is "a black crime, that's horrible to nature!" (I,
149). No less abhorrent to nature is Pharasmanes's treatment of
his sons. For Teribazus, he is an "unnatural father! that would
seize my scepter . . ." (I, 136), while Rhadamistus responds to
Pharasmanes's desire to see him dead: "in wonder/ I view the
unnatural father, who would bathe/ His hand in blood, in a son's
blood . . ." (I, 169).

It is a measure of difference between the sons and their father
that they are constantly aware of what is natural and seek to
govern themselves accordingly, although Pharasmanes's perver-

sion makes that impossible, and the unleashed unnatural powers
can end only in appalling tragedy. Rhadamistus is particularly
sensitive to the commands of nature. Believing that Zenobia has
died as a result of their suicide pact, he accuses himself as a
"traitor to nature" (I, 141). Pondering action against his father,
he mourns its unnaturalness. Not even the prospect of a Roman
victory can bring him delight, for "with a pang of nature [I] shall
behold/ The Roman eagle dart like thunder on thee" (I, 171). He
tries to dissuade Teribazus from slaying their father, since the
"dark insidious deed" would stain his brother's soul (I, 195), and
Teribazus himself knows well the consequences of killing a
parent, for "he's a parent still!" (I, 159) Yet their father's
conduct allows them no recourse, and unnaturalness would seem
to beget the unnatural in order to set things right.

Despite its adherence to outmoded conventions, *Zenobia* was
nevertheless sincerely felt by Murphy, and his passion and
craftsmanship make it one of the successful heroic tragedies of
its period. He did not have to alter it greatly—from acting
version, to first publication, to ultimate inclusion in his *Works*—
because he had effectively expressed his sentiments from the
beginning. His changes constitute no more than the details of
diction (such as changing "and with their limbs/ Manure the
fields of Asia" to "with their scatter'd bones/ Whiten the plains of
Asia" [I, 156]), grammar, and plausibility. For posterity Murphy
merely simplified and corrected his tragedy and appropriately
modified some of its melodrama.[61]

V   The Grecian Daughter

It is difficult today to understand the reasons for the success of
The Grecian Daughter, Murphy's next tragedy. Its plot, suggesting both the artificiality of heroic drama and the excesses of
melodrama, barely offers a clue. Even in summary its weaknesses
seem apparent: an emotional level all but impossible to sustain
after its heroine's opening noble speeches and a climax that
comes far too soon:[62]

Dionysius has seized the throne of Syracuse and imprisoned
old King Evander in a cavern and denied him nourishment.
Through Melanthon—Dionysius's adviser, but loyal to Evander—Euphrasia, the king's daughter, learns of his whereabouts.
While her husband, Phocion, has fled with their child to join the

Greeks, who under Timoleon are coming to Evander's aid, she has remained to care for her father. She persuades Philotus, a guard, to allow her to visit him and, tenderly breastfeeding the old man, she wins over his guards, who permit his escape. Euphrasia's courage rallies the King, and she hides him in the temple tomb where her mother is buried. Confronted by Dionysius, Euphrasia rejects his demands for collaboration and boasts that her husband and the Greeks will overthrow the tyrant, who, unaware of Evander's escape, threatens to execute him. Euphrasia does not know that Phocion has been captured and that only Melanthon's shrewdness has protected her. However, Melanthon brings the couple together in the tomb, where they learn that Dionysius plans to use a truce as a means of slaughtering Timoleon's troops. Phocion goes to warn Timoleon and to instigate an attack, while Melanthon promises to help from within. In the interim, with Philotus's aid, Euphrasia thwarts Dionysius's plot to murder her and Evander. When Timoleon attacks, Melanthon's internal forces join him and they rout Dionysius. He seeks refuge and revenge in the temple, but Euphrasia kills him. She rejoins her husband, and Evander resumes his reign.

Unprepossessing though it seems in summary, Murphy's tragedy was enormously successful. Despite customary production delays by Garrick and threats by political opponents, it opened to acclaim at Drury Lane on February 26, 1772. After three profitable seasons, it continued in stock until 1848,[63] and even as late as 1792 a foreign visitor described the play as one that "drew more tears than the works of [Shakespeare]." [64] Garrick informed Murphy that his wife "was more affected than ever I knew her to be with any play. . . ."[65] In her diary Mrs. Thrale called it "unquestionably the best of all our modern Tragedies, and all its Merit is the Power it has over our Passions too; for nobody I believe ever dream'd of repeating a Line on't. . . ."[66]

Without question, much of the original impact of Murphy's drama may be attributed to Garrick's genius as a producer and the acting talents of Spranger Barry and his wife. Although superior to both *The Orphan of China* and *Zenobia*, it could not have emerged as the most popular tragedy of its period without the combined powers of the actors and the producer-director. Murphy himself acknowledged the lavish production, celebrated Mrs. Barry as a "female Garrick," and credited the dying

Spranger Barry with the most triumphant performance in his career in the role of Evander.[67] As the typical comments of the critic in the *Theatrical Review* suggest, Murphy's views were shared by many of his contemporaries:

Mrs. Barry rose beyond herself. . . . The scenes and decorations were well adapted to the importance of the piece. The representation of the city of Syracuse, with a view of the sea; and the Temple scene, with the mausoleum, in particular are extremely well executed, and do credit to the theatre, and honor to the artists who designed and painted them.[68]

While all this may account for the play's immediate success, however, it fails to explain the continued popularity until about 1795 and then its subsequent decline until nineteenth-and twentieth-century critics dismissed it as an unimportant drama. By reviving the role of Euphrasia in 1782, Sarah Siddons unquestionably enhanced the longevity of the tragedy,[69] but after 1795 audiences no longer shared the enthusiastic responses of Mrs. Garrick and Mrs. Thrale to the emotional exploration of the passions in *The Grecian Daughter*. It seems obvious that Murphy's play fell victim to a change in taste. From 1772 to 1795, a gradual shift in aesthetic values increased emphasis on emotional appeal.[70] After 1795, a surfeit of such appeal had turned Murphy's drama into a set of conventional commonplaces that lacked the spontaneity of uncontrolled romantic expression.

Murphy wrote for the theater of his own time. He responded to changes in taste and tried, while retaining his traditional values, to appease his audience's desires. Murphy's tragedies reflect the increasing demands for greater emotional appeal, for what in the nineteenth century would become melodrama. He had attempted to take advantage of such change as early as *The Desert Island*, but had been entrapped by a conflict between his own values and those of his audience—a conflict expressed in the ambiguity of his theme about the relative worth of primitivism and progress—and could not manage his own discomfiture with the tragicomic form of the play. With *The Grecian Daughter*, he experienced no such difficulties.

Whatever effect the play has had since 1795, before then it provided exactly the proper proportions of classical and romantic characteristics. Modern critical disagreements about its genre, about its conformity to the unities, about its mixture of classical and romantic elements suggest how well Murphy managed to combine traditional tragedy with an appeal to a growing taste for the romantic.[71] In its conclusion, which offers a melodramatic and happy resolution, *The Grecian Daughter* indicates Murphy's willingness to sacrifice his own aesthetic ideals for the sake of popular approval.[72] He recognized what the age demanded and knew that, as Johnson wrote, "those that live to please, must please to live."[73]

Murphy's setting displays his knowledgeable appeal to audience taste for the exotic, wild, and bizarre, while containing the whole within a classical framework.[74] The play's physical details create a romantic aura, particularly in the "subjective Gothic labyrinth" of Evander's prison.[75] The scenic description for Act II, Scene I, reads as though it were drawn from a painting by Poussin, La Rosa, or Lorraine, a landscape of the sublime: "A wild romantic Scene, amidst overhanging Rocks; a Cavern on one side" (I, 228). The temple, with monument, and the sepulcher of Euphrasia's mother in the second scene of the third act, convey a threatening Gothic atmosphere, as do the tombs among which Euphrasia hides her father and holds her clandestine meetings. In Philotus's response to Euphrasia's coming to the cavern of Evander's imprisonment, Murphy, by invoking *Hamlet* for his dialogue, evokes Shakespeare's eerie atmosphere of ghastly presence. In more original dialogue, too, Murphy creates romantic sublimity with all its attendant horror. His language reinforces the earlier stage direction: "The gloom of night sits heavy on the world;/ And o'er the solemn scene such stillness reigns,/ As 'twere a pause of nature: on the beach/ No murmering billow breaks . . ." (I, 228). As in later romantic poetry, nature becomes identified with man's feelings.

Yet Murphy sets his romantic details against a greater backdrop to give his drama classical respectability and appeal. Murphy's primary source—in a play remarkably free of his characteristic liberal borrowing—is a passage (Book V, Chapter 4) from *De Pietate in Parentes* of Valerius Maximus, the Roman historian.[76] Murphy limits it largely to the scene of Euphrasia's nursing Evander, which, as he himself notes, had inspired painters, particularly Rubens, but his use of the material contributes importantly to his purpose. For all his play's romantic elements, Murphy seeks a counterbalance through what he calls in his Postscript an "air of real history."[77] A classical tone controls the romantic excesses of the drama, even though Murphy deliberately falsifies the classical story, placing it in the reign of Dionysius the younger and making Evander the king of Sicily.[78] To bolster its classical characteristics, Murphy uses touches from Plutarch, Cicero, and Virgil, as well as from Belloy's *Zelmire* and Fénelon's *Dialogues des Mort.*[79]

The true duality, however, is conveyed in the character of Euphrasia, the heart and soul of *The Grecian Daughter*. She weeps excessively.[80] From almost the outset, she virtually boasts of her expression of passion. She tells, in words clearly intended to wring the audience's hearts, of how she remained behind when Phocion fled with their child: "Full well thou know'st/ The pangs I suffer'd in that trying moment./ Did I not weep? Did I not rave and shriek/ And by the roots tear my dishevell'd hair?" (I, 220). She cries over her father, bemoaning her "breaking heart" (I, 238). She freely sheds tears, "a weeping pilgrim o'er [her mother's] ashes" (I, 260). She responds gratefully for Philotus's aid, pleading, "These tears attest th' emotions of my heart" (I, 293). Nor does Murphy allow this crying to stand alone as testimony to her display of sentimentalism, a testament of feeling worthy of the beleaguered heroines of romances. Murphy underscores his emotional appeal, setting up a response to the pathetic, as in Philotus's reaction to her plea to see her father: "By Heav'n/ My heart in pity bleeds" (I, 234). To clinch the whole, of course, is Euphrasia's noblest deed, her breastfeeding of her father. Almost two hundred years later, John Steinbeck employed the same device in *Grapes of Wrath* to draw the last vestige of sympathy from *his* audience.

But romantic sentiment is only part of Euphrasia's character. Her warmth and tenderness are balanced by the nobility of the classical heroine. In rather effective blank verse,[81] she expresses sentiments in tones reminiscent of the great female characters of antiquity. Sometimes, as in her vow to cut down the tyrant, Murphy mixes classical strength of character with a blood-lust marked by the ferocity of romantic sensationalism: "Blood is his due, Melanthon; yes, the blood,/ The vile, black blood, that fills the tyrant's veins,/ Would graceful look upon my dagger's point." (I, 226) But generally her language coolly expresses her strong character. Indeed, her conduct is such as to raise questions about her husband's bravery, and Murphy feels compelled to explain why Phocion has left her behind. Compared to her behavior, his conduct ("He is all truth and honour; [she says]/ He fled to save my child" [I, 240]) leaves doubt even after her excuses for him. Euphrasia's courage is in deeds as well as words: she tricks Dionysius, rallies her father, and finally dispatches the tyrant. To her Murphy gives the language that sets forth the theme of the play—oddly its point, though clearly Murphy's message, accords uneasily with the political philosophy of the *Test* and *Auditor* and the fierce foe of the French Revolution. As she scoffs at Dionysius's claim that he had agreed to give the crown to her son, Euphrasia offers the moral of the drama: "Euphrasia's children/ Shall on a nobler basis found their rights,/ On their own virtue, and a people's choice" (I, 276). The republicanism of her sentiments, however inconsistent with Murphy's own arguments elsewhere, appealed strongly to his late-eighteenth-century audience.

That audience appeal was Murphy's overriding concern. It also helps to account for the decline of the play's reputation after 1795. On the one hand, its romantic elements had become commonplaces and a weak expression of the romantic sentiments as they had developed in the last decade of the century. On the other hand, its neoclassical aspects have become identified with everything that a later audience finds unattractive in eighteenth-century heroic tragedy. Although Murphy made stylistic changes from his acting text in both the first printed edition and in his *Works*, they did nothing to alter the tone or effect of his drama.[82] Seeking to please the taste of his contemporaries, Murphy obviously succeeded in *The Grecian Daughter*. However, what appealed to them assured that the play would not endure beyond his own time.[83]

VI Alzuma

Some eleven years after it had been written and well beyond its particular political relevance,[84] *Alzuma*, Murphy's fourth tragedy, appeared at Covent Garden on February 23, 1773. Despite a costly production that included new costumes and impressive music by Dr. Arne for the spectacular "Procession of Virgins of the Sun" in Act II,[85] the tragedy, while benefiting Murphy with three author's nights, proved a failure. It ran nine times and then disappeared for the rest of the century.[86]

National and theatrical politics account for the long delay, which ultimately limited the play's appeal.[87] Designed originally as a lightly veiled allegorical attack on modern Catholic Spain through a depiction of Pizarro's cruel conquest of Peru, *Alzuma* had special relevance in 1762 at the time of Britain's defeat of Spain in Havana.[88] By 1773 it had lost much of its political impact, and only Murphy's own unpopular political activities during the war remained for the audience's notice. Murphy's propagandistic journalism in the *Auditor* had made the play- wright such an attractive target for his political enemies that an appearance then courted theatrical disaster. Even in 1767 Garrick feared a revival of the old controversies and remained uncertain as late as 1770 when he returned the work to the playwright. Bitter enough about Garrick's treatment to berate him and to threaten to withdraw from the theater, Murphy was being unfair.[89] It took three more years for Harris to convince Colman to present the tragedy at Covent Garden.[90]

Yet from the outset, criticism has acknowledged the merits of *Alzuma.* Despite the negative influence of Garrick's supporters and George Steevens's pseudonymous, malicious and personal attack in the *Morning Chronicle,* contemporary evaluations were favorable. Steevens himself in the *Critical,* William Woodfall in the *Monthly,* and the anonymous reviewer in *Town and Country* praised its plot, diction, and sentiments.[91] While noting its deficiencies as characteristic of the genre in the period, modern critics have sustained Murphy's own judgment of its superiority to the *Grecian Daughter* and *Zenobia* and have acclaimed *Alzuma* as his major achievement in tragedy.[92] Were it not for political circumstances and for Murphy's refusal to yield to contemporary taste by allowing Orazia, Alzuma's mother, to live,[93] the work probably would have enjoyed the success it deserved in the theater.

Removed from the personal animosities abundant in Murphy's time, a reader can still feel the power in his strongly classical tragedy. Although Murphy borrowed from Dryden's *Indian Queen* and *Indian Emperor* and from Voltaire's *Alzire* and perhaps *Oreste* and *Merope,*[94] his work derives its power from his own understanding of the forces behind the classical tragedies of Sophocles and Euripides and his ability to adapt their works according to his own English taste and traditions. Even in summary, *Alzuma* suggests the energy drawn from the ancient drama of Orestes's confrontation with the treacherous mother and her lover, who has slain his father and usurped his throne.

Cast for political reasons in the ancient Inca empire during the Spanish conquest, *Alzuma* retains all the psychological tensions of the classical legend that embodies the individual's sub-conscious struggles in gaining maturity. The mythopoeic power of ancient drama forces its way through the restraints of late-eighteenth-century heroic tragedy, and some of its strength may be felt even in a simple account.

Having married Pizarro, her husband's murderer, Orazia, Queen of the Incas, has converted to Christianity and resumed her rule. Her daughter Orellana dreams of the return of Alzuma, her exiled brother, to avenge their father's death and free their country. Withstanding pressures from Pizarro and Orazia to marry his son, Don Carlos, Orellana nevertheless takes advantage of his love. When the disguised Alzuma and his aide, Ozmar, are among the rebels captured by Pizarro, Orellana pleads with Don Carlos to save them. Alzuma, overhearing her plans, reveals his identity to her, but Don Carlos mistakes their embrace as a sign that they are lovers and seeks to kill him. Only Orellana's threatened suicide deters Don Carlos. Orazia, not recognizing her own son, demands that he be slain and that Orellana marry Don Carlos. For the sake of his country, Alzuma demonstrates, through a mark on his breast, that he is her son. The contrite queen seeks to sway Pizarro, but he regards her demands as treacherous. He permits Alzuma to live, but only to be tortured. After Orazia reveals that Alzuma is her son, Pizarro has an unsatisfactory meeting with him, and despite Orazia and the enlightened Don Carlos's intervention, the tyrant vows that Alzuma must die at sunrise. To be alone with Pizarro and his priests, Alzuma pretends a willingness to convert to Christianity. He informs his sister of the truth, however, and prevails on her to keep their mother away. But when Orazia hears the sounds of Alzuma's overcoming Pizarro, she believes her son is being killed and bursts into the temple where Alzuma inadvertently stabs her. Before dying, she offers Christian forgiveness. Alzuma and his sister, overcome by her martyrdom, accept the pardon of Don Carlos and convert to the new faith.

If his Peruvian setting, used to comment on the cruelty and hypocrisy of the Spanish in their conquests, seems unusual for a classical tragedy, it was similar to his choice for the *Orphan of China*. As with his earlier play, Murphy insists that tragedy does not have to be confined by its classical origins: "While GREECE and ROME swell our theatric state,/ And only classic heroes can be great," Murphy says, he "dares trace the virtues of the Torrid Zone" (I, 316-17). Offering a "Peruvian theme . . . in a classic style,"[95] Murphy breaks his complete bondage to classical tradition without yielding the tradition itself. Like *The Orphan of China*, *The Grecian Daughter*, and *Zenobia*, *Alzuma* suggests the changes taking place in the development of late-eighteenth-century classical tragedy.

Yet *Alzuma*, written earlier though produced later than *Zenobia* and *The Grecian Daughter*, is closer than either to classical tragedy. Its romantic elements, despite suggestions of primitivism, are more limited; its adherence to the unities, more pronounced; and its thematic concern for the natural, more decisive. Indeed, Murphy's demand for unified effect in his tragedy led him to object to the common eighteenth-century practice of reducing pathos to comedy and laughter through an anticlimactic epilogue. Having already undermined the custom in his epilogue to *The Grecian Daughter*,[96] in *Alzuma* he chides his audience for allowing playwrights to weaken their tragic effect and asks, "Say, do you wish, ye bright, ye virtuous train,/ That ev'ry tear that fell, should fall in vain?"

Still, *Alzuma* is an eighteenth-century tragedy written for an English audience, and its purpose is political. Murphy must reach his audience through the values of his age, but these, too, he found sufficiently in accord with those of antiquity—particularly in their celebration of and concern for the natural. Like the Greco-Roman playwrights, he condemns excess. The Spaniards, the object of his attack, are associated, because of their Roman Catholicism, with a kind of zealousness unnatural to man, and Murphy makes the most of that association.

Orazia, seeking to protect her son's life, makes the point explicit when she responds to Pizarro's charge that she has reneged on her conversation to the Christian faith: "Zeal in excess is vice, 'tis impious;/ Horrid repugnance to the will of Heav'n;/ Subversion of each virtue; foe to all/ The tender laws of charity and love" . . . (I, 363). Contrasted with Roman Catholicism, the laws of nature are to be celebrated, for the Spaniard's faith perverts true Christianity. The Incas "found their laws/ On the broad base of reason and of nature . . ." (I, 357), while the Spanish conquerors are "fierce barbarian[s] from a world unknown," who would, through their proselytizing, "conquer hearts as you would force our faith" (I, 351).

Orazia's faith denies the specific teaching of Pizarro's Catholicism. From the opening scene, he is a zealot whose "holy work" rests on "Justice [which] calls/ For vengeance on a blind offending world" (I, 320-21). For Orazia, "haughty Spain/ Perverts [God's] holy laws . . ." (I, 366). When Pizarro mocks her people for barbarian human sacrifices, she responds, "Polish'd Barbarian! What dost thou do less?" (I, 379). Rejecting the Spaniard's Catholicism, she joins nature and true Christianity to proclaim her faith in a religion remarkably similar to Murphy's own urbane Anglicanism.

Alzuma, too, ridicules the Spaniards who preach their enlightenment by the sword and for their avarice. Their God is keeper of the confessional and forgives their most heinous crimes despite the hypocrisy of their disavowals. When Alzuma believes his mother will not help him, it is because he regards her as lost to the laws of nature, caught in that "Fanatic fury, [which] blasts each moral virtue" (I, 352), the curse of Catholic zeal. He welcomes her aid as a return to "nature" (I, 369). Finally, in response to Pizarro's proclaiming Spain's laws, Alzuma replies: "Know there's a prior law. . . ./ Great nature's law! that best, that surest guide . . ." (I, 382).

While all this may suggest primitivism, it is actually no more than the use of natural man to ridicule the religion of England's Catholic enemy. Just as English writers during the Seven Years' War used the American Indian as a noble savage whose virtues had been perverted by hypocritical French Catholics,[97] Murphy employs the Incas to ridicule the Spanish. True religion in *Alzuma* expresses the Anglican orthodoxy which during the eighteenth century had absorbed natural religion and latitudinarianism. "Simple reason . . ./ That reason in the paths of nature trod" (I, 316-17) is the guide. Orazia, removed from fanatical Catholic excesses, offers genuine Christianity. Her final words, echoing the putative deathbed proclamation of Joseph Addison, belong safely in the Anglican service: "In me thou seest/ How an expiring Christian suffers death." Her example, sufficient to move her children to faith and Don Carlos to forgiveness, is Christian, not Catholic, virtue. She has, in effect, been converted from the superstitious gods of the Incas, to the vicious God of the Spanish Catholics, and finally to the true God of Christianity, whose virtues are "Love, justice, and humanity . . ." (I, 375).

Like Voltaire, Murphy uses the story of Pizarro for partisan purposes. But, whereas Voltaire sought to denigrate all of Christianity, Murphy makes a political attack on Spain, contrasting its zealousness with the reasonable virtues of the Church of England. Its rational balance coincides nicely with the values of classical antiquity, whose dramatic form he chooses for his vehicle. In its concluding statement, *Alzuma* joins Murphy's political argument with the values that eighteenth-century Englishmen believed they shared with civilized society in antiquity: enlightened tolerance and love of liberty. The freedom Murphy speaks of in his tragedy belongs to true-blue Englishmen and is impossible among the Spanish enemy, goaded by greed and wracked by religious intolerance.

Alzuma had been altered in the years between its composition and its first production, and Murphy revised the acting version immediately for its initial publication. From manuscript through the *Works* in 1786, changes primarily concern diction. Although he unfortunately increased its melodrama, Murphy otherwise strengthened character motivation and plausibility in *Alzuma*. In all, however, the long delay in production minimized the need for extensive revision in any of its printed texts.

VII   The Rival Sisters

Bothered by eye-strain and seeking relief from his labors in translating Tacitus, in 1783 Murphy composed *The Rival Sisters,* a five-act blank-verse tragedy, which was his last play to be produced. As usual, he found his impetus in another drama. Although he agreed with Mme. de Sévigné and Voltaire about the weaknesses of Thomas Corneille's *Ariana* (1672), Murphy believed that the heroine's character provided a worthwhile subject and that a quick dramatic pace, improved dialogue, and heightened characterization would bring forth its "beauties" and remove its "defects." He sought to remodel the classical fable to reveal its universal characteristics.[98]

Murphy essentially retains Corneille's plot, the ancient fable of two sisters' rivalry for the love of Theseus. Ariadne and Phaedra, daughters of King Minos of Crete, have betrayed their father for their love of Theseus. With Theseus, they seek refuge under King Periander on the isle of Naxos. Periander, enamored of Ariadne, rejects the Cretan request to return the trio. With Pirithous's arrival from Athens, however, Periander learns that

Ariadne is to marry Theseus on their return and becomes enraged until Theseus assures him that he plans to wed Phaedra. Pirithous, in turn, regards Theseus and Phaedra's treatment of the unsuspecting Ariadne as villainous, but Theseus insists on using her to retain Periander's protection. He urges Pirithous to try to persuade Ariadne to accept Periander. She refuses and suggests instead that he marry Phaedra. Ultimately Periander and Pirithous inform Ariadne that Theseus loves another, but neither reveals her identity. After Theseus has thwarted Pirithous's attempt to have Phaedra give him up, he is imprisoned by Periander, who threatens to return him to Crete. Ariadne arranges his release, but warns that, if he betrays her, he will be an eternal symbol of infamy. Still Theseus and Phaedra embark without her, even as Ariadne rejects Periander's advice to leave without her sister. When she learns of Phaedra's treachery, she cannot be consoled and tragically takes her own life.

To evoke a greater emotional struggle, Murphy alters details of Corneille's plot. By substituting "a group of virgins" for the confidante in *Ariana*, he focuses more strongly on the turmoil within Ariadne. He intensifies emotion by drawing out his suspense. Responding to Voltaire's criticism of the French play, Murphy prolongs the time of Ariadne's faith in Theseus and develops Theseus's remorse.[99] Murphy increases the tension between King Minos and his daughters to make the girls' defiance more plausible. Yet Murphy also turns their conduct into a moral lesson, which recalls Richardson's message in *Clarissa*, importuning against the sins of parents and their children.[100] This emotional rendering of the thematic relationship to *Clarissa* brings the drama closer to an English audience in its excessively sentimental appeal to late-eighteenth-century taste.

For all its contemporary appeal, however, Murphy clearly conceives of *The Rival Sisters* as a play built upon classical principles, to which he adheres more rigidly than Corneille had done. The sharper focus on Ariadne strengthens a sense of the unities. Ariadne herself recalls those principles when, told of Theseus's treachery, she declares, "Oh! what a change in one disastrous day" (VII, 319). Murphy relies heavily on classical dramatic irony to achieve his effect. Like everything else in the play, it centers around Ariadne, the deceived heroine who speaks without knowledge available to her audience. She misinterprets Phaedra's sentiments about Theseus, thinking her unjust to him and in love with Periander. When Pirithous hesitates to reveal the truth about Theseus and her sister, Ariadne believes that he is withholding information about threats to Theseus, and, on her discovery of Theseus's unfaithfulness, she seeks consolation from Phaedra, the secret cause of her distress. Repeatedly, she accuses characters of villainy, worries about their betraying Theseus, and expresses her fears to the two people who are basest in their relationship to her.

While some of this dramatic irony is effective and several of the speeches are affecting, overall *The Rival Sisters* does not improve greatly on Corneille's play. As with the characters of Mandane in *The Orphan of China* and Rhadamistus in *Zenobia,* Murphy fails to convey the tragic flaw in Ariadne.[101] His treatment of Theseus creates neither a sense of nobility nor attractiveness and makes implausible his appeal to the sisters. Since he had already deceived Ariadne when she betrayed her father for him, Ariadne might be expected to have been prepared for Theseus's conduct with her. Phaedra, too, knows him well enough to remark to Pirithous, "As he once/ With unfelt ardour could delude my sister,/ Bid him once more dissemble, and betray" (VII, 330). Such understanding makes less credible her trust in him, and certainly his conduct throughout does nothing to make him appealing to the audience. At every turn, he willingly sacrifices others for his purpose—whether Ariadne, Phaedra, Pirithous, or Periander. The required nobility of so pivotal a character never emerges in Murphy's portrayal.

Beyond its specific flaws, *The Rival Sisters* demonstrates generally the decline in Murphy's dramatic powers. Never at ease in tragedy, he failed particularly in his final two efforts. Not even his friendliest critics can ignore the slow pace, inadequate character development, and unsatisfactory blank verse in *The Rival Sisters.*[102] Not choosing to have it produced, he published it with an apologetic note in his *Works.* To be sure, he attributes his reluctance to staging the play to his contempt for the Malevoli—evil critics who delighted in charging him with plagiarism—and to his distrust of the vagaries of stage fortune. Yet his preface displays throughout his lack of confidence in the merits of his tragedy.

When on March 18, 1793, John Kemble, the theater manager and Murphy's friend, produced the play at Drury Lane at the

King's Theater in the Haymarket, it created little notice.[103] Introduced as a benefit performance for Kemble's sister, the great Sarah Siddons, who appeared as Ariadne, *The Rival Sisters* ran seven times that season and then quietly departed from the London stage.[104]

VIII   Arminius

Acknowledging the superiority of his political zeal to his diminishing artistic abilities, Murphy published his last play in 1798. Although never performed, *Arminius,* a five-act blank-verse tragedy, contributed to the reactionary climate of opinion hovering over the English theater in response to the French Revolution. Murphy—antidemocratic, monarchical, and conservative—regarded the Revolution's egalitarianism as a threat to order and a subversion of true liberty.[105] His preface berates changes wrought by a "nation of professed Atheists, [who] counteracted the order of Providence in the formation of Civil Society."[106] He deplores the activities of British supporters and damns the Jacobin party, Constitutional Clubs, and Corresponding Societies. In the name of freedom, he defends the anti-civil rights Alien Bill and suspension of habeas corpus and approves a British war for the honor of mankind.

Borrowing from Quintilian, Valerius Maximus, Lucan, and Montesquieu's *Spirit of Laws,* Murphy depends chiefly on Tacitus's account of a first-century German, whose spirit and values he could easily relate to the Saxon heritage of England.[107] To understand Murphy's message, it is sufficient to identify Arminius and the Germans with eighteenth-century Britons and to recognize the treacherous Gauls as contemporary French revolutionaries. His fable, decked out with noble speeches and heroic action, proceeds with the clarity essential to a conventional moral tale:

Segestes, a German nobleman, supports the Roman forces against his own people. While German troops lay siege to his castle, he holds Valeda, his pregnant daughter, prisoner and keeps her from her husband, Arminius, a leader of the free German cause. Segemund, Segestes's son, opposes his father and joins his country's legions, while Flavius, Arminius's brother, defects to the enemy. The traitors argue that their action prevents annihilation, but Arminius insists that they have made

cowardice a virtue by proclaiming it moderation. Before
Arminius arrives on the scene, the Germans have been thwarted
by the Roman Caecina, who has come to Segestes's aid. Over
Segestes's protests, Caecina sends Valeda to the Germans to seek
peace. Instead, Arminius rejects the terms and rallies his
followers. Leading a battle against the Romans, Segemund
unwittingly mortally wounds his father, but before dying,
Segestes attempts to save his son's life. The remorseful
Segemund kills himself. The Gauls within the German camp
assassinate Arminius, but in his final moments, even after
learning that the Romans have withdrawn, he warns his people
that they must prepare for future attacks and advises that, if they
cannot sustain themselves, they must flee to Britain, whose hardy
natives drove mighty Caesar from their shores. When Valeda
attempts to follow her husband to the grave, she is restrained by
a reminder of her unborn child, heir to Arminius, the champion
of his country's liberty.

Murphy's fable presents Arminius as the defender of freedom
against Gaulist treachery. Ascribing a certain nobility to the
Romans, Murphy contrasts it with the conduct of his French
surrogates. At the same time, the behavior of Segestes,
responsible for the discord among the Germans, stands as a
warning to modern British followers of the French revolutionaries. Murphy sees such Britons as stirring up civil discord, and
Arminius's words, when his brother Flavius has departed for the
enemy's camp, warn of the outcome of civil irresponsibility:
" 'Tis ever thus, when discontent and faction/ Brood over fancied
ills, and fire with rage/ Sons against fathers, brothers against
brothers,/ 'Tis horror all, and worse than civil war" (36).

All this propaganda stifles any art in *Arminius.* Blank verse
orations reinforce its pomposity as Murphy's characters make
speeches when they should be expressing their natural feelings.
From Valeda pours forth a veritable anthology of patriotic
homilies: "Your first duty/ You owe your country . . ." (37); "Our
country is our parent: 'tis to her/ Our love, our duty, all our
faculties,/ Our wealth, our pow'r, our very lives are due./ She is
the common mother of us all" (19). Even at the climax, with her
father and brother dead, she speaks like a public orator rather
than a grieving woman: "The dire effects/ That flow from party-
rage," she explains "This day may give/ A lesson to the world,
and teach the nations/That civil union is their truest bliss . . ."

(70). In case her point be missed, she explicates, "And fathers, sons, and families unite/One voice, one heart, to guard their native land" (71).

Arminius's speeches are worse. To a certain extent, Murphy's choice of allegory is inappropriate, and Arminius's counsel underscores its inadequacy. His description of the Gauls as "a traitorous race," applies well enough to them in the play and represents Murphy's view of the modern French, but his next words have little applicability to the Gauls in his drama and inaccurately describe the French revolutionaries, whom Murphy seeks to condemn:

> All civil union was to them unknown.
> Strangers to liberty, and now subdued
> To crouch in bondage; the ambitious slaves
> Would raise the tree of tyranny, and overturn
> In every state, in all the nations round them,
> The laws that hold society in peace. (78)

Without condoning the excesses of the French Revolution, a disinterested observer might well question Murphy's view of events in progress at the time of his writing, and certainly the description inappropriately characterizes the Gauls in the play, who owe no special allegiance to Arminius and the Germans and are merely attempting to unyoke themselves from those who have collared them.

Apart from their inappropriateness, Arminius's didactic speeches have little to do with drama. From the time he first appears, he talks excessively and seemingly endlessly in blank verse that has nothing to do with dialogue. Examples abound, but the closing speeches adequately suggest the character and quality of Arminius's discourse. Dying, he nevertheless offers lessons in history and political science: "Let them embark for Britain; there they'll find/ A brave, a hardy race, who by their valour/ Made Caesar from their coast unfurl his sails,/ and save his legions by inglorious flight." Join those Britons, he advises:

> And from the woods of Germany import
> A form of government, a plan of laws
> Wise, just, and equitable; laws of force
> To guard the gen'ral weal, and on the base
> Of public liberty, of social order,
> And equal justice, raise the noblest fabric
> Of civil union. . . . (87)

But still he is not finished, for Murphy insists on his own propagandistic points. The French "spread rebellion, anarchy, and ruin." Arminius offers a final piece of advice, therefore, to warn not only his followers, but Murphy's contemporaries, to "guard their coast against the Gauls,/ And never,—never let that treach'rous race,/ Nor THEIR DESCENDANTS to the latest time,/ Obtain a footing on their sea-girt isle" (88).

Arminius, Murphy's last play, fails as a drama. Whatever questions may be raised about its political philosophy and sensitivities toward the multitudes of a general population lie outside the province of aesthetic judgment. But its dramatic weaknesses are self-evident. Propaganda need not be destructive of art, but effective propaganda requires great art. Neither as propaganda nor art does *Arminius* succeed. Murphy lived another seven years, but *Arminius* indicates that his dramatic powers had preceded him to the grave.

Notes and References

Abbreviations of Periodicals

BNYPL—*Bulletin of the New York Public Library*
CR—*Critical Review* (18th Century)
GIJ—*Gray's Inn Journal*
JEGP—*Journal of English and Germanic Philology*
MLN—*Modern Language Notes*
MLQ—*Modern Language Quarterly*
MR—*Monthly Review* (18th Century)
PBSA—*Publications of the Bibliographical Society of America*
PMLA—*Publications of the Modern Language Association*
PQ—*Philological Quarterly*
SP—*Studies in Philology*

Chapter One

1. Howard Hunter Dunbar, *The Dramatic Career of Arthur Murphy* (New York, 1946), p. 3; John Pike Emery, *Arthur Murphy: An Eminent Dramatist of the Eighteenth Century* (Philadelphia, (1946), pp. 10-11.
2. Emery, *Arthur Murphy*, p. 10.
3. *Thraliana: The Diary of Hester Lynch Thrale (Later Mrs. Piozzi), 1776-1809*, ed. by Katherine C. Balderston (Oxford, 1942), I, 329.
4. See J. Homer Caskey, "Arthur Murphy's Commonplace Book," *SP* 37 (1940): 598-609. Murphy's Commonplace Book is in the Folger Shakespeare Library.
5. *Thraliana*, I, 168-69.
6. John Taylor, *Records of My Life* (New York, 1833), p. 114.
7. *Thraliana*, II, 1067; Joyce Hemlow, *The History of Fanny Burney* (Oxford, 1958), p. 131.
8. *Thraliana*, II, 973.
9. Taylor, *Records of My Life*, pp. 114-15.
10. *Boswell's Life of Johnson*, ed. by G. B. Hill and L. F. Powell (Rev. ed., Oxford, 1934), II, 127.
11. Jesse Foot, *The Life of Arthur Murphy, Esq.* (London, 1811), p. 11. Foot's biography includes Murphy's autobiographical sketch.

12. For the complex history of the *Gray's Inn Journal* and for discussions of its various editions, I am indebted to Ronald B. Botting, "The Textural History of Murphy's *Gray's Inn Journal*," *Research Studies of the State College of Washington* 25 (1957): 33-48. My discussion covers the 1754, 1756, and 1786 editions of the work and notes the particular edition cited.

13. Murphy in (1754), #52, p. 311, describes the relationship of his journal to the *Tatler* and *Spectator*, but drops the passage in subsequent editions.

14. Charles H. Gray, *Theatrical Criticism in London to 1795* (New York, 1931), p. 122.

15. *New Essays by Arthur Murphy*, ed. by Arthur Sherbo (East Lansing, 1963), p. 3.

16. For a fuller description, see Botting, "Textual History," p. 39.

17. Emery, *Arthur Murphy*, p. 31; *GIJ* (1756): II, 451.

18. Botting, "Textual History," p. 39.

19. *Life of Johnson*, I, 309.

20. See Botting, "Textual History," p. 33; Emery, *Arthur Murphy*, pp. 23-24.

21. Dunbar, *Dramatic Career*, pp. 7-8; Roy E. Aycock, "Shakespearian Criticism in the *Gray's Inn Journal*," *Yearbook of English Studies* 2 (1972): 68.

22. Arthur Murphy, *The Works of Arthur Murphy, Esq.* (London, 1786), V, 209. Hereafter referred to as *Works*.

23. *Works*, V, 29, 315-17. See, too, V, 208-14, 298, 310ff.; VI, 143ff.

24. Thomas W. Perry, *Public Opinion, Propaganda, and Politics in Eighteenth-Century England: A Study of the Jew Bill of 1753* (Cambridge, Mass., 1962), p. 76.

25. See Robert D. Spector, "The *Connoisseur*: A Study of the Functions of a Persona," *English Writers of the Eighteenth Century*, ed. by John H. Middendorf (New York, 1971), pp. 109-22.

26. *Works*, V, 391.

27. *Ibid.*, V, 178.

28. *Ibid.*, V, 411.

29. *Ibid.*, VI, 318.

30. *Ibid.*, V, 411.

31. *Ibid.*, VI, 319-20.

32. *Ibid.*, VI, 318.

33. *GIJ* (1756), I, 293.

34. *Works*, VI, 378-79. Cf. Gray, *Theatrical Criticism*, p. 123.

35. *GIJ* (1754), #69, p. 158; *Works*, V, 113.

36. *GIJ* (1756), I, 244.

37. *Works*, V, 255.

38. Dunbar, *Dramatic Career*, p. 6; Emery, *Arthur Murphy*, p. 14.

39. See Arthur Sherbo, *English Sentimental Drama* (East Lansing, 1957), pp. 4ff.; J. Homer Caskey, "Arthur Murphy and the War on Sentimental Comedy," *JEGP* 30 (1931): 563-77.

40. *GIJ* (1754): #93, p. 369.

41. See Gray, *Theatrical Criticism*, p. 124; Caskey, "Murphy and the War on Sentimental Comedy," p. 569; Emery, *Arthur Murphy*, p. 23.

42. *GIJ* (1754): #76, p. 219.

43. *Works*, VI, 332-33.

44. *Ibid.*, V, 184; VI, 333, 336. See Emery, *Arthur Murphy*, p. 23.

45. Aycock, "Shakespearian Criticism," p. 68. See, for example, *GIJ* (1756): II, 49-50, 55-56.

46. *Works*, V, 120ff.

47. Aycock, "Shakespearian Criticism," pp. 70-71; *Johnson on Shakespeare*, ed. by Arthur Sherbo, in *Yale Edition of the Works of Samuel Johnson* (New Haven, 1968), VII, 304-305.

48. *Works*, VI, 338.

49. *Ibid.*, VI, 248.

50. *Ibid.*, VI, 337.

51. *GIJ* (1754), #8, p. 46; *Works*, VI, 408ff.

52. *Works*, VI, 247.

53. *GIJ* (1754), #8, p. 47.

54. Aycock, "Shakespearian Criticism," p. 69; David Nichol Smith, *Shakespeare in the Eighteenth Century* (Oxford, 1928), p. 83. See *GIJ* (1754): #8, pp. 43ff.; (1756): I, 244; II, 237, 265ff., 344.

55. See Emery, *Arthur Murphy*, pp. 12-13, and Sherbo, *New Essays*, pp. 1 and 174ff. However, Dunbar, *Dramatic Career*, p. 4, is unconvinced of Murphy's connection.

56. See Sherbo, *New Essays*, but compare Henry Knight Miller's review in *BNYPL* 69 (1965): 459-70 and Sherbo's rejoinder.

57. Sherbo, *New Essays*, pp. 179-84, 189-90.

58. *Ibid.*, pp. 99-168.

59. Dunbar, *Dramatic Career*, p. 39 and Appendix A; John Pike Emery, "Murphy's Criticism in the *London Chronicle*," *PMLA* 54 (1939): 1099-1104; Sherbo, *New Essays*.

60. For Murphy's contributions, see Benjamin C. Nangle, *The "Monthly Review," Second Series, 1790-1815* (Oxford, 1955).

61. See *MR* 76 (April 1787): 273-82; (May: 369-84; 77 (July 1787): 56-70; (Aug.): 131-40; 78 (April 1788): 324-31.

62. *MR* 78 (Feb. 1788): 148 and (June): 521. Caskey, "Murphy's Common-place Book," p. 608, incorrectly assesses Murphy's dramatic criticism in the *Monthly*.

63. Foot, *Life*, p. 240.

64. Robert Donald Spector, *English Literary Periodicals and the Climate of Opinion during the Seven Years' War* (The Hague, 1966), *passim*.

65. *Test* (July 9, 1757):#35.

66. See *Test* (April 23, 1757): #24. Cf. Emery, *Arthur Murphy*, p. 33, and Dunbar, *Dramatic Career*, p. 36. For more details on the *Test*, see Spector, *English Literary Periodicals, passim.*

67. For a full account of Murphy's work on the *Auditor*, see Spector, *passim.*

68. Robert R. Rea, *The English Press in Politics, 1760-1774* (Lincoln, 1963), pp. 30-31.

69. *Auditor* (July 29, 1762).

70. *Ibid.*, August 19, 1762.

71. For a full discussion of the episode, see George Nobbe, *The North Briton: a Study in Political Propaganda* (New York, 1939), Ch. XII.

72. Foot, *Life*, pp. 189ff. and 240; Dunbar, *Dramatic Career*, pp. 137, 157.

73. *Works of Henry Fielding, Esq. with the Life of the Author*, ed. by Arthur Murphy (London, 1762), I, 7. Further references appear parenthetically in the text. Murphy's essay has been dealt with harshly by most Fielding scholars and by Dunbar, *Dramatic Career*, pp. 137ff. Susan M. Passler's recent article, "Arthur Murphy's 'Essay on the Life and Genius of Henry Fielding, Esq.': Re-reading a Slighted Critic," *New Rambler* 14 (Spring 1973): 15-23, does greater justice to Murphy's work.

74. See Matthew Grace, "Introduction," *The Lives of Henry Fielding and Samuel Johnson together with Essays from the Gray's-Inn Journal* (Gainesville, Florida, 1968), pp. xiii-xiv.

75. *Ibid.*, p. vii, and *Henry Fielding: The Critical Heritage*, ed. by Ronald Paulson and Thomas Lockwood (London, 1969), pp. 17-18.

76. Cf. Emery, *Arthur Murphy*, p. 82; *CR* 14 (July 1762): 1-21.

77. Grace, "Introduction," p. xvi.

78. Emery, *Arthur Murphy*, p. 86.

79. Dunbar, *Dramatic Career*, p. 138.

80. See Emery, *Arthur Murphy*, pp. 152-53; *Johnson: The Critical Heritage*, ed. by J. T. Boulton (New York, 1971), pp. 15, 35.

81. James L. Clifford and Donald J. Greene, *Samuel Johnson: A Survey and Bibliography of Critical Studies* (Minneapolis, 1970), p. 48.

82. Grace, "Introduction," p. xviii, xvi. See, too, *Johnson: The Critical Heritage*, p. 68.

83. *The Works of Samuel Johnson, LL.D.*, ed. by Arthur Murphy (London, 1792), I. Further references appear parenthetically in the text.

84. Murphy was setting himself apart from Hawkins and Boswell.

85. Donald A. Stauffer, *The Art of Biography in Eighteenth Century England* (Princeton, 1941), I, 410.

86. *Ibid.*, I, 410-11.

87. W. K. Wimsatt, Jr., *Philosophic Words: A Study of Style and Meaning in the "Rambler" and "Dictionary" of Samuel Johnson* (New Haven, 1948), p. 81.

88. See *Johnson: The Critical Heritage*, p. 22.

89. See Foot, *Life*, pp. 424ff.; Taylor, *Records of My Life*, p. 120; Emery, *Arthur Murphy*, pp. 163ff.; Carola Oman, *David Garrick* (Suffolk, 1958), p. xvi.

90. Arthur Murphy, *The Life of David Garrick* (London, 1801). References appear parenthetically in the text.

91. See Emery, *Arthur Murphy, passim,* and Dunbar, *Dramatic Career, passim.*

92. For a different view of Rich, see Paul Sawyer, "John Rich's Contribution to the Eighteenth-Century London Stage," *Essays on the Eighteenth-Century English Stage,* ed. by Kenneth Richards and Peter Thomson (London, 1972), pp. 85–104.

93. See Emery, *Arthur Murphy*, pp. 165ff.

94. References to Murphy's poems, unless otherwise indicated, are to his *Works* and are given parenthetically.

95. Cf. Mary E. Knapp, *Prologues and Epilogues of the Eighteenth Century* (New Haven, 1961), p. 133.

96. For a recent discussion of the subject, see Robert D. Hume, "Goldsmith and Sheridan and the Supposed Revolution of 'Laughing' against 'Sentimental' Comedy," *Studies in Change and Revolution,* ed. by Paul J. Korshin (Menston, Yorkshire, 1972), pp. 237–76.

97. Emery, *Arthur Murphy,* p. 14 and "The Notes of Smart's *Hilliad,*" *MLN* 61 (1946): 162–65.

98. Dunbar, *Dramatic Career,* p. 76; Emery, *Arthur Murphy,* p. 54; *CR* 10 (Oct. 1760): 319–20; *MR* 23 (Nov. 1760): 412.

99. Dunbar *Dramatic Career,* pp. 112–13, and Emery, *Arthur Murphy,* p. 77, are appalled by its strong language. Churchill's attacks on Murphy, apart from that in the *Rosciad,* are in the *Apology,* the *Author,* the *Candidate, Independence,* and the *Journey.*

100. The original publication in London was in 1761; Foot, *Life*, pp. 196ff., presents the revision and notes that even Churchill praised the poem.

101. Dunbar, *Dramatic Career,* p. 112, notes that Shirley had attacked Murphy in the *Craftsman.* Murphy's quarrels with Churchill, Lloyd, and Colman were part of the political controversy he was engaged in, and with Colman there was an additional theatrical rivalry.

102. Foot, *Life,* p. 203n., erroneously reports that Murphy's poem silenced his opponents. *The Murphiad: A Mock Heroic Poem* appeared in London in 1761.

103. See n. 101 and discussion of the *Auditor* and plays.

104. The poem, originally entitled *The Expostulation,* was published as *The Examiner,* but appeared again as *The Expostulation* in Murphy's

Works. For responses to the work, see Dunbar, *Dramatic Career,* p. 119. Emery, *Arthur Murphy,* p. 78, cites Boileau's *Satire IX* as a model. Both Dunbar, p. 118 and Emery, p. 78, react more favorably to the poem than to Murphy's *Ode.* For contemporary praise, see *MR* 25 (Nov. 1761): 398 and *CR* 12 (Nov. 1761): 400.

105. For example, his translation of Pope's "Ode on Solitude" appeared in *GIJ,* April 13, 1754; his dedication of "Epistle to Lord Halifax" was in gratitude to Lord Loughborough (Emery, *Arthur Murphy,* p. 161); and his rendering of Sallust's *History of Cataline's Conspiracy* expresses his opposition to the French Revolution (J. Homer Caskey, "The First Edition of Arthur Murphy's *Sallust,*" *PQ* 13 [1934]: 404-408). For a favorable view of Murphy as translator, see H. MacL. Currie, "Arthur Murphy, Actor and Author," *New Rambler* 14 (Spring 1973): 9-13.

106. Foot, *Life,* p. 323. See *Literary Magazine* 2 (May-June 1757): 259-60.

107. Foot, *Life,* pp. 315-16.

108. Emery, *Arthur Murphy,* pp. 98, 149.

109. *Ibid.,* pp. 156-57; for contemporary praise, see *CR* 23 (March 1767): 179, and *MR* 36 (April 1767): 298.

Chapter Two

1. For general background, see *The London Stage, 1660-1800,* ed. by G. W. Stone, Jr. (Carbondale, Ill., 1962), Pt. 4, I, "Introduction"; Allardyce Nicoll, *A History of English Drama, 1660-1800* (Cambridge, 1961), III, *passim;* Cecil Price, *Theatre in the Age of Garrick* (Totowa, N.J., 1973), *passim.*

2. See H. L. Bruce, "Voltaire on the English Stage," *University of California Publications in Modern Philology* (June 1918): #1, pp. 69, 92; *The Private Correspondence of David Garrick with the Most Celebrated Persons of His Time,* ed. by James Boaden (London, 1831-32), I, 66.

3. See, for example, Nicoll, *History of English Drama,* III, 110-11, 123; Willard A. Kinne, *Revivals and Importations of French Comedies in England, 1749-1800* (New York, 1939), p. 248; Elizabeth Stein, *David Garrick, Dramatist* (New York), Chapter 3; Peter A. Tasch, *The Dramatic Cobbler, The Life and Works of Isaac Bickerstaff* (Lewisburg, Pa., 1971), pp. 46, 221.

4. See Tasch, *Dramatic Cobbler,* pp. 46, 287.

5. Kinne, *Revivals and Importations,* p. 58.

6. Foot, *Life,* p. 445.

7. *London Stage,* Pt. 4, I, xxiv; Price, *Theatre in the Age of Garrick,* pp. 142ff.; Dunbar, *Dramatic Career,* p. 150; *Eighteenth Century Drama: Afterpieces,* ed. by Richard W. Bevis (London, 1970),

p. viii; Philip K. Jason, "The Afterpiece: Authors and Incentives," *Restoration and 18th Century Theatre Research* 12 (May 1973): 4.

8. Price, *Theatre in the Age of Garrick*, p. 154.

9. *London Stage*, Pt. 4, I, cxlv; Hume, "Goldsmith and Sheridan," p. 257.

10. Hume, "Goldsmith and Sheridan," p. 257; Eugene R. Page, *George Colman the Elder* (New York, 1935), p. 50.

11. Bevis, *Afterpieces*, p. xiv; Harry W. Pedicord, *The Theatrical Public in the Time of Garrick* (New York, 1954), p. 147.

12. Jason, "The Afterpiece," pp. 4, 9.

13. Emery, *Arthur Murphy*, p. 28.

14. For attacks, see *CR* 1 (Jan.-Feb. 1756): 78-82, and *MR* 14 (Jan. 1756): 78. The *Monthly* reviewer was Sir Tanfield Leman (for all attributions, see B. C. Nangle, *The Monthly Review, First Series* [Oxford, 1934]). The quotation is from *London Magazine* 25 (Jan. 1756): 39. The German visitor was Theodor von Schön (see John A. Kelly, *German Visitors to English Theaters in the Eighteenth Century* [Princeton, 1936], p. 156). See, too, *London Chronicle* 20 (Oct. 18-20, 1756): 388; and *Theatrical Review* 1 (1772): 176-77.

15. See "Advertisement" in *The Way to Keep Him and Five Other Plays by Arthur Murphy*, ed. by J. P. Emery, p. 9. My further parenthetic references are to this text based on Murphy's *Works*.

16. For alterations from an earlier draft, see Emery, *Arthur Murphy*, p. 18 and Dunbar, *Dramatic Career*, pp. 21-22. For additional scene, see *London Stage*, Pt. 4, II, 533, 540.

17. Both Emery and Dunbar discuss Murphy's changes, but my discussions throughout are based on my own examination of the various states of Murphy's plays, including those manuscript copies of the acting versions in the Larpent collection of the Huntington Library.

18. See Christopher Smart's "Epilogue," in Emery, *Plays*, p. 59.

19. See Nicoll, *History of English Drama*, III, 179; Caskey, "Murphy and the War on Sentimental Comedy," p. 571; Emery, *Arthur Murphy*, p. 29.

20. Dunbar, *Dramatic Career*, pp. 21-22.

21. *Ibid.*, p. 25 and Emery, *Arthur Murphy*, p. 29.

22. See Emery, *Arthur Murphy*, p. 29 and *Plays*, pp. 18-19, 56ff.

23. The only edition was in London, by W. Reeve, 1756. Further references are parenthetic.

24. Dunbar, *Dramatic Career*, p. 28; Emery, *Arthur Murphy*, p. 29.

25. Dunbar, *Dramatic Career*, p. 26. But cf., Simon Trefman, *Sam. Foote, Comedian, 1720-1777* (New York, 1971), p. 74.

26. See Trefman, *Foote*, p. 74 and Emery, *Arthur Murphy*, pp. 29-30.

27. See Emery, *Arthur Murphy*, p. 29 and his "Murphy's Authorship of the Notes of Smart's *Hilliad*," *MLN* 61 (March 1946): 162. See *CR* 1 (March 1756): 146-47 and Foot, *Life*, p. 107.

28. Trefman, *Foote*, pp. 76-77; Emery, *Arthur Murphy*, p. 29; Dunbar, *Dramatic Career*, p. 26.

29. For identifications, see Dunbar, *Dramatic Career*, p. 28.

30. See Dunbar, *Dramatic Career*, p. 26; Trefman, *Foote*, p. 75; *CR* 1 (March 1756): 146-47.

31. Trefman, *Foote*, p. 75.

32. *MR* 14 (Jan 1756): 67, 78.

33. *London Stage*, Pt. 4, II, 524, 536.

34. See *Literary Magazine* 1 (March-April 1756): 29; Foot, *Life*, pp. 106-107. The play, with an introduction by Simon Trefman, was published by the Augustan Reprint Society (Los Angeles, 1969), #137. Further references are parenthetic.

35. For prior discussion, see Dunbar, *Dramatic Career*, pp. 31-32. See Trefman's introduction, but compare his comments in *Foote*, pp. 73ff.

36. Trefman, "Introduction," p. v. emphasizes Murphy's criticism of English prejudices.

37. Murphy's treatment of Shaftesbury is to be contrasted with his later attitude expressed in *Know Your Own Mind*. In *GIJ* Murphy deals with both Shaftesbury and Akenside. See Trefman, "Introduction," pp. iv-v.

38. *Ibid.*, p. iv.

39. Dunbar, *Dramatic Career*, pp. 41-42.

40. For initial indifferent reaction, see *London Stage*, Pt. 4, II, 657. For praise, see *CR* 5 (April 1758): 330-33; *MR* 18 (May 1758): 415-20; *London Magazine* 27 (April 1758): 167.

41. See his letter to Garrick, Emery, *Plays*, p. 72. Parenthetic references are to this edition. For other sources, see, Emery, *Arthur Murphy*, pp. 36-37; Bevis, *Afterpieces*, pp. 164, 197; Dunbar, *Dramatic Career*, p. 45.

42. John Genest, *Some Account of the English Stage* (Bath, 1832), IV, 517; Nicoll, *History of English Drama*, III, 116, 180.

43. Nicoll, *History*, p. 181; Emery, *Plays*, p. 65; Dunbar, *Dramatic Career*, p. 46.

44. Genest, *English Stage*, IV, 517; Dunbar, *Dramatic Career*, p. 47. See *GIJ* (1756): II, 163-64.

45. Bevis, *Afterpieces*, p. xi.

46. See Emery, *Arthur Murphy*, p. 38; Dunbar, *Dramatic Career*, p. 43.

47. See, for example, Emery, *Arthur Murphy*, p. 38.

48. As noted earlier, observations depend on my own study of the texts, but see, too, Bevis, *Afterpieces*, p. 194; Emery, *Plays*, pp. 65-68; Dunbar, *Dramatic Career*, pp. 48, 54.

49. A note in the 1758 edition indicates that Codicil's scene and *"a few Passages in the second Act"* had been omitted from the original production.

50. The manuscript for a 1791 Covent Garden production is in the Huntington Library.

51. Dunbar, *Dramatic Career*, p. 122.

52. See Emery, *Plays*, p. 245, and *Arthur Murphy*, p. 70.

53. Dunbar, *Dramatic Career*, pp. 134–35.

54. See *CR* 12 (Dec. 1761): 437–38; *Biographica Dramatica* (London, 1812), III, 96; Dunbar, *Dramatic Career*, pp. 134–35; Kinne, *Revivals and Importations*, pp. 82–83.

55. *MR* 25 (Dec. 1761): 473. See Dunbar, *Dramatic Career*, p. 135, which speaks of Mrs. Griffiths's review as a "petticoat view of the ridiculing of Miss Harlow."

56. Emery, *Plays*, p. 280. Further references are parenthetic.

57. See Dunbar, *Dramatic Career*, p. 133.

58. The point is Dunbar's *Dramatic Career*, p. 133.

59. Emery, *Arthur Murphy*, p. 71.

60. Dunbar, *Dramatic Career*, p. 133.

61. Kinne, *Revivals and Importations*, pp. 82–83.

62. *Ibid.*

63. For disagreement about the genre, see Nicoll, *History of English Drama*, III, 181; Emery, *Arthur Murphy*, p. 71; Dunbar, *Dramatic Career*, pp. 132–33, 301.

64. See page 2 of the 1761 London edition, published by P. Vaillant.

65. Emery, *Arthur Murphy*, p. 63.

66. See *London Stage*, Pt. 4, II, 874ff., 944–45. For nature of the abridgment, see Dunbar, *Dramatic Career*, p. 145, who cites article in *St. James's Chronicle* (July 6, 1761).

67. See Preface to the play.

68. See *MR* 28 (Feb. 1763): 166–67 and *CR* 15 (Feb. 1763): 113–19.

69. See Dunbar, *Dramatic Career*, pp. 146, 148, 295; Emery, *Arthur Murphy*, pp. 74–75.

70. Emery, *Arthur Murphy*, p. 184, n. 44.

71. Nicoll, *History of English Drama*, III, 181; Emery, *Arthur Murphy*, p. 73; Dunbar, *Dramatic Career*, p. 301.

72. Dunbar, *Dramatic Career*, p. 145.

73. See Price, *Theatre in the Age of Garrick*, p. 171. See n. 71 above.

74. Text is *Works*, II. Further references are parenthetic.

75. See Foot, *Life*, p. 184; Dunbar, *Dramatic Career*, p. 145. Nicoll, *History of English Drama*, III, 181, exaggerates Murphy's indebtedness.

76. See Dunbar, *Dramatic Career*, p. 146 and Kinne, *Revivals and Importations*, pp. 81–82.

77. See particularly, *St. James's Chronicle* (Jan. 25, 1763), #295. Even the *Critical* and *Monthly* (see n. 68) make this charge.

78. Such a reference as "Canada must be restor'd" (1763 ed., p. 13) had to be altered for lack of topicality in his *Works*.

79. Genest, *English Stage*, v, 55. See, too, *CR* 17 (Jan. 1764): 52.

80. *London Stage*, Pt. 4, II, 1030, notes that the original production was delayed from a scheduled opening on December 31.

81. Dunbar, *Dramatic Career*, p. 165. See *St. James's Chronicle* (Jan. 10, 1764), #445; *London Chronicle* 15 (Jan. 10-12, 1764): 37 *London Magazine* 33 (Jan 1764): 38-39; *Universal Magazine* 34 (Jan. 1764): 42. Only John Langhorne, who pointed out the political attack on Murphy, praised the play in the *MR* 31 (Jan. 1764): 70.

82. *London Stage*, Pt. 4, II, 1032, 1034; Dunbar, *Dramatic Career*, pp. 167-68.

83. Dunbar, *Dramatic Career*, p. 169.

84. *London Stage*, Pt. 4, III, 1965ff.

85. Paul Vaillant's reissue altered the title page, but kept the old title in the running heads. George Kearsley published a new edition in 1776.

86. See *St. James's Chronicle* (Jan. 10, 1764), #445 and *London Chronicle* 15 (Jan. 10-12, 1764): 37.

87. Stein, *David Garrick*, p. 29; Dunbar, *Dramatic Career*, p. 166f; Emery, *Arthur Murphy*, p. 90.

88. Dunbar, *Dramatic Career*, p. 167; see Murphy's "Advertisement" to the first edition.

89. For a discussion of the type, see Nicoll, *History of English Drama*, III, 181-82; Dunbar, *Dramatic Career*, pp. 164, 171-72; Emery, *Arthur Murphy*, pp. 90ff. and *Plays*, pp. 285-86. Further parenthetic references are to Emery, *Plays*.

90. *London Stage*, Pt. 4, II, 1070, 1104; III, 1621. The 1772 performance was entitled *Merit before Money*.

91. Dunbar, *Dramatic Career*, p. 172, suggests this, but fails to note that Murphy's anonymity would have defeated his purpose.

92. Foot, *Life*, pp. 198-99.

93. Parenthetic references are to the *Works*.

94. Dunbar, *Dramatic Career*, p. 196.

95. Emery, *Arthur Murphy*, p. 94, attributes her conduct to Murphy's yielding to sentimental taste.

96. *Ibid.*, p. 94; Dunbar, *Dramatic Career*, p. 175, cites *London Chronicle* 17 (March 28-30, 1765): 309-10.

97. Cf. Genest, *English Stage*, V, 67; Dunbar, *Dramatic Career*, p. 175; Emery, *Arthur Murphy*, p. 94.

98. Foot, *Life*, pp. 283-85; *London Stage*, ed. by C. B. Hogan, Pt. 5, I, 12, 18-21. Dunbar, *Dramatic Career*, p. 259, describes the prelude as a competitive work to George Colman's *New Brooms!* at Drury Lane.

99. Dunbar, *Dramatic Career*, pp. 264-65.

100. D. F. Smith, *The Critics as the Audience of the London Theatres from Buckingham to Sheridan* (Alburquerque, 1953), p. 113; Stein, *David Garrick*, p. 25.

101. Parenthetic references are to Murphy's *Works*.

102. Dunbar, *Dramatic Career*, p. 198.

103. For a discussion of these points see Hume, "Goldsmith and Sheridan."

104. The Huntington Ms., apparently in a later addition, includes the character of Mrs. Gamut to ridicule comic opera. Murphy berates its neglect of wit and sentiment.

105. The work is published in Foot, *Life*, to which further parenthetic references are made. Dunbar, *Dramatic Career*, p. 226, notes the parody is of Act I, Sc. 1, 2 (part), 4, 5.

106. Emery, *Arthur Murphy*, p. 115.

107. Spector, *English Literary Periodicals*, passim; Foot, *Life*, pp. 252–53. Yet Emery, *Arthur Murphy*, p. 117, points out that both Johnson and Murphy approved of Nahum Tate's adaptation of *King Lear* with its happy ending.

108. See *London Stage*, Pt. 4, III, 1680; Dunbar, *Dramatic Career*, p. 226.

109. See G. W. Stone, Jr., "Garrick's Long Lost Alteration of *Hamlet*," *PMLA* 49 (Sept. 1934): 897ff.

110. Foot, *Life*, p. 254.

111. *Ibid.*, p. 252; Emery, *Arthur Murphy*, p. 117.

112. Foot, *Life*, p. 254; Dunbar, *Dramatic Career*, p. 232.

113. Dunbar, *Dramatic Career*, p. 227.

Chapter Three

1. Dunbar, *Dramatic Career*, pp. 296, 300; Emery, *Arthur Murphy*, p. vii; Caskey, "Murphy and the War on Sentimental Comedy," p. 577; Hume, "Goldsmith and Sheridan," p. 265.

2. For background, see Hume, "Goldsmith and Sheridan"; Price, *Theatre in the Age of Garrick;* Arthur Friedman, "Aspects of Sentimentalism in Eighteenth-Century Literature," *The Augustan Milieu*, ed. by Henry Knight Miller *et. al.* (Oxford, 1970), pp. 247–61; Sherbo, *English Sentimental Drama*.

3. Caskey, "Murphy and the War on Sentimental Comedy," p. 571.

4. Nicoll, *History of English Drama*, III, 156; Murphy, *Life of Garrick*, II, 53.

5. Caskey, "Murphy and the War on Sentimental Comedy," pp. 575–76.

6. *Letters of David Garrick*, ed. by David M. Little and George M. Kahrl (London, 1963), III, 985.

7. Dunbar, *Dramatic Career*, pp. 85-86. See "Advertisement" to the 1760 edition of the play.

8. Emery, *Arthur Murphy*, p. 58; Bevis, *Afterpieces*, p. 197.

9. Bevis, *Afterpieces*, pp. xi, 197; Emery, *Arthur Murphy*, pp. 58ff.; Dunbar, *Dramatic Career*, p. 87. For contemporary opinion: *London Magazine* 29 (Jan. 1760): 42; *London Chronicle* 7 (Jan. 24-26, 1760): 95; *MR* 22 (Feb. 1760): 143-45; *CR* 9 (Feb. 1760): 141-43.

10. Bevis, *Afterpieces*, p. 187; Dunbar, *Dramatic Career*, p. 86; Emery, *Arthur Murphy*, p. 53; *London Stage*, Pt. 4, II, 808.

11. Emery, *Arthur Murphy*, p. 54.

12. Dunbar, *Dramatic Career*, pp. 88-90.

13. *London Stage*, Pt. 4, II, 837.

14. Dunbar, *Dramatic Career*, p. 91.

15. *Ibid.*, p. 100. For contemporary opinion, see *MR* 24 (Feb. 1761): 159; *CR* 11 (Jan. 1761): 48-49.

16. Nicoll, *History of English Drama*, III, 112. See Murphy's "Advertisement" to the published play.

17. Bevis, *Afterpieces*, p. 201.

18. For a comparison of the two, see Kinne, *Revivals and Importations*, p. 59.

19. Foot, *Life*, p. 162; Emery, *Arthur Murphy*, pp. 57ff.; Dunbar, *Dramatic Career*, pp. 95f.

20. Kinne, *Revivals and Importations*, p. 63.

21. Dunbar, *Dramatic Career*, p. 103.

22. Parenthetic references are to Emery, *Plays*, which presents the text from Murphy's *Works*.

23. See Murphy's "Advertisement" in Bevis, *Afterpieces*, p. 201, in which he affects the characteristic "amateurishness" of Restoration dramatists.

24. See *MR* 22 (Feb. 1760): 144.

25. Caskey, "Murphy and the War on Sentimental Comedy," p. 571, describes it as a weak imitation of Restoration comedy.

26. See Kinne, *Revivals and Importations*, p. 64; Dunbar, *Dramatic Career*, p. 103; Nicoll, *History of English Drama*, III, 162.

27. See Prologue in Emery, *Plays*, p. 136. For contemporary responses, see *CR* 9 (Feb. 1760): 142-43; *London Chronicle* 7 (Jan. 24-26, 1760): 95. Cf. Emery, *Arthur Murphy*, p. 62; Dunbar, *Dramatic Career*, p. 86.

28. See Dunbar, *Dramatic Career*, p. 102; F. S. Boas, *An Introduction to Eighteenth-Century Drama, 1700-1780* (Oxford, 1953), p. 314.

29. See Emery, *Plays*, p. 129; Dunbar, *Dramatic Career*, p. 102.

30. *London Stage*, Pt. 4, II, 902ff.; Dunbar, *Dramatic Career*, pp. 128-29; Emery, *Arthur Murphy*, p. 66.

31. Dunbar, *Dramatic Career*, p. 130; Gray, *Theatrical Criticism in London to 1795*, p. 163.

32. *MR* 25 (Dec. 1761): 472-73; *CR* 12 (Dec. 1761): 431-37. See, too, *Court Magazine* 1 (Nov 1761): 118-19.

33. *Garrick Letters*, I, 334; Foot, *Life*, p. 171.

34. See Nicoll, *History of English Drama*, III, 117.

35. See Murphy's "Advertisement" to the first edition. Nicoll, *Ibid.*, exaggerates Murphy's use of Molière's play.

36. See Dunbar, *Dramatic Career*, p. 127. Comparison with James Miller's *The Picture: or, The Cuckold in Conceit* (London, 1745), a faithful adaptation of Molière's farce, suggests how little Murphy's work is indebted to the play.

37. See Emery, *Arthur Murphy*, p. 67; Kinne, *Revivals and Importations*, p. 65; Foot, *Life*, p. 182.

38. Foot, *Life*, p. 182; Dunbar, *Dramatic Career*, p. 130; Boas, *Eighteenth-Century Drama*, p. 314.

39. Foot, *Life*, p. 171.

40. Dunbar, *Dramatic Career*, p. 130.

41. *Garrick Letters*, I, 334.

42. Ernest Bernbaum, *The Drama of Sensibility* (Cambridge, Mass., 1915), p. 252.

43. See Nicoll, *History of English Drama*, III, 163; Emery, *Arthur Murphy*, p. 67.

44. See Emery, *Arthur Murphy*, p. 69.

45. See Dunbar, *Dramatic Career*, p. 131.

46. Foot, *Life*, p. 308.

47. *London Stage*, Pt. 4, II, 1030ff.

48. *CR* 17 (Jan. 1764): 51; *MR* 30 (Jan. 1764): 70.

49. See, for example, *Gentleman's Magazine* 24 (Jan. 1764): 22; *London Magazine* 33 (Jan. 1764): 38; *Royal Magazine* 10 (Jan. 1764): 28; *Universal Magazine* 34 (Jan. 1764): 39; *London Chronicle* 15 (Jan. 10-12, 1764): 36.

50. See Foot, *Life*, p. 194; Dunbar, *Dramatic Career*, p. 162; Nicoll, *History of English Drama*, III, 181; Bruce, "Voltaire on the English Stage," pp. 81, 88-89.

51. Foot, *Life*, p. 192, is followed in his opinion by Emery, *Arthur Murphy*, pp. 86-87; Dunbar, *Dramatic Career*, pp. 158, 163; Nicoll, *History of English Drama*, III, 7.

52. *London Stage*, Pt. 4, III, 1844ff. My discussion emphasizes the full-length comedy, but considers, as well, Murphy's abridgment.

53. Foot, *Life*, pp. 192ff. and Dunbar, *Dramatic Career*, p. 161.

54. Bruce, "Voltaire on the English Stage," pp. 79ff. Bruce notes that Murphy had available Smollett's and Francklin's translated edition of the play (*The Babbler*).

55. See *Works*, II, 315; Foot, *Life*, p. 192; Stein, *David Garrick*, p. 46; Emery, *Arthur Murphy*, p. 88.

56. *Works*, II, 303-304. Where there are differences from the first edition published in London in 1764, they are presented in my notes.

57. *Works*, II, 349. 1764: "Why this is enough to spoil a man's dancing, indeed" (p. 86).

58. *Works*, II, 352. 1764: p. 88.

59. *Works*, II, 354. 1764: "Then let us dance away reflection for the present" (p. 94).

60. *Works*, II, 306. 1764: "contracted into a narrow attention to self, and his understanding acts the subservient part to schemes of interest" (p. 2).

61. Dunbar, *Dramatic Career*, p. 162.

62. *Works*, II, 332.

63. *Works*, II, 308. 1764: after "a damn'd high story"—"and so a friend is sacrificed to the sport of the next company" (p. 4).

64. *London Stage*, Pt. 4, II, 1210-12, 1223.

65. *London Stage*, Pt. 5, I, 108. Kinne, *Revivals and Importations*, p. 122, notes that much of the dialogue was replaced by song.

66. The "Advertisement" to the first edition notes that one of the scenes printed in the text had been eliminated from the production. Parenthetic references are to *Works*, IV.

67. *Court Miscellany*, 3 (Jan. 1767): 45.

68. See, for example, *MR* 36 (Jan. 1767): 72, Colman's review; *CR* 23 (Jan. 1767): 59-60; *London Chronicle* 21 (Jan. 10-13, 1767): 48; *St. James's Chronicle* (Jan. 22-24, 1767), #920.

69. Dunbar, *Dramatic Career*, p. 183.

70. *Letters of Laurence Sterne*, ed. by L. P. Curtis (Oxford, 1935), p. 297.

71. See Murphy's "Advertisement" and Dunbar, *Dramatic Career*, pp. 176ff. and Emery, *Arthur Murphy*, p. 95.

72. Foot, *Life*, p. 204.

73. Emery, *Arthur Murphy*, p. 97, finds the revision more interesting, but Dunbar, *Dramatic Career*, p. 185, sees it as no improvement.

74. See Emery, *Arthur Murphy*, p. 95.

75. Dunbar, *Dramatic Career*, pp. 182ff.; Emery, *Arthur Murphy*, p. 97; Kinne, *Revivals and Importations*, pp. 71-72.

76. Foot, *Life*, p. 212; Nicoll, *History of English Drama*, III, 163.

77. *London Chronicle*, see note 68 above.

78. Kinne, *Revivals and Importations*, p. 71, describes the material as "thrown in for good measure."

79. *London Stage*, Pt. 5, I, 60ff. and later references. Dunbar, *Dramatic Career*, p. 281, is inaccurate about performance information. See Emery, *Arthur Murphy*, p. 125.

80. For contemporary opinion: *London Magazine* 46 (Feb. 1777): 64; *Town and Country* 9 (March 1777): 149-50. *London Chronicle* 41 (Feb. 22-25, 1777), raises objections about plot; *Westminster Magazine* 5 (Feb. 1777): 85, is a personal attack on Murphy. For Steevens's response, see Dunbar, *Dramatic Career*, p. 289.

81. *MR* 58 (June 1778): 435.

82. Foot, *Life*, p. 301.

83. For an account, see Foot, *Life*, pp. 228 ff.; Dunbar, *Dramatic Career*, p. 268; Emery, *Plays*, p. 333.

84. Dunbar, *Dramatic Career*, p. 269; Emery, *Arthur Murphy*, p. 125.

85. Dunbar, *Dramatic Career*, p. 273.

86. Dunbar, *Dramatic Career*, p. 283; Emery, *Plays*, p. 333.

87. Foot, *Life*, p. 294; Emery, *Plays*, p. 334; Dunbar, *Dramatic Career*, pp. 286-87.

88. Emery, *Arthur Murphy*, p. 137; Bernbaum, *Drama of Sensibility*, p. 256.

89. Foot, *Life*, p. 294; Dunbar, *Dramatic Career*, pp. 287ff.

90. Bernbaum, *Drama of Sensibility*, pp. 255-56.

91. Dunbar, *Dramatic Career*, p. 285.

92. See Foot, *Life*, p. 294 and Bernbaum, *Drama of Sensibility*, p. 256.

93. Nicoll, *History of English Drama*, III, 118.

94. See Dunbar, *Dramatic Career*, pp. 276ff.; Emery, *Arthur Murphy*, pp. 121-27; Kinne, *Revivals and Importations*, p. 145, fails to recognize the differences between Murphy's play and its source.

95. Parenthetic references are to Emery, *Plays*, which uses *Works*, IV.

96. See Emery, *Arthur Murphy*, p. 134.

97. See, especially, Dunbar, *Dramatic Career*, p. 288.

98. See Trefman, *Foote*, pp. 260-61.

99. Cf., Nicoll, *History of English Drama*, III, 164.

100. Dunbar, *Dramatic Career*, p. 283.

101. Emery, *Arthur Murphy*, pp. 127ff.

102. The changes are fewer than Dunbar, *Dramatic Career*, p. 275, suggests.

Chapter Four

1. See Pedicord, *Theatrical Public*, pp. 65-66, 119-20, 138 ff. and Nicoll, *History of English Drama*, III, 56.

2. Nicoll, *History of English Drama*, III, 53.

3. Price, *Theatre in the Age of Garrick*, passim.

4. Sybil Rosenfeld, "Landscape in English Scenery in the Eighteenth Century," *The Eighteenth Century English Stage*, ed. by Kenneth Richards and Peter Thomson (London, 1972), pp. 171-78.

5. See Emery, *Arthur Murphy*, pp. 171ff.; Dunbar, *Dramatic Career*, p. 295.

6. Emery, *Arthur Murphy*, p. 173; Dunbar, *Dramatic Career*, pp. 295-96.

7. Pedicord, *Theatrical Public*, p. 138.

8. *London Stage*, Pt. 4, II, 771-72.

9. Foot, *Life*, p. 162; Genest, *English Stage*, IV, 581-82; Emery, *Arthur Murphy*, p. 172.

10. For Murphy's difficulties with Garrick, see earlier discussion.

11. See *Poems of Charles Churchill*, ed. by James Laver (London, 1933), I, 4 n. 62, 53.

12. See Emery, *Arthur Murphy*, pp. 77-78.

13. Foot, *Life*, p. 119.

14. Nicoll, *History of English Drama*, III, 70, 222, overestimates Murphy's indebtedness to his sources. Cf., Dunbar, *Dramatic Career*, p. 83 and Emery, *Arthur Murphy*, p. 52.

15. The edition used is in *Works*, III. Further references are parenthetic.

16. Emery, *Arthur Murphy*, pp. 52-53.

17. Dunbar, *Dramatic Career*, pp. 82-83.

18. Foot, *Life*, p. 159; *Garrick Letters, passim.*

19. Dunbar, *Dramatic Career*, p. 85; Emery, *Arthur Murphy*, p. 53; Nicoll, *History of English Drama*, III, 51, 222.

20. For some discussion of these characteristics, see Emery, *Arthur Murphy*, pp. 52-53; Dunbar, *Dramatic Career*, pp. 84-85; Nicoll, *History of English Drama*, III, 51, 222.

21. See, particularly, Murphy's addition to Constantia's first speech in his printed versions of the play. Overall, however, his revisions do not amount to much.

22. Dunbar, *Dramatic Career*, p. 84.

23. See *London Magazine* 29 (Feb. 1760): 93; *CR* 9 (Feb. 1760): 133-40; *MR* 22 (Feb. 1760): 137ff. Emery, *Arthur Murphy*, p. 182, n. 47, cites borrowings from Gray's *Elegy* and from *King Lear* and *Hamlet*.

24. Cf. Dunbar, *Dramatic Career*, p. 83 and Genest, *English Stage*, IV, 581-82.

25. William W. Appleton, *A Cycle of Cathay* (New York, 1951), pp. 78ff.; Kalman A. Burnim, *David Garrick Director* (Carbondale and Edwardsville, Ill., 1973), pp. 12-13, 70.

26. *Garrick Letters*, I, 253f., 272f., 300f.

27. Foot, *Life*, pp. 146-50, gives Whitehead's analysis of the play. See, too, pp. 143ff. and 152-53.

28. Dunbar, *Dramatic Career*, p. 62.

29. *London Stage*, Pt. 4, II, 722. See, too, Foot, *Life*, p. 151; Dunbar, *Dramatic Career*, p. 68; Price, *Theatre in the Age of Garrick*, pp. 70-71.

30. Emery, *Arthur Murphy*, p. 49. Genest, *English Stage*, IV, 550, says 1777 production was less well received.

31. See Dunbar, *Dramatic Career*, pp. 70-71. Henry Fox advised the dedication to Bute as a political maneuver.

32. For some estimates, see Emery, *Arthur Murphy*, pp. 50-51; Appleton, *A Cycle of Cathay*, p. 86; Genest, *English Stage*, IV 550; Price, *Theatre in the Age of Garrick*, pp. 159-60; Dunbar, *Dramatic Career*, p. 74.

33. See Spector, *English Literary Periodicals*, p. 339; Appleton, *Cycle of Cathay*, pp, 77, 112, 140.

34. See *Works*, I; further references are parenthetic.

35. Such references are scattered throughout the play.

36. See Price, *Theatre in the Age of Garrick*, p. 159; Emery, *Arthur Murphy*, pp. 48-49; Dunbar, *Dramatic Career*, pp. 71-73.

37. Dunbar, *Dramatic Career*, p. 74, describes Goldsmith's as the "best contemporary estimate." But Appleton, *Cycle of Cathay*, pp. 86-87, see Goldsmith as less favorable than a superficial reading of his words indicates.

38. *Collected Works of Oliver Goldsmith*, ed. by Arthur Friedman (Oxford, 1966), I, 170-79. See *CR* 7 (May 1759): 430-40.

39. For the genesis of the play and discussion of its sources, see Appleton, *Cycle of Cathay*, pp. 82ff. For further details see Nicoll, *History of English Drama*, III, 60.

40. *MR* 20 (June 1759): 575.

41. See Bruce, "Voltaire on the English Stage," pp. 70ff., for many of the details in this paragraph. Dunbar, *Dramatic Career*, pp. 65ff.

42. Foot, *Life*, p. 155.

43. Nicoll, *History of English Drama*, III, 18, calls it "a patriotic epistle." See Dunbar, *Dramatic Career*, p. 72.

44. Cf. Hurd's *Discourse on Poetical Imitation* (1751). Dunbar, *Dramatic Career*, pp. 65-66, describes the indebtedness to Corneille, Racine, and classical dramatists.

45. A response to Murphy—"A Letter from M. Voltaire to the Author of the *Orphan of China*"—is spurious and fails to deal with the issues Murphy raised. See Bruce, "Voltaire on the English Stage," p. 75.

46. See, for example, Dunbar, *Dramatic Career*, p. 61; Nicoll, *History of English Drama*, III, 75; Emery, *Arthur Murphy*, p. 50.

47. For background, see Dunbar, *Dramatic Career*, pp. 187ff.

48. Barry and Miss Dance threatened to withdraw from Drury Lane and go to Ireland. Then Miss Dance, claiming illness, did leave the cast. See Dunbar, *Dramatic Career*, pp. 190ff.

49. *London Stage*, Pt. 4, III, 1331-33; Emery, *Arthur Murphy*, p. 101.

50. Dunbar, *Dramatic Career*, p. 196.

51. *MR* 38 (March 1768): 244; *CR* 25 (April 1768): 314; *Court*

Miscellany 4 (March 1768): 140. But see Johnson's criticism of the artificiality of such plays, Thrale, *Anecdotes*, pp. 216-17.

52. Pedicord, *Theatrical Public*, p. 138.

53. Emery, *Arthur Murphy*, p. 101; Dunbar, *Dramatic Career*, pp. 196-97; Nicoll, *History of English Drama*, III, 76.

54. Dunbar, *Dramatic Career*, p. 193.

55. Further references to the play from *Works*, I, are given parenthetically.

56. See Foot, *Life*, p. 219.

57. Genest, *English Stage*, V, 165; Emery, *Arthur Murphy*, p. 103.

58. Nicoll, *History of English Drama*, III, 76, overemphasizes the importance of the source.

59. For general details of Murphy's use of sources, see Emery, *Arthur Murphy*, pp. 103-104; Dunbar, *Dramatic Career*, pp. 194-95.

60. Emery, *Arthur Murphy*, p. 105, fails to judge the character in context.

61. Dunbar, *Dramatic Career*, p. 196, accurately notes that changes are more numerous in the final act.

62. Emery, *Arthur Murphy*, pp. 113-14, places the climax in the second act.

63. See *London Stage*, Pt. 4, III, 1610ff.; Dunbar, *Dramatic Career*, pp. 210, 221; Emery, *Arthur Murphy*, p. 111; Foot, *Life*, pp. 226-28. For contemporary reponses, see some of the following (which include comment on the flaws in plot): *MR* 46 (March 1772): 259-60; *CR* 33 (March 1772): 224-29; *Gentleman's Magazine* 42 (March 1772): 139; *Town and Country Magazine* 4 (Feb 1772): 97-98; *London Chronicle* 31 (Feb. 25-27, 1772): 200; (Feb. 27-29): 204.

64. Kelly, *German Visitors to English Theatres*, p. 135.

65. *Garrick Letters*, II, 784.

66. *Thraliana*, I, 248.

67. See dedication to the 1772 edition.

68. *Theatrical Review* is quoted in *London Stage*, Pt. 4, III, 1610.

69. Roger Manvell, *Sarah Siddons: Portrait of an Actress* (New York, 1970), p. 347.

70. See Dunbar, *Dramatic Career*, p. 221; Genest, *English Stage*, V, 324; Nicoll, *History of English Drama*, III, 76.

71. Emery, *Arthur Murphy*, pp. 113-14; Foot, *Life*, p. 225 and n. 70.

72. Dunbar, *Dramatic Career*, p. 214; J. W. Donohue, Jr., *Dramatic Character in the English Romantic Age* (Princeton, 1970), pp. 81-82.

73. "Prologue" for the opening of Drury Lane, September 1747.

74. Nicoll, *History of English Drama*, III, 52, 76.

75. Donohue, *Dramatic Character*, p. 68n. Parenthetic references to Murphy's plays are to *Works*, I.

76. Foot, *Life*, pp. 223-34.

77. See 1772 edition.

78. Cf. Genest, *English Stage*, V, 324.

79. Emery, *Arthur Murphy*, pp. 112-13; Dunbar, *Dramatic Career*, pp. 214-15.

80. Emery, above, makes the point, but fails to recognize that there is more to the character.

81. Dunbar, *Dramatic Career*, p. 222, compares Murphy's verse favorably to that in the drama of his time.

82. Although Dunbar, *Dramatic Career*, p. 216, asserts that the revisions of Acts III and V in the first edition make the play less melodramatic, their verboseness actually adds to the sense of melodrama.

83. Dunbar, *Dramatic Career*, p. 223.

84. See *Works*, I, 311. Further references are parenthetic.

85. Dunbar, *Dramatic Career*, p. 235, says that the play was "ill staged, ill acted, and barely successful." However, there seems to be no real evidence for this judgment.

86. *London Stage*, Pt. 4, III, 1696ff.

87. Dunbar, *Dramatic Career*, p. 235, describes it thus.

88. *Ibid.*, p. 234, notes the original title was *Conquest of Peru*, but was changed by 1768.

89. *Ibid.*, p. 240.

90. See "Advertisement" in *Works*, I, 314-15.

91. *MR* 48 (March 1773): 212-15; *CR* 35 (March 1773): 229; *Town and Country Magazine* 5 (March 1773): 129-30; *London Chronicle* 33 (Feb. 23-25, 1773): 191. Dunbar, *Dramatic Career*, pp. 243, 247ff., attributes some unfavorable attitudes to Murphy's feud with Garrick and notes that Steevens, who reviewed the work in the *Critical*, probably attacked it in the *Morning Chronicle* because Murphy had refused to take his advice.

92. Foot, *Life*, p. 280; Dunbar, *Dramatic Career*, pp. 235, 245; Nicoll, *History of English Drama*, III, 77; Emery, *Arthur Murphy*, p. 119; Genest, *English Stage*, V, 365.

93. Dunbar, *Dramatic Career*, p. 246.

94. See Bruce, "Voltaire on the English Stage," pp. 86ff.; Nicoll, *History of English Drama*, III, 76-77; Genest, *English Stage*, V, 365; Dunbar, *Dramatic Career*, p. 239. Emery, *Arthur Murphy*, pp. 118-19 stresses Murphy's essential originality.

95. Nicoll, *History of English Drama*, III, 76.

96. See Knapp, *Prologues and Epilogues*, p. 277.

97. See Spector, *English Literary Periodicals*, *passim*.

98. See Murphy's discussion of the play, *Works*, VII, 244-48. Further references are parenthetic.

99. Emery, *Arthur Murphy*, p. 155.

100. This point is most apparent in Act I and in Ariadne's dying lament in Act V.

101. Emery, *Arthur Murphy*, p. 173.

102. Nicoll, *History of English Drama*, III, 77; Emery, *Arthur Murphy*, pp. 155-56.

103. Published on March 20, 1793, as it was performed, the play has changes that increase the pathos in Ariadne's character.

104. Emery, *Arthur Murphy*, p. 149; *London Stage*, Pt. 5, III, 1477.

105. Nicoll, *History of English Drama*, III, 54; Dunbar, *Dramatic Career*, p. 315.

106. *Arminius: A Tragedy* (London, 1798), pp. vi-vii. Further references are parenthetic.

107. See "Preface" and Emery, *Arthur Murphy*, p. 160.

Selected Bibliography

PRIMARY SOURCES

1. Collected Works

The Works of Arthur Murphy, Esq. London: T. Cadell, 1786. 7 Vols.

The Way to Keep Him and Five Other Plays. Ed. by J. P. Emery. New York: New York University Press, 1956.

New Essays by Arthur Murphy. Ed. by Arthur Sherbo. East Lansing: Michigan State University Press, 1963.

The Lives of Henry Fielding and Samuel Johnson, together with Essays from the Gray's-Inn Journal. Ed. by Matthew Grace. Gainesville: Scholar's Facsimiles and Reprints, 1968.

2. Individual Works

The Gray's Inn Journal. London: W. Faden and J. Bouquet, 1753-1754.

———. London: P. Vaillant, 1756. 2 Vols.

The Apprentice. London: P. Vaillant, 1756.

The Spouter, or, The Triple Revenge. London: W. Reeve, 1756.

An Englishman from Paris (1756). Ed. by Simon Trefman. Los Angeles: University of California (Augustan Reprint Society, #137), 1969.

The Test. London: S. Hooper, 1756-1757.

The Upholsterer, or What News? London: P. Vaillant, 1758.

———. In *Eighteenth-Century Drama: Afterpieces.* Ed. by Richard W. Bevis. London: Oxford University Press, 1970.

The Orphan of China. London: P. Vaillant, 1759.

The Desert Island. London: P. Vaillant, 1760.

The Way to Keep Him. 3 Acts. London: P. Vaillant, 1760.

———. In *Eighteenth-Century Drama: Afterpieces,* 1970.

———. 5 Acts. London: P. Vaillant, 1761.

All in the Wrong. London: P. Vaillant, 1761.

The Old Maid. London: P. Vaillant, 1761.

Ode to the Naiads of Fleet-Ditch. London: M. Cooper, 1761. For revision, see Foot, *Life of Arthur Murphy.*

The Examiner. London: J. Coote, 1761.

An Essay on the Life and Genius of Henry Fielding, in *Works of Henry Fielding.* London: A. Millar, 1762. Vol. I.

185

The Auditor. See *Political Controversy.* London: S. Williams, 1762-1763.
The Citizen. London: G. Kearsly, 1763.
No One's Enemy but His Own. 3 Acts. London: P. Vaillant, 1764. For later two acts, see *Works.*
What We Must All Come To. London: P. Vaillant, 1764. See *Three Weeks after Marriage,* 1776.
The Choice (1765). See *Works.*
The School for Guardians. London: P. Vaillant, 1767.
Zenobia. London: W. Griffin, 1768.
Hamlet with Alterations (1772). See *Works.*
Three Weeks after Marriage. London: G. Kearsly, 1776.
The Rival Sisters (1783). See *Works.* See, too, below.
Seventeen Hundred and Ninety-One. London: G. G. J. and J. Robinson, 1791.
An Essay on the Life and Genius of Samuel Johnson. In *Works of Samuel Johnson.* London: T. Longman, 1792.
The Rival Sisters. London: John Bell, 1793.
The Works of Cornelius Tacitus; with an Essay on His Life and Genius. London: For the Author, 1793. 4 Vols.
Arminius. London: J. Wright, 1798.
The Life of David Garrick, Esq. London: J. Wright, 1801. 2 Vols.

SECONDARY SOURCES

ANON. *A Letter from Mons. De Voltaire to the Author of the Orphan of China.* London: I. Pottinger, 1759. An attack on Murphy.
APPLETON, WILLIAM W. *A Cycle of Cathay.* New York: Columbia University Press, 1951. Discusses the sources of the *Orphan of China.*
AVERY, EMMET L. *Congreve's Plays on the Eighteenth-Century Stage.* New York: Modern Language Association, 1951. Describes influences during Murphy's period.
AYCOCK, ROY E. "Arthur Murphy, the *Gray's-Inn Journal,* and the *Craftsman:* Some Publication Mysteries," *PBSA* 67 (1973): 255-62. Bibliographical background. Offers nothing beyond Botting's discussion.
———. "Shakespearian Criticism in the *Gray's-Inn Journal,*" *Yearbook of English Studies* 2 (1972): 68-72. General discussion of Murphy's dramatic principles and critical attitudes.
BAKER, DAVID E. *Biographica Dramatica.* London: Rivingtons, 1812. 2 Vols.
BEATTY, JOSEPH M., JR. "The Battle of the Players and Poets, 1761-1766," *MLN* 5 (1919): 449-62. Churchill's attack on Murphy in the *Rosciad.*

BELLOY, PIERRE LAURENT BAYRETTE DE. *Zelmire.* Naples: J. Gravier, 1777.

BERNBAUM, ERNEST. *The Drama of Sensibility: A Sketch of the History of English Sentimental Comedy and Domestic Tragedy, 1696-1780.* Cambridge, Mass.: Harvard University Press, 1915. Old-fashioned treatment of sentimental drama, but offers perceptive comments on Murphy's plays.

BOAS, F. S. *An Introduction to Eighteenth-Century Drama.* Oxford: Oxford University Press, 1953. A chapter on Murphy, devoted largely to summary.

BOTTING, ROLAND B. "Bolingbroke and Murphy's Aboulcasem," *MLQ* 5 (March 1944): 89-91. Sees Murphy's Oriental tale in *Gray's Inn Journal* as an attack on Bolingbroke.

———. "Christopher Smart's Association with Arthur Murphy," *JEGP* 43 (January 1944): 49-56. Describes their friendship and their joint attack on John Hill.

———. "The Textual History of Murphy's *Gray's Inn Journal,*" *Research Studies of the State College of Washington,*25 (March 1957): 33-48. An excellent article describing the differences among the editions.

BRADFORD, CURTIS B. "Arthur Murphy's Meeting with Johnson," *PQ* 18 (July 1939): 318-20. Offers support and adds details to Mrs. Thrale's account.

BRUCE, HAROLD L. "Voltaire on the English Stage," *University of California Publications in Modern Philology* 8 (June 1918): #1. Provides a chapter on Murphy's attitude toward Voltaire and use of his work.

BURNIM, KALMAN A. *David Garrick Director.* Carbondale and Edwardsville: Southern Illinois University Press, 1973.

CASKEY, J. HOMER. "Arthur Murphy's Commonplace-Book," *SP* 37 (1940): 598-609. Describes Murphy's comments on drama in Murphy's manuscript.

———. "Arthur Murphy and the War on Sentimental Comedy," *JEGP* 30 (October 1931): 563-77. Sees Murphy as using French comedy to combat sentimentalism.

———. "The First Edition of Arthur Murphy's *Sallust,*" *PQ* 13 (October 1934): 404-408. Describes publication under a pseudonym in 1795.

CHURCHILL, CHARLES. *Poems.* Ed. by James Laver. London: Methuen, 1933. 1 Vols. Contains attacks on Murphy.

CIBBER, COLLEY. *Three Sentimental Comedies.* Ed. by Maureen Sullivan. New Haven: Yale University Press, 1973.

COLMAN, GEORGE. *Dramatick Works.* London: Becket, 1777. 4 Vols.

CORNEILLE, THOMAS. *Ariana.* Paris: Petite Bibliothèque des Théâtres, 1786. Vol. I.

CRÉBILLON, PROSPER JOLYOT DE. *Rhadamiste et Zénobie.* Paris: Chez
  Fuges, 1800.
CURRIE, H. MACL. "Arthur Murphy, Actor and Author," *New Rambler*
  14 (Spring 1973): 9–13. Some interesting comments on Murphy's
  translations.
DAVIS, BERTRAM H. *A Proof of Eminence: The Life of Sir John Hawkins.*
  Bloomington: Indiana University Press, 1973.
DESTOUCHES, PHILIPPE NERICAULT. *Oeuvres Dramatiques.* Paris:
  Lefèvre, 1811. 6 Vols.
DUNBAR, HOWARD HUNTER. *The Dramatic Career of Arthur Murphy.*
  New York: Modern Language Association, 1956. An excellent
  account of Murphy and his work with particular emphasis on his
  dramatic writing.
EMERY, JOHN P. *Arthur Murphy: An Eminent English Dramatist of the
  Eighteenth Century.* Philadelphia: University of Pennsylvania
  Press, 1946. A detailed account of Murphy's life and work.
———. "Murphy's Authorship of the Notes of Smart's *Hilliad,*" *MLN* 61
  (March 1946): 162–65. Gives an account of Murphy's battles with
  Hill and attributes the notes to Smart's work to Murphy.
———. "Murphy's Criticisms in the *London Chronicle,*" *PMLA* 54
  (1939): 1099–1104. Attributes to Murphy articles written during
  1757–1758.
———. "An Unpublished Letter from Arthur Murphy to Oliver
  Goldsmith Concerning *She Stoops to Conquer,*" *PQ* 17 (1938):
  88–90. Letter of 1773 on a proposal for an epilogue.
FAGAN, CHRISTOPHE BARTHÉLEMY. *L'Étourderie.* Paris: Petite Bibliothe-
  que des Théâtres, 1789. Vol. 9.
FERGUSON, OLIVER W. "Sir Fretful Plagiary and Goldsmith's 'An Essay
  on the Theatre': The Background of Richard Cumberland's
  'Dedication to Detraction,'" *Quick Springs of Sense,* ed. by Larry
  S. Champion. Athens, Georgia: University of Georgia Press, 1974,
  pp. 113–20. Discussion of sentimental comedy.
FONE, B. R. S. "*Love's Last Shift* and Sentimental Comedy,"
  Restoration and 18th Century Theatre Research 9 (May 1970):
  11–23. Characteristics of sentimental comedy.
FOOT, JESSE. *The Life of Arthur Murphy, Esq.* London: J. Faulder, 1811.
  Account of Murphy's life and career, with documents, letters, and
  unpublished writing. Foot was executor of Murphy's estate.
FOOTE, SAMUEL. *Dramatic Works.* London: A. Millar, 1797. 2 Vols.
———. "Samuel Foote's Primitive Puppet-Shew." Ed. by Samuel N.
  Bogorad and R. G. Noyes, *Theatre Survey* 14 (Fall 1973): #1a.
FRIEDMAN, ARTHUR. "Aspects of Sentimentalism in Eighteenth-Century
  Literature," *Augustan Milieu.* Ed. by H. K. Miller *et al.* Oxford:
  Clarendon Press, 1970, pp. 247–61. Good general discussion of
  sentimental characteristics.
GARRICK, DAVID. *Dramatic Works.* London: R. Bald *et al.,* 1774. 2 Vols.

———. *Letters of David Garrick.* Ed. by D. M. Little and G. M. Kahrl. London: Oxford University Press, 1963. 3 Vols. Correspondence with Murphy and comments about his work.

———. *Private Correspondence of David Garrick with the Most Celebrated Persons of His Time.* Ed. by James Boaden. London: H. Colburn and R. Bentley, 1831–1832. 2 Vols.

GENEST, JOHN. *Some Account of the English Stage from the Restoration in 1660 to 1830.* Bath: H. E. Carrington, 1832. 10 Vols. Anecdotal and critical material.

GILLILAND, THOMAS. *The Dramatic Mirror.* London: C. Chapple, 1808. 2 Vols.

GOLDSMITH, OLIVER. *Collected Works.* Ed. by Arthur Friedman. Oxford: Oxford University Press, 1966. 5 Vols.

GRAY, CHARLES H. *Theatrical Criticism in London to 1795.* New York: Columbia University Press, 1931. Important material on Murphy's journalism, particularly the *Gray's Inn Journal.*

HILL, AARON. *Alzira.* London: John Osborn, 1736.

HOGAN, CHARLES BEECHER, ed. *The London Stage.* Carbondale: Southern Illinois University Press, 1968. Pt. 5, 3 Vols. Important information on production of Murphy's plays.

HUME, ROBERT D. "Goldsmith and Sheridan and the Supposed Revolution of 'Laughing' against 'Sentimental' Comedy," *Studies in Change and Revolution. Aspects of English Intellectual History, 1640–1800.* Ed. by Paul J. Korshin. Menston, Yorkshire: Scolar Press, 1972, pp. 237–76. Revision of traditional attitudes toward the dominance of sentimental comedy in the eighteenth century.

JASON, PHILIP K. "The Afterpiece: Authors and Incentives," *Restoration and 18th Century Theatre Research* 12 (May 1973): 1–13. Describes the practical and commercial considerations motivating authors to write afterpieces.

KELLY, JOHN ALEXANDER. *German Visitors to English Theaters in the Eighteenth Century.* Princeton: Princeton University Press, 1936. Some foreign reactions to Murphy's work.

KINNE, WILLARD AUSTIN. *Revivals and Importations of French Comedies in England, 1749–1800.* New York: Columbia University Press. 1939. Important material on Murphy's use of French comedy.

KNAPP, MARY E. *Prologues and Epilogues of the Eighteenth Century.* New Haven: Yale University Press, 1961. Discusses some of Murphy's work in these genres.

KNIGHT, JOSEPH. *David Garrick.* London: Kegan Paul *et al.*, 1894.

LA CHAUSSÉE, PIERRE-CLAUDE NIVELLE DE. *Le Préjûgé à la Mode.* Naples: J. Gravier, 1777.

LAFF, LEONARD J. "Sheridan and Sentimentalism," *Restoration and 18th Century Theatre Research* 12 (May 1973): 36–48. Discusses characteristics of sentimentalism.

LEE, NATHANIEL. *The Rival Queens; or, the Death of Alexander the Great.* London: R. Wellington and E. Rumbal, 1702.

LEHNERT, MARTIN. "Arthur Murphy's *Hamlet*-Parodie (1772) auf David Garrick," *Shakespeare-Jahrbuch* 102 (1966): 97-167. Prints Murphy's text and gives details of its composition.

MARMONTEL, JEAN FRANCOIS. *Belisaire.* Paris: Merlin, 1767.

METASTASIO, PIETRO. *Dramas and Other Poems.* Tr. by John Hoole. London: Otridge and Son, 1800.

MILLER, HENRY KNIGHT. "Internal Evidence: Professor Sherbo and the Case of Arthur Murphy," *BNYPL* 69 (1965): 459-70. Disputes Sherbo's evidence for attributing *Entertainer* and other essays to Murphy.

MILLER, JAMES. *The Picture: or, The Cuckold in Conceit.* London: J. Watts, 1745.

MOCULLOCH, PHILIM [pseud.]. *The Murphiad.* London: J. Williams, 1761. An attack on Murphy.

MOISSY, ALEXANDRE GUILLAUME MOUSLIER DE. *La Nouvelle École des Femmes.* Paris: Didot l'aîné, 1772.

MOLIÈRE, JEAN BAPTISTE POQUELIN. *Oeuvres Complètes.* Paris: Nelson, 1913. 6 Vols.

NANGLE, BENJAMIN C. *The Monthly Review, First Series, 1749-1789. Indexes of Contributors and Articles.* Oxford: Clarendon Press, 1934.

———. *The Monthly Review, Second Series, 1790-1815. Indexes of Contributors and Articles.* Oxford: Clarendon Press, 1955.

NICOLL, ALLARDYCE. *History of English Drama, 1660-1900.* Later Eighteenth Century. Cambridge: Cambridge University Press, 1961. Vol. 3. A general study, somewhat dated in its treatment of Murphy.

NOBBE, GEORGE. *The North Briton: A Study in Political Propaganda.* New York: Columbia University Press, 1939. Important discussion of Murphy's political journalism.

OMAN, CAROLA. *David Garrick.* Bungay, Suffolk: Hodder and Stoughton, 1958. Unsympathetic treatment of Murphy in his relations with Garrick.

PAGE, EUGENE R. *George Colman the Elder: Essayist, Dramatist, and Theatrical Manager.* New York: Columbia University Press, 1935. Discusses Murphy's personal and professional relationships with Colman.

PASSLER, SUSAN M. "Arthur Murphy's 'Essay on the Life and Genius of Henry Fielding, Esq.': Re-reading a Slighted Critic," *New Rambler* 14 (Spring 1973): 15-23. A fair appraisal of Murphy's treatment of Fielding.

PEDICORD, HARRY WILLIAM. *The Theatrical Public in the Time of Garrick.* New York: King's Crown Press, 1954. Contains interesting material on the popularity of Murphy's plays.

PERRY, THOMAS W. *Public Opinion, Propaganda, and Politics in Eighteenth-Century England: A Study of the Jew Bill of 1753.* Cambridge, Mass.: Harvard University Press, 1962. Describes Murphy's anti-Semitism in the *Gray's Inn Journal.*

PIOZZI (THRALE), HESTER LYNCH. *Anecdotes of the Late Samuel Johnson, LL.D., during the Last Twenty Years of His Life.* Ed. by S. C. Roberts. Cambridge: Cambridge University Press, 1925. Anecdotes about Murphy in relation to Johnson.

PRICE, CECIL. *Theatre in the Age of Garrick.* Totowa, N.J.: Rowman and Littlefield, 1973. Discussion of all aspects of stage productions in Murphy's time.

REA, ROBERT R. *The English Press in Politics, 1760-1774.* Lincoln: University of Nebraska Press, 1963. Discusses Murphy's *Auditor.*

RICHARDS, KENNETH, and THOMSON, PETER, eds. *The Eighteenth-Century Stage.* London: Methuen and Co., 1972. Essays on the theater, playwrights, and actors in Murphy's period.

SHERBO, ARTHUR. *English Sentimental Drama.* East Lansing: Michigan State University Press, 1957. A good discussion of the characteristics of sentimental drama.

———. "Imitation or Concealment: Who Wrote the *Entertainer* Essays," *BNYPL* 69 (1965): 471-86. Supports claims for Murphy's authorship.

SHERIDAN, RICHARD BRINSLEY. *Dramatic Works.* Ed. by Cecil Price. Oxford: Clarendon Press, 1973. 2 Vols.

SMART, CHRISTOPHER. *The Hilliad.* London: J. Newbery, 1753. Contains Murphy's notes.

SMITH, DANE FARNSWORTH. *The Critics as the Audience of the London Theatres from Buckingham to Sheridan: A Study of Neoclassicism in the Playhouse, 1671-1779.* Albuquerque: University of New Mexico Press, 1953. Offers some comments on responses to Murphy's plays.

SPECTOR, ROBERT DONALD. *English Literary Periodicals and the Climate of Opinion during the Seven Years' War.* The Hague: Mouton and Co., 1966. Discusses Murphy as a political writer.

STEIN, ELIZABETH. *David Garrick, Dramatist.* New York: Modern Language Association, 1938. Discussions of Garrick's plays show parallels and perhaps borrowings in Murphy's.

STONE, GEORGE WINCHESTER, JR. "Garrick's Long Lost Alteration of *Hamlet,*" *PMLA* 49 (September 1934): 897ff. Discusses the work that Murphy parodied.

———, ed. *London Stage.* Carbondale: Southern Illinois University Press, 1967. Pt. 4, 3 Vols. Important information on production of Murphy's plays.

STRATMAN, CARL J. et al., eds. *Restoration and Eighteenth Century Theatre Research: A Bibliographical Guide, 1900-1968.* Carbondale: Southern Illinois University Press, 1971.

TASCH, PETER A. *The Dramand Works of Isaac Bickerstaff.* Lewisburg, Pa.: Bucknell University Press, 1971. Comments on Murphy's personal and professional relationships.

TAYLOR, JOHN. *Records of My Life.* New York: J. and J. Harper, 1833. 2 Vols. Anecdotes about Murphy.

THRALE, HESTER LYNCH. *Thraliana: The Diary of Mrs. Hester Lynch Thrale (Later Mrs. Piozzi), 1776-1809.* Ed. by Katherine C. Balderston. Oxford: Clarendon Press, 1942. 2 Vols. Important contemporary accounts of Murphy's personality and talents.

TREFMAN, SIMON. "Arthur Murphy's Long Lost *Englishman from Paris:* A Manuscript Discovered," *Theatre Notebook* 20 (Summer 1966): 137-41. Account of the discovery of the manuscript and description of its original production and its contemporary relationships.

———. *Sam, Foote, Comedian (1720-1770).* New York: New York University Press, 1971. Murphy's relationships with Foote.

VOLTAIRE, FRANÇOIS-MARIE AROUET DE. *Works.* Tr. by Tobias Smollett, Thomas Francklin, *et al.* London: J. Newberry, 1761-74. 38 Vols.

Index

193